ETHOS

Joe,
Blessings!

Alan

ETHOS

How Should We Then Think?
A Biblical Worldview of Issues Facing Our Culture
Alan Sargent

TATE PUBLISHING
AND ENTERPRISES, LLC

Published by Tate Publishing & Enterprises, LLC
127 E. Trade Center Terrace | Mustang, Oklahoma 73064 USA
1.888.361.9473 | www.tatepublishing.com

Tate Publishing is committed to excellence in the publishing industry. The company reflects the philosophy established by the founders, based on Psalm 68:11,
"The Lord gave the word and great was the company of those who published it."

Book design copyright © 2015 by Tate Publishing, LLC. All rights reserved.
Cover design by Junriel Boquecosa
Interior design by Honeylette Pino

Published in the United States of America

ISBN: 978-1-63449-135-8
Religion / Christian Life / General
14.11.14

...prepare your minds for action...

—1 Peter 1:13, NASU

Brethren, do not be children in your thinking...but in your
thinking be mature.

—I Corinthians 14:20, NASU

This book is dedicated to Hettie Lue Brooks, who first mentioned to me over thirty years ago: "Someone needs to write a book that deals with the Scriptural basis for the stuff we deal with every day." I guess I'm the "someone."

It is also dedicated to the relentless seeker of truth; to that person who wants more than perfunctory answers to probing questions. May he or she find some truth here.

Acknowledgement

Thanks are to be heaped on those who made contributions to my life and specifically to this volume: my proofreader and constant support these 40+ years, my wife, Lynn; and thanks also to Rev. Guy C. Ames, III, who led me, more than anyone, to a saving and empowered relationship with the Lord. The ideas and beliefs of this book would not have been possible without the input of "Brother Bob" Stamps, Pastor Dave Walker, Morris Cerullo, Dave Cerullo, Terry Law, Pastor Tim Brooks, David Barton, Gary Hanvey, Don and Hettie Lue Brooks, and my pastor, Ricky Jones.

Contents

Introduction

Ethos, according to *Webster's*, refers to the distinguishing character, sentiment, moral nature, or guiding beliefs of a person, group, or institution; it comes from the Greek and Latin words by the same spelling. Whatever a culture's ethos, so will be its practice or default. This book attempts to help readers determine what a "Christian ethos" would look like.

Humans have been made differently than animals. They are rational creatures; their actions and, more importantly, their reactions are supposed to be more rational—less instinctive. Their decisions to marry, what vocation they shall pursue, and what behavior they consider acceptable—or unacceptable—are governed by the parameters they have subscribed to mentally, not by some blind drives for survival or dominance, which are instinctive in nature.

Belief systems have consequences...in the way we live, the way we love, and the way we worship. Samuel Smiles said it best: "Sow a thought, and you reap an act; sow an act, and you reap a habit; sow a habit, and you reap a character; sow a character, and you reap a destiny." It all starts with the way we think.

Right thinking precedes right action; or as the Scripture relates, As a man "thinketh in his heart, so is he" (Prov. 27:3, KJV). Can we control our thoughts? Is it possible to only think righteously and therefore act righteously or are we, at our core, instinctive creatures that cannot be held responsible for our thoughts or actions? This book presumes the truth of Scripture—books have already been written that establish both the veracity and the reliability of the Bible—and the fact that humans have been created in God's image. If it was not possible to control what is thought, the Scripture giving us a list of thoughts we *should* choose would be purposeless.

> Finally, brethren, whatsoever things are true, whatsoever things are honest, whatsoever things are just, whatsoever things are pure, whatsoever things are lovely, whatsoever things are of good report; if there be any virtue, and if there be any praise, think on these things.
>
> —Phil. 4:8, KJV

It is possible to think AND act righteously, but it is not automatic. Although Man is called to be holy (Lev. 11:44, 19:2, 20:7; 1 Pet. 1:15–16), he is not left to do this without the help of the One Who has such high expectations. "Also, the Spirit helps us with our weakness" (Rom. 8:26, NCV). "For it is God who is at work in you, both to will and to work for His good pleasure" (Phil. 2:13, NASU).

This book was written first and foremost as a reference work (that is why the topics were alphabetized and an index was included). However, it also may be used as a weekly devotional (there are fifty-two chapters) or read straight through. An effort was made to be as entertaining as possible (sorry if my own anecdotal experiences were referenced too often, but my life is at least amusing to me).

When is a book like this ever finished? The simple answer is never. As long as there are new issues facing our culture, the Christian community must derive answers from a biblical worldview. As the need continues, I will keep adding another chapter on my Web site: www.mintchocolatechip.org. I've already added ones on immigration, capital punishment, adoption, and tattoos, and I plan on many other topics. Is there another volume coming out? Perhaps.

It should be said that there is a temptation to deal only with those topics upon which I have "landed" in my own belief systems; I acknowledge there is also a temptation to write in such a way as to justify my own behavior; but let me also state in unequivocal terms that the biblical "Ethos" communicated here far exceeds my actions and this caveat is in no way an attempt to escape the accusations of hypocrisy that would normally follow such an ambitious undertaking. Rather, let me here fully confess that everything written is my aspiration, not my performance. If I were to limit my writing to only those areas where I felt some confidence in my own integrity of thought, it would be a short tome indeed.

One other disclaimer, I have made a concerted effort to quote accurately and, in the interest of readability, have attributed internally. Sometimes my memory may have been inaccurate, or the way I reasoned may be flawed, but Scripture and its flawless basis are the foundation of the credibility and timelessness of this work, not my own efforts, anyway.

So what should Christians think? That is what this book is all about. This book gives those who are more than nominal Christians—in name only—insight into what the Bible says about the issues of the day. The Word of God is as relevant to today as it was the day God inspired its authors to write it...and, if it is relevant, those who claim to follow its tenets should make every effort to apply it.

> How can a young man keep his way pure? By keeping it
> according to Your Word. With all my heart I have sought
> You; do not let me wander from Your commandments.
> Your Word I have treasured in my heart, that I may not sin
> against You.
>
> —Prov. 119:9, NASU

1

Abortion

I'd like to say I was in love, but in retrospect, I was just "in lust." In any case, the resultant pregnancy came as a surprise to us both. We were both unmarried Bible college students and both too old to act so irresponsibly—but using protection does not make fornication right...carrying protection in your wallet or purse only makes your sin premeditated; it does, however, ameliorate the immediate consequences and limit the collateral damage...don't take that as an endorsement for birth control.

We had been dating for some time, both of us loved the Lord, but the one indiscretion that passionately occurred in the back seat of my car betrayed the sinful natures that still lurked within us. Ironically, there is only one thing you can do to cover up a sin... commit more sin. When pregnancy is the result of your lust, you can do one of two things...have the child or commit murder. To be candid, I don't know what went through my mind. I knew that what I did might be legal, but never was there any doubt that what I did was immoral.

I will never—in this life—know the sex or name of the child we aborted. We never got married—it was later that I married my wife of forty years—and I chose conveniently to believe the lie that the six-week-old fetus was just a blob of protoplasm. Proof of the sin of abortion is the struggle I've had personally to forgive myself. Receiving the Savior's forgiveness was a little easier, but not much.

Susan (not her real name...why bring injury or pain to someone who might have had the same struggles and why give glory to the enemy?), wherever you are, I'm sorry. I pray you have found the same peace through the forgiveness of a Savior who nailed that sin and others to a cross on a lonely hill two thousand years ago.

I assume all the blame. I cannot lay the blame on Roe v. Wade, an errant culture, my stepmother who loaned me the money, or the young woman I talked conspiratorially into the dark deed meant to hide my sin.

Maybe there is some redeeming value of the experience in the hundreds I've been able to subsequently counsel over the years. Still, I believe that abortion is murder...those that call it "choice" have removed the right to choose that the unborn cannot voice. There is no statute of limitation on murder, and I am prepared to surrender myself should it ever be designated as the self-centered violent act that it is.

Is abortion biblical? What about those laws that legalize behavior that God does not support? What should the attitude of Christians be toward those who get pregnant outside of marriage? What about abortion in the case of rape, incest, or if the life of the mother is at risk? Can we be "pro-choice" and still be a Christian? What about RU-483 (the so-called morning after pill) or other abortifacients? What about partial-birth abortions or other late-term abortions? What about miscarriage? These and other questions need to be addressed.

According to the medical dictionary, *abortion* is the premature exit of the products of conception (the fetus, fetal membranes, and placenta) from the uterus. It is the loss of a pregnancy and does not refer to why that pregnancy was lost. A spontaneous abortion is the same as a miscarriage; a miscarriage of three or more consecutive pregnancies is termed habitual abortion. *Webster's* defines abortion thusly: The act of giving premature birth; particularly, the expulsion of the human fetus prematurely, or before it is capable of sustaining life; miscarriage. (From *Webster's Revised Unabridged Dictionary of the English Language*, PC Study Bible formatted electronic database Copyright © 2011 by Biblesoft, Inc. All rights reserved.)

Roe v. Wade, the defining moment legalizing this life-ending procedure, occurred as a court case before the US Supreme Court in 1973. Winning this case made abortion the guaranteed right of any woman in the United States; making her pregnancy primarily a privacy issue: an interpretation of the Due Process Clause of the Fourteenth Amendment to the Constitution as a privacy guarantee. Fifty-three million abortions later, we have a lack of taxpayers and an abundance of therapy seekers.

Answering questions:

1. Is abortion biblical?

    The Bible doesn't use the word translated in English as "abortion," though the Hebrew word *nephel* and the Greek word *ektroma* come close (these words are usually translated as "miscarriage"—Job 3:16, Eccl. 6:3; or as "untimely born"—I Cor. 15:8, NASU). In both cases, there is a negative connotation attached. Life was considered as precious and a gift. Barrenness was even considered as a curse (Gen 29:31; Deut. 7:14), and abortion or miscarriage was seen as a violation of the first command given to all of creation (Gen. 1:28).

    There is a mention of God-ordained retribution against the "sons of Ammon" for "ripping open the pregnant women of Gilead" in Amos 1:13. One can see there a definite aversion from God's perspective for this heinous practice.

2. What about those laws that legalize behavior that God does not support?

    Although this is really a much larger question—we are called "to obey God rather than men" (Acts 5:29, NKJV)—the fault really lies with an electorate who continues to elect representatives that make ungodly laws. They make those laws from ignorance, but it is the mature Christian's responsibility to make sure the men running for office know God's law and believe that it should have preeminence. Our early Supreme Court justices often cited the Bible when seeking a precedence in their rulings. In Roe v. Wade, the justices could cite no law as precedent—that is called "legislating from the bench."

In fact, in 1976, when I had the birth of my firstborn, I decided to move out of California because the state legislature passed AB289, a bill legalizing sex between any two consenting adults: in one stroke legalizing five acts the Bible prohibits—sodomy (Gen 18:16), homosexuality (Lev. 18:22), fornication (Eph. 5:3), adultery (Ex. 20:14), and incest (Lev. 18:17).

3.   What should the attitude of Christians be toward those who get pregnant outside of marriage?

There was only one immaculate conception—Mary was impregnated by the Holy Spirit (Matt. 1:18)—anyone else getting pregnant outside the context of marriage has a challenge. This is not to say that Joseph and Mary did not face challenges. In fact, Joseph thought to do what many men of his time did and quietly send Mary away (Matt. 1:19)—good thing abortion was not an option or we'd all have been in trouble.

Yes, there are many challenges to raising a child as a single parent (whether made a single parent by an act of another's sin—as in rape or incest, by your own sin—as in fornication, a victim of divorce, experiencing the death of a spouse, or making the choice as an unmarried person to visit a sperm bank.) How one gets to single parenthood does not make single parenting any easier, but Christians don't need to look down a pious nose and condemn. Single parents need help, not self-righteous judgment.

Young women who get pregnant outside of marriage need love, appropriate forgiveness, compassion, and encouragement... from parents, from peers, and from the Church. The time for judgment and discipline is past—when applicable, that should have happened when a promiscuous lifestyle first showed itself. If Christians are going to reject abortion as an option—and I'm saying we should, except when advised by a qualified medical professional that the health of the mother is at risk—then we must be supportive of adoption, raising children with our help, and providing the care, counsel, and other help unwed mothers may need.

4. What about abortion in the case of rape, incest, or if the life of the mother is at risk?

    The conceived child had no say in the matter. He or she didn't choose the manner of his or her conception. By my mother-in-law's account, my wife was the product of a rape...that doesn't make her existence any less valuable to God or to me. As Christians, we should encourage purity, fidelity, and sexual integrity...but we should never take our frustration with someone's lapse in those areas out on the innocent nor should we think God any less capable of working His purposes out in spite of it all.

5. Can we be "pro-choice" and still be a Christian?

    Of course. How we believe on any political issue may not affect our relationship with God. It may, however, create an internal conflict that has consequences in the way we live our lives. Right thinking precedes right action.

    God is all about life (John 10:10).

6. What about RU-483 (the so-called morning after pill) or other abortifacients?

    Some methods of abortion may be more or less reprehensible to our culture, but ease and convenience are not the standards by which they should be judged. Biblically speaking, life does not begin at conception. It begins in the heart of God (Jer. 1:5).

    In fact, anything that makes it easier to avoid the consequences of sin should be suspect. As Christians, we don't need to make any "provision for the flesh" (Rom. 13:14)...our lust needs to be hobbled, not enabled. This has to do with anything that encourages or feeds our baser animal drives...pornography, sensual movies or books, and of course anything that weakens the will (drugs, excessive alcohol consumption, etc.).

7. What about partial-birth abortions or other late-term abortions?

Any abortion that occurs post-viability—after the baby can survive outside the womb; this varies with the pregnancy, but generally twenty-first or later weeks—is more difficult, but is still an abortion. Called, technically speaking, an "intact dilation and evacuation," this procedure has been outlawed in most states and accounts for less than 1 percent of abortions annually. Sometimes it is only seconds away from being infanticide.

8. What about miscarriage?

Sometimes, this is how God deals with an unviable pregnancy. Something has gone wrong in the biological process and the body refuses to bring the child to full term. As Christians, we should comfort those who mourn a loss, and this certainly includes those who have lost a child through miscarriage. Christians should always recommend medical and psychological care of those who have suffered a miscarriage.

Who knows why? Some things are left for only God to know (Isaiah 55:8–9; I Cor. 13:12). Sometimes, medical science can help; sometimes prayer; sometimes adoption is the answer.

Recommended reading list:

- *I'll Hold You In Heaven: Healing and Hope for the Parent Who Lost a Child through Miscarriage, Stillbirth, Abortion or Early Infant Death*, Jack Hayford
- *Grieving the Child I Never Knew*, Kathe Wunnenberg
- *Abortion and the Conscience of the Nations*, Ronald Reagan

Web sites:

- www.crisispregnancy.com
- www.focusonthefamily.org
- www.4AbortionAlternatives.com

2

Affirmative Action

Sitting out in the car all alone in the parking lot, I wept with great wracking sobs, repenting of all that had been done to the Native American as if I had been the one *personally* to perpetrate all the atrocities I had just seen in the film. Kevin Costner had done a marvelous job in his 1990 film *Dances with Wolves*, and I felt as guilty as the director and producers wanted me to.

The scripture that comes to mind, known to more as a song ("Turn, Turn, Turn"—written by Pete Seeger in the late 50s and popularized by the UK group The Byrds), is that passage which says, "To everything there is a season, and a time to every purpose under heaven" (Eccles. 3:1, KJV). To me, the question is not should there be affirmative action, but should there *still* be affirmative action? There was a time when affirmative action was necessary, but that time has since passed.

The concept of affirmative action says that minorities (especially blacks and women) need extra consideration (particularly in college admission percentages and employment) to deal with the fact that they have been repressed for so long. There are quotas for admission and employment that must be filled to bring college and labor force populations to a more representative number (reflecting the same percentages as the general population). This may require that criteria be different for these applicants.

Simple and straightforward, this concept has been acceptable to me and a large portion of America…in the past. I mean, I was never a slave and I am willing to see inequities made right. But that time is past. I didn't personally enslave anyone (nor pick my gender), and a case can certainly be made that continued affirmative action does more to hold back minorities than it does to help them advance. Affirmative action is today only encouraging racism and sexism by creating a double standard—I can't imagine the self-esteem of the minority applicant being well served by the inference that he or she only got accepted or hired by virtue of an un-level playing field.

Is affirmative action biblical? Should minorities be given a "leg up," so to speak? What's wrong with the government mandating equality if equity is not rendered? How do we right the wrongs of the past? Are there other inequities that exist that require our attention? These and other questions are the ones thinking Christians should be asking themselves.

According to a combination of what many dictionaries say, *Affirmative Action* is the process by which positive action has been taken to alleviate the inequalities that exist for women and minorities in the areas of employment, education, or society; a temporary preference to make up for a past prejudice. Generally, efforts have pursued two courses: (1) legally through the courts and the legislatures and (2) culturally through public discourse, movies, books, and other organs of social change.

Answering questions:

1. Is affirmative action biblical?

    In one sense no, for God is not a respecter of persons (Acts 10:34–35). In another sense, yes; to ask if "a temporary preference to make up for a past prejudice" is biblical, you don't have to go very far. Jesus, in His famous Sermon on the Mount, said, "It was said, 'WHOEVER SENDS HIS WIFE AWAY, LET HIM GIVE HER A CERTIFICATE OF DIVORCE'; but I say to you that everyone who divorces his wife, except for the reason of unchastity, makes her commit adultery; and whoever marries a divorced woman commits adultery" (Matt. 5:31–32, NASU).

The Lord made this passage even more clear when the Pharisees approached Him later:

> Some Pharisees came to Jesus, testing Him and asking, "Is it lawful for a man to divorce his wife for any reason at all?" And He answered and said, "Have you not read that He who created them from the beginning 'MADE THEM MALE AND FEMALE', and said, 'FOR THIS REASON A MAN SHALL LEAVE HIS FATHER AND MOTHER AND BE JOINED TO HIS WIFE, AND THE TWO SHALL BECOME ONE FLESH'? So they are no longer two, but one flesh. What therefore God has joined together, let no man separate." They said to Him, "Why then did Moses command to GIVE HER A CERTIFICATE OF DIVORCE AND SEND HER AWAY." He said to them, "Because of your hardness of heart Moses permitted you to divorce your wives; *but from the beginning it has not been this way.*" And I say to you, whoever divorces his wife, except for immorality, and marries another woman commits adultery." (Matt. 19:3–10, NASU)

Yes, affirmative action is biblical, but it is also biblical to set things back on their proper course. And I believe, whether it's all the preferences we have given to Native Americans or to blacks—my brother-in-law was a doctor who had to give free health care to the Native Americans in Montana—we do their descendants a disservice if we continue this double standard to assuage our guilt. That is what confession and forgiveness is for. Affirmative action and free health care were our repentance. The only question to be debated is our timing. When does repentance become enablement?

2. Should minorities be given a "leg up," so to speak?

As I said, we must be careful we don't enable them. When does treating someone preferentially actually cease to be the helping hand it was intended to be (one could lump Food

Stamps and Aid to Dependent Children in here, too)? One can argue the decision that resulted in The Trail of Tears, the Three-fifths Compromise or Japanese Internment Camps…I'm sure they seemed right at the time…and the retrospect of history makes them rightfully reprehensible; but somewhere along the line, we all have to see ourselves equally as un-hyphenated Americans. Mercy-driven Christians are the most susceptible to guilt manipulation. The result is an interrupted confession–forgiveness cycle that handicaps both the majority and the minority they wanted to help.

3. What's wrong with the government mandating equality if equity is not rendered?

Nothing, as long as adequate debate for all parties is allowed and a preset time to reconsider is determined—a sunset clause. Forced integration—bussing—was a terrible, *but necessary*, provision to eliminate discrimination in education. And I'm not naïve enough to believe there aren't racial prejudices left to be conquered. But today, we have blacks occupying important positions in every area of our culture and mixed marriages of all races pointing toward a time when we are more focused on what unites us than on what divides. Christians need to champion this worldview.

4. How do we right the wrongs of the past?

First, we recognize they are wrong—*confession*. Depending on how egregious, there may be some necessary groveling or public humility that is required. As cultural change happens slowly, those truly guilty of an offense are likely no longer present. This may require their descendants (read hapless recipients of their prejudices) to sincerely confess in absentia… and sincere patience from the descendants of those wronged.

Second, there must be an attempt to make some allowance (read "Affirmative Action") for those disadvantaged—*repentance* (proof of repentance is changed behavior—it was not enough to make the Emancipation Proclamation or the Civil Rights Act of 1964; the concept of hyphenated Americans must disappear from our culture).

Lastly, there must be an acceptance of the repentant acts—when they become counter-productive—*forgiveness*. When the descendants of those disadvantaged are fully compensated—of course this can never really happen any more than toothpaste can be put back in the tube—a general reconciliation must occur.

Although Christ has paid in full for all our sins and satisfied the need for equity in the world to come (that is what Heaven and Hell are for), that does not alleviate the call for equity in this world.

5. Are there other inequities that exist that require our attention?

Of course…the plight of the Coptic Christians, the refugee crisis in the Middle East, the starving in Ethiopia and Sudan, those disenfranchised in North Korea–China–Iran, Pakistan–Afghanistan, those in the world with poor health or not enough to eat, etc.…and that doesn't even cover the present inequities in America…but that is why He left us here (not just to pray or wring our hands, but to do)!

> What use is it, my brethren, if someone says he has faith but he has no works? Can that faith save him? If a brother or sister is without clothing and in need of daily food, and one of you says to them, "Go in peace, be warmed and be filled," and yet you do not give them what is necessary for their body, what use is that? Even so faith, if it has no works, is dead, being by itself. (James 2:14–17, NASU)

Recommended reading list:

- *Productive Christians in an Age of Guilt Manipulators: A Biblical Response to Ronald J. Sider*, David Chilton
- *Emotional Blackmail: When the People in Your Life Use Fear, Obligation and Guilt to Manipulate You*, Susan Forward

- *Affirmative Action: Social Justice or Reverse Discrimination,* Francis Beckwith and Tom E. Jones

Web sites:

- www.christianpost.com/...relations-affirmative-action-
- www.patheos.com/blogs/anxiousbench/... and-affirmative-action

3

Alcohol, Marijuana, and Other Controlled Substances and the Fight for the Will

"I'm proud to be an Okie from Muskogee, a place where even squares can have a ball…" Surely, a song that put my hometown on the map—mine, not singer Merle Haggard's—everyone remembers, right? It told of a place where "white lightnin's still the biggest thrill of all." This country song wasn't too accurate when it was penned back in 1969. Although the album it was on won Country Album of the Year when I was a junior in high school, we *did* have a drug problem on campus. Sure, alcohol, the more acceptable redneck alternative, was king, but "Mary Jane" got more than her fair share of dates! Me? I was too much of a nerd to be in with the "cool crowd" that did drugs.

Fast forward—on your iPad, not your 8-track—and the question for teens is not whether your friends are occasionally drinking alcohol or smoking marijuana, but are they high *every* day at school? As of 2013, marijuana is legal (for medicinal use only—and for adults over eighteen) in eighteen states with ballot initiatives in ten more. Although only Washington and Colorado have approved it for recreational use (as of this date), federal officials are eyeing legalization on a national level to generate billions in tax revenue. With thoughts that savings on the cost of regulation and then tax revenue generated may be one of the solutions to our budget crisis, there's no doubt that lawmakers may be consumers already!

Their argument is the same every teenager offers: "Everybody's doing it!" or "They tried limiting alcohol consumption—a reference to Prohibition—and look how that turned out!" Of course, most parents used to offer the age-old comeback: "Well, obviously not *everyone*...because *you're* not!"

Dictatorial methods may have worked when corporal punishment was more in vogue or grounding more practical, but today's reasoning teens demand more meaty explanations—and fewer authoritarian edicts. Besides, Christianity must be relevant here, too.

Is alcohol or drug consumption biblical? I am freer when I feel uninhibited...how can that be a bad thing? What's the big deal with marijuana...if we legalize it, won't that make the price go down? What about the savings in law enforcement and incarceration? What about the potential for tax revenue? If it's wrong for teens, why is it right for adults? These, and other questions, are the ones thinking Christians must answer.

Consumption of anything that surrenders the decision-making power of the will must be suspect. What separates Man from animals is our reasoning capacity. You never hear of any other creature weighing options, deliberating possibilities, or setting goals. No, all decisions made by animals are on an instinctive level; they have no ability to take a reasoned course of action. Why should we lower ourselves to their level by consuming substances that compromise our will?

According to a dictionary amalgamation, a *controlled substance* is generally any chemical, drug, or alcohol-containing beverage whose manufacture, possession, or use is controlled by a government. Limits for its sale or consumption may vary from state to state or, in the cases of the Eighteenth and Twenty-First Amendments to the US Constitution, may be prohibited or allowed on a national basis. According to the Bible, our bodies are the temple of the Holy Spirit (1 Corinthians 6:19) and we must be careful to consume only those things that won't desecrate them.

Answering questions:

1. Is alcohol or drug consumption biblical?

    One would have to think that Jesus changed the water into grape juice at the wedding feast in Cana for anyone to think that drinking alcoholic beverages is unbiblical—and from the context (John 2:9–10, 4:46), it was clearly alcoholic. Besides, it was not grape juice Jesus Himself drank from the cup mentioned at the Last Supper mentioned in Luke 18:17–18, it was wine; again, read the context. However, we are told specifically to not get drunk:

    > And be not drunk with wine, wherein is excess; but be filled with the Spirit. (Ephesians 5:18, KJV)

    Another admonition is given for those who would seek a leadership position:

    > The overseer then must be irreproachable, husband of one wife, *sober*, discreet, decorous, hospitable, apt to teach; *not given to excesses from wine*, not a striker, but mild, not addicted to contention, not fond of money, conducting his own house well, having [his] children in subjection with all gravity; (but if one does not know how to conduct his own house, how shall he take care of the assembly of God?) (1 Tim. 3:2–5, Darby)

2. I am freer when I feel uninhibited…how can that be a bad thing?

    Inhibition is an inner feeling that what one wants to do may not be acceptable. Perhaps that is the voice of the Holy Spirit. Ignoring that voice—or drowning it out by alcohol or drugs—may have you doing things you shouldn't; listen to Solomon's wisdom on that:

    > Who has woe? Who has sorrow? Who has contentions? Who has complaining? Who has wounds without cause? Who has redness of eyes? Those who linger long over

wine, those who go to taste mixed wine. Do not look
on the wine when it is red, when it sparkles in the cup,
when it goes down smoothly; at the last it bites like a
serpent and stings like a viper. Your eyes will see strange
things and your mind will utter perverse things. (Proverbs
23:29–33, NASU)

3. What's the big deal with marijuana…if we legalize it, won't
    that make the price go down?

    Just because the cost to purchase marijuana is less or legal,
    does not make it wise. Besides, the *initial* cost is only part of
    the story. Many who are addicted to harder drugs got their start
    on the "gateway drug," marijuana. As a Christian, it is hard to
    allow the Holy Spirit to control you when you are controlled by
    an addiction to alcohol or drugs.

    The real problem with marijuana, drugs, or even alcohol
    in excess is that you capitulate in the fight for the will. Your
    ability to be in control of your mind or body is greatly impaired
    by controlled substances…that's why they are controlled!
    Mothers Against Drunk Driving (MADD) aren't just kill-joy
    parents wanting to spoil party-goers' good times. They have a
    legitimate concern that drunk driving—whether it's alcohol
    or marijuana—is going to put others at risk. And the statistics
    vastly support them!

4. What about the savings in law enforcement and incarceration?

    For any new law to be a real savings, it has to more than
    offset the other costs that no longer enforcing the old law might
    cause. You might put fewer people in jail for buying or selling
    drugs, but you might incarcerate more for the irresponsible
    things they'll do when their inhibitions disappear…rape, abuse,
    burglary, violence, kidnapping, murder…all very costly to a
    peaceable society.

5. What about the potential for tax revenue?

That our lawmakers would be willing to consider surrendering a peaceable society just because they cannot control their own addiction to spending is hypocritical at best. You cannot tax something addictive into non-use. Tobacco use is proof of that. Lawmakers think so-called sin-taxes diminish their practice, all the while they know their increasing revenue from taxing those "vices" is an indication of the hold they have on some people. It is kind of like gambling revenues going to education…it is nothing other than a thinly veiled attempt to justify something that is a net loss economically, socially, and culturally.

6. If it's wrong for teens, why is it right for adults?

There are many activities that are appropriately restricted for younger people. Movie ratings come to mind. I will say, however, there are also some activities that are not appropriate at any age. We generally have laws against these things. I will also say that you can't make laws fast enough to corral a lawless society. People who cannot control themselves usually end up in jail…society's attempt at sequestering those who refuse to grow up and act responsibly.

Recommended reading list:

- *Changing Your Stars: Empowerment for a Different Destiny*, Alan E. Sargent
- *Breaking Free: Making Liberty in Christ a Reality in Life*, Beth Moore
- *Addiction: The Master Keys to Recovery*, Dr. Michael J. De Vito

Web sites:

- www.addictionrecoverykeys.com/
- www.pachills.com
- www.teenchallengeusa.com

4

Angels and Demons

I can close my eyes and I still feel the wind in my hair, the sun on my cheeks…the same things I felt as I laid there after the wreck, waiting for the ambulance—you know, the noise of a wreck is deafening, but it cannot compare in magnitude to the silence that reigns after.

We had been travelling all night. I drove till breakfast, but now that we were back on the road again and the heater was blowing hot air on my feet, I fell to a much-needed sleep. We had just spent the Christmas holidays of 1985 in Massachusetts, my wife's old stomping grounds, and were making our way back to Tulsa. The boys, seven and nine, were asleep in the back of our brand new Jeep Wagoneer, the last vestige of a once-prosperous lifestyle. My wife's rotund seven-and-a-half-month pregnant bulge—containing my daughter—left little room for steering, but my sleepiness had forced her to take over the driving.

About 9:00 a.m., on January 2, 1986, somewhere on Interstate 40 in the mountains of Crossville, Tennessee, I was awakened to my wife's screams…the car was sliding out of control on a black-ice-covered section of asphalt. Instinctively, seeing the rapidly approaching edge of the three-hundred-foot embankment that went down to the other two east-bound lanes, I grabbed the steering wheel and turned it hard to the right. Suddenly, the patch of black ice came to an abrupt end and the sliding tires caught on cold dry asphalt; the vehicle careened into the opposite mountain cut, going instantly from 65 mph to zero on a sheer face of rock.

That any of us survived is a miracle. Lynn only had a few cuts (one small scar on her forehead is all that remains); one boy twisted his ankle, the other had a sprained knee, and Anna ended up a ten-month baby (the pregnancy went into shock); I sustained the bulk of the injuries—the impact was on the front right corner of the car—later they diagnosed me with a broken back (T2), a fractured pelvis, a shattered right sub-talus (heel), all the ribs and cartilage tissue in my chest separated and internal bleeding. Although I never lost consciousness, the pain was tremendous.

Initially, shock from the impact was sufficient to shield me from the pain, and with the help of my wife, I was able to get out and at least lay on the ground. My older son, Jeremy, prayed in the Spirit as fast as he could, Jon was crying...a trucker stopped and called 911...a bearded man in a flannel shirt and jeans comforted the kids (we assumed he was with the trucker) while the EMTs put me on a gurney. I heard the bearded man say to Jeremy, "You just keep praying, son; everything is going to be alright."

The rest is history...the arguing of the emergency room doctors in Crossville over my blood type (O+), the cursing of one doctor as they realized they didn't have any (because it was the most in demand), the doctors telling my wife to tell me good-bye because they didn't think I would survive the life flight to the University of Tennessee hospital...and hobbling out of the hospital five days later!

While I was recovering back in Tulsa, we decided to thank all those people that had helped at the wreck site. We called the trucking company, the highway patrol, and the ambulance folks. Although they graciously received our thanks, none of them remembered the man in the flannel shirt. Even the trucker said he never traveled with a partner. Yet our family all remembered that man being there. We could only conclude we had been blessed by an angelic visitation (Heb. 13:2).

The more I share that story, the more I find out that others have similar stories of special visitations in their hours of need or during especially challenging situations. Angels, who do the bidding of God (Ps. 91:11), are the messengers of God (Gen. 28:12), are extremely strong (Ps. 103:20), and assigned individually to us (Matt. 18:10), often show up when we least expect them.

Are angels and demons real and biblical or just legendary and mythical? What is the purpose of angels? What is the purpose of demons? Where do angels and demons come from? Do angels and demons still work on the earth? These are the questions that thinking Christians must ask.

According to a dictionary amalgamation, an *Angel* is a celestial intermediary, affecting the will of heaven on the earth, and usually in humanoid form. A *Demon* is a malevolent spiritual being, often depicted as an afflicting agent of evil. According to the Bible, angels were created by God, though some fell—the origin of demons—in a great rebellion against God, led by Lucifer, the leader of the angels (see Isaiah 14 and Ezekiel 28).

Answering questions:

1. Are angels and demons real and biblical or just legendary and mythical?

   To give the reader a starting place for an understanding of something movies and stories are quick to communicate and facts are slow to corroborate, let me begin with some basic knowledge.

Angels:

A. Angels have only a male designation, at least as far as they are discussed in Scripture (although they are depicted in pop culture often as female in gender, the only named angels {actually archangels or "ruling angels"}—Michael {Jude 9}, Gabriel {Luke 1:26}, Lucifer {Isaiah 14:12; Rev. 2:5}, and Abaddon [Hebrew] or Apollyon [Greek]{Rev. 9:11}are always male in gender.

B. Angels have been assigned to be witnesses of creation (Job 38:7), messengers of God to Mankind (2 Chron. 36:16), and as individual helpers on a mission (Gen. 19:1–28).

C. Angels have the power to destroy (2 Kings 19:35), but they do the bidding of God when they do (Ps. 103:21).

D. Angels are numerous (Ps. 68:17), strong (Ps. 03:20), and protect us (Ps. 91:11).

E. Synonyms for angels:
   1. Ministering spirits (Heb. 1:13–14)
   2. Sons of God (Gen. 6:20; Job 38:7)
   3. Morning stars—actually archangels—(Job 38:7; Is. 14:13)
   4. The angel of the Lord—many theologians believe this is a name assigned to Jesus as He appeared to men in the Old Testament (Gen. 16, 22; Ex. 3, Num. 22, Judges 2, etc.)

Demons:

A. As fallen angels, they rebelled with Lucifer and were ejected from heaven (in fact, most of what we know about the origin of Lucifer and the rebellion against God he led, taking one-third of the angels with him, etc., we learn from two passages of Scripture in Isaiah 14 and Ezekiel 28; in Is. 14, an analogy is drawn between the complete destruction of the king of Babylon and Lucifer, likening his sin with Lucifer's, and his destruction; in Ez. 28, God has the "prince of Tyrus" in the crosshairs—his destruction will be like the "king of Tyrus" [another name for Lucifer] because his sin was like Lucifer's).

B. Demons fathered bastard offspring with the "daughters of men," creating the mutant giant race (Gen. 6:1–4)—many theologians think this is where some of the Greeks got their mythological heroes; and the origin of Goliath and his brothers—the last offspring of this race.

C. Demons have a hierarchy to which they answer (Eph. 6:12), but they generally have the purpose of destruction that Lucifer (Satan) has (John 10:10).

D. Demons fall into different categories based on the kinds of afflictions they bring, a source of some their synonyms (this is a partial list; Legion had thousands of demons in him [Mk. 5:9]):

1. Satan (also known as the *Devil*—Matt. 4:5, *Lucifer*—Is. 14:12, Rev. 2:5, the *Dragon* or the Serpent—Rev. 12:9, the *Prince of devils*—Matt. 9:34, *Beelzebub*—Luke 11:14 [which literally translated means: "the lord of the flies"], the *prince of demons*—Matt. 12:24, the *Prince of this World*—John 12:31 and *Leviathan*—Is. 27:1).

2. Familiar spirits—Lev. 19:31

3. Unclean spirits—Matt. 10:1

4. Seducing (or deceitful) spirits—I Tim. 4:1

5. Evil spirits—Luke 8:2

6. Spirit of infirmity—Luke 13:11

7. Spirit of jealousy—Num. 5:14

8. Spirit of distortion—Is. 19:14

9. Spirit of divination—Acts 16:16

10. Spirit of fainting—Is. 61:3

11. Spirit of harlotry—Hosea 4:12

2. What is the purpose of angels?

The primary purpose of angels or "ministering spirits" is to do just that: minister. The real question is to whom are they to minister and by Whom are they sent? Both questions find their answer in the passage in Hebrews 2:13–14. They are sent *by* God and sent *to* us, those who are to "inherit salvation."

3. What is the purpose of demons?

Just as Jesus came to "destroy the works of the Devil" (I John 3:8), so also the purpose of demons is to destroy the work of God (John 10:10). Everywhere they can, they will thwart God's work. Since we are His workmanship (Eph. 2:10), his primary strategy is to deceive us into thinking we are worthless—can you see why Christians believe every life has value?

4. Where do angels and demons come from?

The short answer is: The heart of God. The obvious response to that is: How could a good God create something so evil? The answer to that is: He did not create Lucifer or any of the demons in their "fallen state." Isaiah 14 and Ezekiel 28 tell us of a spiritual battle before man was created between Lucifer, who had been created "perfect" (Ezek. 28:15), and God. When we first see Lucifer in the Garden of Eden, he is already in a fallen state. As a serpent, he tempts Eve and Adam—who was "with her" (Gen. 3:6). By believing him and disobeying God, they traded what they had—authority over their realm—for a place subservient to Satan, for whom you obey is your master. This is how Satan came to be the Prince of this World…Adam, who had been given authority over the earthly realm (Gen. 1:28), gave over this authority when he obeyed the serpent rather than God (Gen 3:1–19).

The demons are "fallen" angels who do the bidding of their master, Satan, the prince of demons (Matt. 12:24). They rebelled with Lucifer (which literally translated means "bearer of light") and fell with him (Isaiah 14:12–15)…numbering in their horde one-third of all the angels (Rev. 12:7, 9).

5. Do angels and demons still work on the earth?

Of course they do. Although the demons' and the Devil's fate is sealed (Matt. 25:41), they still struggle against us (John 10:10). What we must remember, is that this is a spiritual battle (Eph. 6:12), not a physical one. Although there are real consequences in the physical world—Hitler did exterminate over six million Jews—the battle is first spiritual.

When I was in Belize once leading a mission team, one of our evening's activities was to join the small local body of believers in a "prayer march." They were marching each night around the 'dagoo,' a grass hut built for the 'worship' services of the traveling voodoo witch doctor from Miami. The witch doctor would often charge these impoverished villagers thousands for a few moments of 'connection' with dead relatives. They would allegedly 'communicate' with the spirits of the dead who would 'manifest' through her—the witch doctor—to the relative...they're called spiritists or mediums in the Bible (Lev. 19:21; 20:6) and encouraging the activity of demons is strictly forbidden (demons would masquerade as the departed spirits).

We found out later that the witch doctor had been run out of town as a fraud because she couldn't get the demons to manifest all that week—the week that we had been praying.

We have been given spiritual weapons that are very effective against the enemy, but they are not wielded in the same way (2 Cor. 10:4).

Recommended reading list:

- *Angels*, Billy Graham
- *The Unseen World: Christian Reflections on Angels, Demons and the Heavenly Realm*, A. N. S. Lane
- *The Screwtape Letters*, C. S. Lewis

Web sites:

- www.evangelicaloutreach.org/angels
- www.focusonjerusalem.com/angelsanddemons.html
- www.spiritualwarfaredeliverance.com/html/christian

5

Astrology, Horoscopes, and the Occult

Some people joke about a wicked stepmother...I don't. Although my first stepmother was emotionally abusive of my mentally handicapped older brother and me, I do not consider her as wicked...just the product of her dysfunctional family. I cannot say the same about my second stepmother. I mean, she had a crystal ball, used tarot cards, astral projection, and was convinced she was the reincarnation of a nine-year-old girl from fourteenth-century Scotland...what would you say?

Now, in her defense, I have to say she meant well—she even said that she only performed "white witchcraft"—little comfort to me, a Christian. I didn't take her too seriously until my wife and I picked up our emotionally distraught two-year-old we had left with grandma and grandpa to babysit. He was by the front door whimpering in abject terror when we arrived...to this day, we don't know what happened that night, but Jeremy was inconsolable for hours.

Things finally came to a head when she called about six months later asking if they could have Jeremy stay overnight. I responded that he could, if I accompanied him. She asked, "Don't you trust us?" She was baiting me and I knew it. I didn't care. I was not about to subject my son to her spiritual influence for a minute, let alone overnight. "Frankly, no," I blurted out. "After all, you're a witch." She hung up on me.

My wife, who had been privy to my side of the conversation, just looked at me in shock. Ten seconds later, the phone rang again. This time it was my dad. "You are going to regret what you just said the rest of your life." And then he hung up, too. A week later we moved out of town.

Is astrology biblical? What about Ouija boards, séances, and mediums...aren't they just innocent forms of magic—parlor tricks to entertain and amuse? What about reading your horoscope? What about the occult? Is there any power in an inanimate object or is that just superstition? These are the questions that the thinking Christian must answer.

Astrology, according to the dictionary, consists of a belief system where there is an influence exerted by celestial objects on human behavior; it is not to be confused with astronomy. According to the Bible, many of these "dark-side" spiritual activities are an abomination to the Lord (Deut. 18:10–12).

Answering questions:

1. Is astrology biblical?

   The word "astrology" comes from two words—*aster* (star) and *logos* (word). Earlier, in the dictionary definition, I said, "Not to be confused with *astronomy*." Astronomy has to do with the message behind the "names" of the stars (*aster* + *nomen*).

   Actually, astrology comes from ancient Greek tradition and was based on a geocentric perspective; most of the calculations have been carried down to contemporary times through this faulty view...since Copernicus, we've known that the sun—Sol—was the center of our *Sol*ar System.

   Being born "under" a certain zodiacal sign does not indicate proclivities for certain behaviors, nor are there certain activities that should be avoided during certain times. Our desire to seek an "oracle" rather than God's wisdom in our decision making is a testimony to our impatience and our susceptibility to superstition. Much of the wisdom of Scripture does not get gleaned by the casual reader, but only is revealed to the serious student of the Word. Perhaps another reason we seek an oracle—read: "an easier route"—is that we are just too lazy.

2. What about Ouija boards, séances, and mediums…aren't they just innocent forms of magic—parlor tricks to entertain and amuse?

We Christians, being spiritually alive, have a tendency to be drawn to the spiritual. But we must keep in mind that for every good thing, there is an evil counterpart…not equal in power or authority, for indeed the greater force is God (1 John 4:4); yet a force that exists in the absence of good. (Just as cold is the absence of heat and darkness is the absence of light, so evil is the absence of good). As Edmund Burke once said, "All that is necessary for the triumph of evil is that good men do nothing."

Ouija boards, séances, tarot cards, fortune tellers…all have one thing in common: They all seek to reveal the unknown by encouraging the activity of demons. Demons—the Bible calls them in Hebrew: *shed* from which we get "shade" or the image produced when the light is blocked—have been around since the fall of Lucifer (Isaiah 14 and Ezekiel 28). The rebellion he led resulted in one-third of the angels falling (Rev. 12:4). Their longevity gives them increased knowledge and they often use that knowledge to masquerade as those that have departed this life (I Sam. 28:7). Those that are adept at encouraging the activity of demons are called mediums or spiritists or those that operate with "familiar spirits."

Do those mediums have real power? Yes, but their power is rooted in their ability to deceive through imitation, intimidation, and fear. More about this in the article on "Angels and Demons."

If these things reveal real truth, why shouldn't we seek knowledge in this way? *Because God is the only authorized fount of truth.* What is revealed through Ouija boards, tarot cards, séances, and mediums will be intended to deceive or gain a hold in some way. Besides, the soul has a latent power that was locked inside of man for a reason. Adam possessed much intelligence, but his fall caused God to take control of this from him. Disconnected from God, the soul only devises self-seeking purposes. The power of the Holy Spirit, in some measure, returns this power to the Christian in the gifts of the Spirit (I Cor. 12).

3. What about reading your horoscope?

It may seem a harmless amusement, but those that read their horoscope open a door to its deception. To act on that deception only gives the Deceiver (read: Satan) power, and the legal right to accuse you in the courtroom of heaven. Lucifer is called the "Accuser of the brethren" (Rev. 12:10) for a reason.

4. What about the occult?

The root of the word "occult" means "to block the light of." In fact, in astronomy, an "occultation" occurs when a celestial object passes in front of another celestial object. (Occultations can reveal much to the astronomer and the astrophysicist about the atmosphere, if any, surrounding the occluding object.)

Anything that blocks the light of God is occultic, inferior, and deceptive and should never be preferred to the true revelation only brought about by the unimpeded light of God's Word (Psalms 119:105).

5. Is there any power in an inanimate object or is that just superstition?

Demons seek to find their highest form of expression— human possession, if possible; if not, a herd of pigs may suffice (Matt. 8:31; again more in the article on "Angels and Demons"— an inanimate object is almost no expression at all. Although there may be some demonic power in an inanimate object our fear of that only enables the enemy. We should remember, "You are from God, little children, and have overcome them; because greater is He who is in you than he who is in the world" (I John 4:4, NASU).

Recommended reading list:

- *The Latent Power of the Soul*, Watchman Nee
- *A Christian Response to Dungeons and Dragons*, Peter Leithart and George Grant
- *The Heavens Declare*, William D. Banks

Web sites:

- www.northforest.org/ChristianTopics/Astrology
- www.biblestudysite.com/astrol
- www.gospelway.com/religiousgroups/astrology

6

Authority and Submission

My dad was a disciplinarian back when "Grab your ankles!" was not an invitation to change your shoes...back when the Decalogue was the Ten Commandments, not the Ten Suggestions! However, I am a believer in the carrot *and* the stick, the rod *and* the staff. You can either drive the sheep or lead them...usually, some of both are required.

As a Boy Scout, I learned that hierarchy—the flow of authority—is necessary, that leadership is earned, that rank has its privileges...and responsibilities, and that chaos reigns when those called to lead don't. Sometimes we would elect a popular patrol leader everybody liked, but we would then do poorly in competitions. We performed best when we had a leader that led. We may not always have liked the orders he gave, but submitting to them won us more ribbons and the occasional "at-a-boy" from our Senior Patrol Leader John Ashby.

It was the same way in high school. When Mr. Huffer, our marching band director, said to turn right, obedience led to order...and the accurate spelling of the right word on the football field at half-time. When Mr. Dunn or Mr. Jeffries said to study a certain chapter for the upcoming chemistry or physics test, submission to that directive was self-preservational and wise.

College and later the work-a-day world were no different. There were those placed in authority and those who had to submit to that authority. It was easier to submit to those who had learned the value of "servant leadership." Truly, John C. Maxwell was right when he said, "People don't care how much you know, until they know how much you care."

Life has a tendency to bless right behavior. Of course, there are always exceptions to which one can point...where injustice has triumphed or obedience has been rewarded with persecution...but even that seems to be temporary—justice finally being served by the vacuum of righteousness created.

There is a *right* hierarchy—a *proper* flow of authority—in almost everything. Although sometimes it seems arbitrary, there is usually a reason the person in charge is so. Even in the Holy Trinity there is a hierarchy. The Son submitted to the sending of the Father and the Holy Spirit submitted to the sending of the Son (John 20:20–21). Man, created in God's image (Gen. 1:26), is also under a hierarchy; the spirit rules over the soul, and the soul—reason, will, and emotion—rules over the body.

Man was created to rule over the earth (Gen. 1:28–30) but gave up that authority to Satan by obeying the serpent rather than God (Gen. 3). When Jesus, the second Adam (I Cor. 15:45–48), died for our sins (Rom. 5:8), He took back that authority (Matt. 28:18) and He will ultimately restore it all to us (2 Tim. 2:12).

Even in the Christian home, there is a proper hierarchy. The husband rules over the wife (Gen. 3:16), together they rule over the children (Col. 3:20, Eph. 6:1)...and the kids pick on the dog, right? Actually, the same grace that gives those in authority the wisdom to rule justly provides those who submit with the patience and respect required not to rebel...or pick on the dog.

Is authority and submission a biblical concept? It is easier to be in authority, isn't it? It's easier to order other people around than to have to be the one submitting to those orders, isn't it? Why do we live in a male-dominated society...or is that an assumption that reveals my misogynistic perspective? Why does anyone have to be in charge? I mean, who died and left you king? Surely the one most knowledgeable should be in authority, right? These and other questions are the ones thinking Christians should be asking.

According to a combination of what many dictionaries say, *Authority* is the power to command obedience or determine what is right. *Submission* is the acknowledgement of inferiority in position or the willingness to acquiesce to someone's superiority of position. Note that inferiority and superiority are purely positional considerations, not a judgment of the person. I believe that the one who is in submission to someone in authority over them actually has an underlying mission—a sub-mission—which is vital and supportive to success.

Answering questions:

1. Is authority and submission a biblical concept?

    Of course it is, as evidenced by my introductory remarks on this subject. But what gives God the right to be the Ultimate Authority? In a word, creation (Gen. 1:1). Whoever invents, creates, or makes something knows best how it works. Authority comes from the same Latin word *auctoritas* as author does. As the "Author and Finisher of our faith" (Heb. 12:2), His authorship gives Him the exclusive right of control of His "work."

    Christians are required to submit to those in authority (Rom. 13:1–5), except where obedience to that authority might require disobedience to God (Acts 5:29).

2. It is easier to be in authority, isn't it? It's easier to order other people around than to have to be the one submitting to those orders, isn't it?

    Actually, the one in ultimate authority is also the one in ultimate responsibility. Although one may delegate power or control over some aspect of his task, the responsibility for that task remains his…that's what President Harry Truman meant when he said, "The buck stops here."

    It may be easy to say that you are the one in authority, but to assume the responsibility for anything is not so easy. Giving orders to others may mean that you are sharing the task with those who are submitting to your authority, but it does not absolve you of your responsibility for completing that task successfully. If you can't bear the responsibility, don't covet the authority.

3. Why do we live in a male-dominated society...or is that an assumption that reveals my misogynistic perspective?

Blame God, right? I mean, He's the One Who set it up that way (Gen. 3:16; Eph. 5:23), didn't He? That's right, He did; and for a reason. From the beginning, God chose Adam to be the one in charge. He drew Eve from Adam's side (Gen. 2:21–23), not the other way around (1 Cor. 11:8–9). Someone had to have responsibility, and it would have been unfair for God to hold him responsible for that over which he had no authority. That's why He only uses one verse to pronounce His curse upon the Woman (Gen. 3:16) and three verses to pronounce His curse on the Man (Gen. 3:17–19).

Authority in the home is a reflection of the relationship of Christ and the Church (Eph. 5:22–33). Even as Christ is to be the Head of the Church, so is the husband to be the head of the wife (Eph. 5:22). Some have argued that both are to be submitted to each other, quoting Ephesians 5:21, but that is taking this verse out of context. Read it for yourselves. This verse comes at the end of Paul's instruction to the Church brethren. His instructions concerning the relationship between husbands and wives do not begin till verse 22. Besides, anything with two heads is a monster!

4. Why does anyone have to be in charge?

Simply, because responsibility must be singular, so must authority. When everybody's responsible, nobody's responsible. Chaos reigns when nobody's in charge. Anarchy reigns when everyone's in charge. When everybody does what is right in his own eyes, only the strongest prevails...and might does not make right, it only makes fright!

5. I mean, who died and left you king?

In fact, Jesus! His death and resurrection will put us all—who believe—in a royal way (2 Tim. 2:12; Rev. 20:6). Right now, we're in training; that's why salvation occurs at a moment in time, but redemption is a process. I have a T-shirt that has half the truth…it says, "IT IS WHAT IT IS." That may be true, but it's not the Truth. One day I'm going to print on the back, "BUT IT'S NOT WHAT IT'S GOING TO BE!"

There is a lot of transformation that is going to be required before we'll be ready to take the reins of anything that is substantial. That's what Church leaders are for (Eph. 4:11–15)—bringing us to the "unity of the faith." That's what the Word is for (Eph. 5:26). And we need this process of preparation for *as the king goes, so goes the kingdom.*

6. Surely the one most knowledgeable should be in authority, right?

Well, that's one of the prerequisites, for sure; which is why the constituency needs to do its homework. We don't need to invest the unqualified with a position of authority. However, integrity and experience both count for even more than knowledge… and all of that before party affiliation. A spoils system only leads to cronyism, favoritism, and injustice.

Authority and submission require each other to operate successfully. Authority must operate within the bounds of the rule of law…and with humility, patience, and gentleness (Eph. 4:2). Submission must be wise, won, and willing.

Recommended reading list:

- *Authority from God*, Randy Clark
- *Spiritual Authority*, Watchman Nee
- *The Authority of the Believer*, J. A. MacMillan
- *Roman 13: The True Meaning of Submission, 2nd Edition*, Timothy Baldwin, JD and Dr. Chuck Baldwin

Web sites:

- www.victorious.org/authority.html
- www.durrance.com/FrAl/CHRISTIAN%20AUTHORITY. html
- www.characterbuildingforfamilies.com/authoritybeliever. html

7

Birth Control

Before I say anything, I must caution you to read to the end.

"I am so sorry, babe. Perhaps if we had come to this conclusion sooner, things would have been different." This is the remark I made to my wife, after we had our late-life miscarriage. To say we were devastated is an understatement.

I'd like to think we were mature enough Christians to arrive at the decision earlier—the decision to allow God to rule in the area of our procreativity—but we weren't. Maybe it was our hedonistic culture that was so self-indulgent…maybe it was everyone who said it would cost too much to bring another child into this world… maybe it's the fact that I had always looked down on others who had a lot of children (I mean, didn't they know what was causing them to get pregnant all the time?!)…maybe it was Dr. Ehrlich's book (*The Population Bomb*)…or a combination of these.

In any case, I didn't arrive at this conclusion until I was forced to consider what might be God's view. This happened in the summer of 1987…I remember it because I was looking at the prospects of becoming a full-time teacher at Applied Life Christian College… and I knew the greater responsibility I would have to communicate the truth. I was scared spitless! What if I taught a lie? What if I were to teach one thing, only to find out later that I was teaching heresy?! There were many things in my personal theology that were still "up in the air." I determined to spend that summer coming to some conclusions.

The conclusion I arrived at in the area of birth control was not politically correct. In fact, there were many Christians that espoused quite a different view. I told no one what I discovered in the Scriptures. Partly because I was afraid to...partly because I knew my wife would say, "That's easy for *you* to say!" Others would say I had been converted to Roman Catholicism (they are not in favor of contraception), or I had gone off the deep end, or that I must have come into some money (it has been totaled by some that you will spend $180,000 per child...before they get to college).

So, what did I find in the Scriptures regarding birth control? Nothing. In fact, everything I found only had encouragement to reproduce. For example:

> And God blessed them: and God said unto them, *°be fruitful, and multiply*, and replenish the earth, and subdue it; and have dominion over the fish of the sea, and over the birds of the heavens, and over every living thing that moveth upon the earth." (Gen. 1:28, ASV)

In fact, God uses this phrase "be fruitful, and multiply," five more times in Scripture (Gen. 8:17, 9:1, 35:11; Jer. 23:3; Ezek. 36:11). I didn't even include His command to all creation in Genesis 1:22 to "be fruitful and multiply"—a general attitude, not just a command.

> As arrows are in the hand of a mighty man; so are children of the youth. Happy is the man that hath his quiver full of them: they shall not be ashamed, but they shall speak with the enemies in the gate. (Ps. 127:4–5, KJV)

> The godly always give generous loans to others, and their children are a blessing. (Ps. 37:26, NLT)

> Lo, children are a heritage of Jehovah; (and) the fruit of the womb is (his) reward. (Ps. 127:3, ASV)

I challenge anyone and everyone: *find me a scripture that condemns fruitfulness.* Barrenness in Scripture is a sign of *disfavor* (Gen 26:1; Deut. 7:24; 2 Kings 2:21; Ps. 107:34), *never of favor.*

To say that Lynn and I were instant converts is to warp the truth. True, I came to that conclusion as I began teaching that fall, but the conviction grew until I began to try to get my wife to see it from my perspective…one has to understand she was an only child and had not spent much time baby-sitting growing up; when we had our first child, she was already twenty-eight…by the time she arrived at my conclusion on the matter, her abilities to conceive and carry to full term had been diminished (her age then, forty-nine). We both knew the risks, but surrendered that area in time to experience the agony of a false start. Regret is where the past meets the present to guide the future.

Is birth control biblical? What are the options for Christians? Isn't it better for single Christians to carry a condom (in the purse or wallet) than to have an unwanted pregnancy? Where do aborted babies and miscarriages go, heaven or hell? What about non-Christians; what are their options? Isn't the earth replenished yet? These, and other questions, are the ones thinking Christians should be asking themselves.

According to a combination of what many dictionaries say, *Birth Control* is the act of preventing birth. But more definition is needed. Some birth control is really abortion…whether by abortifacient drugs (the "morning after pill") or by physical removal; some is by judicially managing the exposure of the ovum to the sperm (called "the rhythm method"), or impeding their progress (the use of a condom and diaphragm)…then there's the IUD (intrauterine device)—both the copper clad and hormonal types—Novaring, "The Pill" (hormonal or progestin-only type or "mini-pill"), the injection, the patch, etc., but I am not a gynecologist nor a medical doctor of any kind—a qualified medical professional is always a good place to start when seriously considering any kind of contraception.

Answering questions:

1. Is birth control biblical?

    No; again I challenge anyone to find me a scripture that even hints of birth control in a positive context. God is, of course, in favor of completely turning everything over to Him (Acts 10:36; Romans 10:12). The concept of Lordship is unconditional surrender—one might even say, "If He's not Lord of all, He's not Lord *at all*."

    Now, I know this is a hard saying. We want to obey when it's convenient. But if there's anything inconvenient—even with nine months to prepare—it is bringing a child into this world! Talk about upsetting the apple cart! From less sleep, to increased expenses, to planning everything around the realities of a new baby...nothing could be more of an interruption. Of course that could be the point...or at least a part of it. Nothing makes us humans identify with God's frustration with us, than being parents ourselves.

    And just think about the ills it might solve: less debt and deficit with more people to tax; more consumers—and our economy is consumer-based; fewer parents dependent on the government in old age—maybe this is how it was handled before Social Security and Medicare; and maybe no more vendetta against the US by radical Islam—one of the reasons they call us "The Great Satan" is our abortion-on-demand policy. Who knows, maybe we would have more disease, less food, and more unemployment...but maybe our disease curers, food inventors, and job creators were all aborted or never even conceived!

2. What are the options for Christians?

    There are many who don't want children. Is it possible to be married and not have kids...and still not be sexually frustrated? Of course. Besides the other ways to satisfy your mate's sexual desires—volumes have been written on this subject (even from a Christian perspective)—there is also the possibility that sexual satisfaction, contrary to popular opinion, might not be the most important factor in a happy marriage. People hate abstinence because it means saying no to yourself...and yes to self-control, which is a fruit of the Spirit (Gal. 5:22).

Also, many have successfully monitored their mean body temperature to determine optimum fertility in order to avoid intercourse at these times—or to plan a pregnancy by coming together opportunely. Again, consult your physician.

And, of course, you may choose to control outcomes by taking it more out of God's hands—as your faith is, so be it unto you. If your subsequent revelation condemns you, you are only a prayer away from forgiveness. Just remember, that proof of repentance is changed behavior.

3. Isn't it better for single Christians to carry a condom (in the purse or wallet) than to have an unwanted pregnancy?

Gee, I don't know. On the one hand, we *are* making a provision for the flesh, and we are told never to do that (Romans 13:14). The time to pray for self-control is before the date—not when we are scouring our brains to think of some comfortable place where we can be privately alone together. As the old saying goes, it is not good to sow our wild oats on Saturday night, and then pray for a crop failure on Sunday morning.

On the other hand, it would be great if we could be excited over the prospects of a child rather than filled with dread. The best advice is this: Don't be sexually intimate until you're married; don't get married until you're ready to get pregnant (of course, you're never really ready); and trust God with your procreativity.

4. Where do aborted babies and miscarriages go, heaven or hell?

Whether caused by a rape, a sin on yours or someone else's part, or by happenstance or something genetic, it was not the baby's fault. Heaven is well populated with such and the Supreme Judge is merciful (Matt. 19:14; Mk. 10:14; Lk. 18:16).

5. What about non-Christians—what are their options?

This is being written to Christians; non-Christians may have more "options," but the Bible says eternity in hell is a certainty if they don't make Jesus Lord (Rom. 3:23, 6:23, 10:9–10). Again, I'm not a medical doctor, but they can choose a Pro-Life approach to birth control or a pro-death approach (since such self-condemning terms are not pleasant or PC, they choose to call their position: Pro-Choice).

Pro-Choice folks (and I don't mean to say that you can't be a Christian and have a Pro-Choice stand…just not for long; we are all on a learning curve; but make no mistake about it; in my opinion—and I think Scripture supports me—God is pro-life and His children will come to see it as He does) have many "options."

In addition to the other obvious ones previously mentioned, there is the abortion and the abortifacients. Whether it's in the first, second or third trimester, the abortion is still taking a life. Some may make an exception in the case of rape or incest—though my wife and I might disagree with them (she was the product of a rape). The abortifacients are those drugs—including the "morning after pill"—that prevent a fertilized egg from implantation on the uterine wall. Christians believe that life begins at conception. In fact, life begins in the heart of God (Jer. 1:5).

The most heinous form of abortion—though one could argue that all abortion is murder—is the dilation and extraction procedure where the late-term child is delivered except for the head. The cranial cavity is then collapsed and its contents extracted—which of course results in the painful and immediate death of the infant—and the now deceased infant's delivery is completed (the infant is discarded). As of this writing, this barbaric procedure has been outlawed in many states.

6. Isn't the earth replenished yet?

Hardly…for my answer to this, see my article on "Abortion," where I actually do the math for the statement that every person on the face of the earth would fit in the state of Texas.

There is a huge paradigm shift coming everywhere Christians have bought into the philosophy of managing their own birth rates (check the incidence of births by ethnic group and country in Europe—you'll find the top birth rates *and the future voting majorities* are held by Muslims or others who do not believe in or practice contraception). Besides, God is well able to control our birth rates if we give him the chance (check out the increase in male births after WWII).

Answering other questions:

1. What about cost?

Some say they can't afford to have more children. I thought God was the ultimate provider! Besides, I don't know of any large Christian families that don't have their needs met, do you?

2. What about unwed mothers?

Good thing they didn't regularly practice abortion when Joseph and Mary had their experience, huh?

3. What about being one of those late-life births? Wouldn't that inherently disadvantage you?

I don't know…I guess I'll ask John and Charles Wesley when I see them…they were the fifteenth and seventeenth (of nineteen) children of Samuel and Susannah, herself the twenty-fifth of twenty-five children. Charles, the younger brother of the founder of the Methodist Church, wrote and published over six thousand hymns. His son, Samuel, was known as "the English Mozart"; his grandson Samuel Sebastian was one of the foremost composers of the nineteenth century.

My wife and I recovered from our loss and have been delighted with the adoption of four children by one of our sons and his wife. Although we have made many mistakes in our own decisions about birth control, we have been forgiven and continue to advocate what we have come to believe is a Christian ethos.

Recommended reading list:

- *Godly Seed: American Evangelicals Confront Birth Control, 1873–1973*, Allan Carlson
- *Taking Charge of Your Fertility: 10th Anniversary Edition*, Toni Weschler
- *Hannah's Hope: Seeking God's Heart in the Midst of Infertility, Miscarriage and Adoption Loss*, Jennifer Saake

Web sites:

- www.site.themarriagebed.com/biology/birth-control
- www.not-the-pill.com
- www.christiancontraception.com

8

The Church

It is a little bit strange—at least it was in those days—to attend the wedding ceremony of your parents, but I distinctly remember it. Grace Episcopal Church, I think, in Muskogee, Oklahoma…I especially remember the smells—burning candles and oldness (probably came from their need to replace the upholstery on the massive dark-stained wooden pews). I don't remember much else—I was only four—my stepmother, Betty, wore white (I think she wore a cap-looking hat with a veil on the front, covered here and there with white pearls); my dad wore a black suit with shiny lapels and a thin straight back tie. I remember the priest standing in the front of a very long aisle.

So we became Episcopalians; my dad didn't care much…one church was as good as another and he wanted his new bride to be happy, I'm sure. I had been born a Presbyterian—I mean, my mom *was* the daughter of the pastor of the Pastor of First Presbyterian Church—but she died of Hodgkin's lymphoma when I was two. The Vacation Bible School I attended in the summer was put on by the Baptists; the church I attended after my mother got sick was a Disciples of Christ church where my grandmother on my father's side sang in the choir; later, after my dad remarried (Betty), we joined another Episcopal church (St. Edward's), a little closer to home; later, I was born again at First Methodist (and I've ministered in churches in at least thirty other denominations and even met the Pope). I guess you would say I was a "Heinz 57" Christian.

Who is the Church?

However, I said all of that to say this: Sitting in a church doesn't make you any more a Christian than sitting in a garage makes you a car. It just doesn't work that way. There are churches...and then there is *the* Church. Let me explain. There are many groups of "Christians" who are members of those churches and their respective denominations; and some of them (only God really knows who they are—Matt. 7:21–23) are members of the Church Universal...*the* Church.

In other words, there are many who call themselves Christians who are *Chr*istians *in* n*ame* o*nly*: "Chr-inos" I call them. Maybe they are Baptists, Methodists, Episcopalians, Presbyterians, Mennonites, Quakers (they call themselves "the Society of Friends" today), Evangelicals (although seen more as a group designation, there is a denomination called "Evangelical Free" today), Assemblies (I don't know what the members of "Assemblies of God" call themselves; except Pentecostals perhaps...but not to be confused with those in the Pentecostal Holiness denomination, of course), Completed Jews (those who were Jews, but now claim Jesus as Messiah), or Non-denominationals...but are they Christian? Have they made Jesus Lord (Rom. 10:9–10)?

The question is really an important one as Christ is not coming back for anyone except His Bride, the Church (Rev. 19:7–9). There will be many who will be surprised on that day.

The Mission of the Church

Now that we have established who the Church is—the blood-bought redeemed, all who have been saved by making Jesus the Lord of their lives—let us proceed to our mission. In a word: *sacrifice*. Although some particular churches may be called to different aspects of the Church's mission—inner city missions, international missions, etc.—we are all called to "go into every man's world" (from a quote by Oral Roberts...see also, Matthew 28:18–20). It is our sacrifice that makes us credible. Without it, we'll never leave the comfort of the familiar.

What does sacrifice look like? Basically, that means that we are to find a need and fill it (Phil. 4:19). We earn the right to be heard by meeting the needs of a spiritually lost and dying world. Some cannot hear what the Church has to say for the loudness of their growling stomachs…so we must feed them; some cannot hear what we have to say because of the distraction of their pain… so we must heal them; some cannot hear us for the distraction of their shivering…so we must clothe them. Whether they need clean drinking water for their thirst, shelter from the weather for their bodies, education for their minds, fellowship for their loneliness, comfort for their loss…the Church's mission is the same as Christ's, Who came to seek and save the lost (Luke 19:10).

> One guy complained to his friend, "The poor are getting poorer, the rich only want to spend their excess on themselves, crime is skyrocketing, there are natural disasters happening all around us, the economy is terrible, parents are not accepting responsibility for their kids…isn't it horrible?"
>
> "Yeah," his Christian friend replied. "What a great time to be alive!"

Show me a growling stomach and I'll show you a feeding center. Show me someone sick and I'll show you a hospital. Show me someone in need of an education and I'll show you a Christian school. The real and mature Church is busy doing good works (Eph. 2:10) and communicating their message humbly and sacrificially… *and* their message is transforming (Matt. 16:18).

The Church's Message

What is our message? The same as Christ's: *love*. In fact, love is *measured* in sacrifice. Listen to how the Apostle John puts it in the most famous of all scriptures:

For God so loved the world that He gave His only begotten Son, that whosoever believes on Him should not perish, but have eternal life. (John 3:16)

Knowing that sending His Son would inevitably lead to His death (Heb. 9:24–28), He decided to send Him to the earth anyway. Our message is the same as His. Listen to what Jesus said:

By this all men shall know you are my disciples, that you have love, one for another. (John 13:35)

Again, the Apostle John delineates not just what our (God's and ours) mission is, but also our message. Just as Jesus came to destroy the works of the Devil (1 John 3:8), we have been left here to do the same. All the hunger, nakedness, sickness, and ignorance experienced by Man are a result of the Devil's deceptions...sin and its attendant curses. So the sacrifices we make to feed, clothe, heal, and educate communicate our message...and His: *love*.

Is "The Church" a biblical concept? How do good works translate into our message? If we point to our good works, aren't we really boasting? How is the Church different from just another social club or humanitarian organization? Can't I just as well meet God out in nature or on the golf course? These and other questions are the ones thinking Christians should be asking themselves.

According to a combination of what many dictionaries say, *The Church* is that group of individuals that see themselves as the exclusive recipients of "the truth" of God. Sometimes they have a denominational label—sometimes a lack of a label *is* their label as in "non-denominational" churches—but always "Christian"; it can also refer to the meeting place of a group of Christians if they gather in a structure of some sort. As you can see, the dictionaries miss the point. Just as a family is defined as those with the same last name, so also the Church, as God's family, is defined as those that are related to Him.

Our last name in the family of God is "Christian." "Christian" means "little Christ" (it was actually first given to the early believers in Antioch as an epithet—Acts 11:26). All who claim to be members of the Church, who take the last name, must also take on His mission of *sacrifice* for which He was anointed—*Christos* means "anointed"—and the message He came to deliver—*love* (John 3:16).

Answering questions:

1. Is "The Church" a biblical concept?

    Yes; from the time God spoke to Moses designating that he was to build the tabernacle (Ex. 25:8–39:32) as a specific place to meet Him, God has always dealt with us spatially. Although God is a Spirit (John 4:24), He recognizes Man lives in a world of three-dimensional reality. From the moment God first dealt with Man, he used three-dimensional objects as symbols to communicate abstract truths. Even the tabernacle itself, with all of its symbolic intricacies, was only to point to the reality of man's physical intricacies as He chose to dwell ultimately in us.

    The relationship we have with God, however, is both personal and corporate (Rom. 14:12); and it is intimate and interdependent (Eph. 5:22–32); not that He needs us, but He *chooses* to not exist apart from us. Even though we must each have a personal relationship with God, it is this corporate relationship of interdependency (1 Cor. 12:14–27) that is unique about the Church.

2. How do good works translate into our message?

    When a villager has to walk ten miles round trip to get water, he is ready to listen to anyone who wants to drill a well for his community. I was blessed to help a children's home in Belize build some playground equipment. When I spoke to them, there was rapt attention. When our team helped a village build a hurricane-proof structure for the whole community, it was easy to have a listening audience for our message of God's love. Obvious sacrifice yields obvious fruit…again, as John Maxwell said, "People don't care how much you know until they know how much you care."

Whether it's the Mercy Ships (operating since 1978) bringing free medical care, the Missionaries of Charity (founded by the late Mother Teresa—currently working in 133 countries) feeding the poor, or the unselfish efforts of countless missionaries across the world, the platform for their Gospel message is earned by the good works they do. Although not motivated by the megaphone they have been rightfully given, their message of God's love is heard loud and clear.

3. If we point to our good works, aren't we really boasting?

Yes…but that doesn't mean we shouldn't do them, just that we shouldn't point. The Pharisees were Jesus's target in many of His verbal assaults against the religious establishment of His day (Matt. 23:13–39). He called them many things, but mostly hypocrites. They were great about using one standard for themselves and another for everyone else (if that reminds you of a Congress who often votes to exempt themselves of the very laws they perpetrate on the American public…then you understand the meaning of the word *hypocrite*). Together with the scribes and many of the religious leaders, they were famous for making a great show of their "righteousness" (Matt. 12:38–44).

Boasting has no place in the Church (Rom. 3:27), unless you want to boast of God's goodness in the midst of your unworthiness (1 Cor. 1:31); that is not to say we can't be proud of what God has wrought in others (2 Cor. 7:14, 8:24).

4. How is the Church different from just another social club or humanitarian organization?

In fact, some churches are, sadly, not much different. Social clubs and humanitarian organizations do good—they are many times focused on helping the blind or some disadvantaged segment of society; they raise money for their cause—by dues, fundraisers, or coercing their members; they have speakers that inform and inspire…kind of sounds like many churches, huh? Don't get me wrong; I'm not against social clubs or humanitarian organizations; they do a good work, but Jesus isn't coming back for them.

The Church is much different. It teaches (Matt. 28:20), exhorts (Heb. 10:25), disciplines Heb. 12:5–11), comforts (2 Cor. 1:4–7), encourages (1 Thess. 5:14), rebukes (2 Tim. 4:2), heals (James 5:13–15), *and* identifies the needs of others, meeting them where advisable and possible. It is also the place of worship. Why? Because God is manifestly present when we gather in His Name (Matt. 18:20).

5. Can't I just as well meet God out in nature or on the golf course?

God *is* everywhere present (omnipresent), you are right (Ps. 139:7–12); but why just meet Him on the golf course or at the lake? Why not the office or the grocery store? Let's make Him a part of everything we do. And let's meet Him not just on Sunday, but all seven days a week (Gal. 4:1–10). No, what is really going on in the mind of those arguing for Sunday golf games in lieu of going to church, is an excuse for going golfing *rather* than to gather with other believers! There is a scripture I want to share with those who want to meet God elsewhere.

> …and let us consider how to stimulate one another to love and good deeds, not forsaking our own assembling together, as is the habit of some, but encouraging one another… (Heb. 10:24–25, NASU)

And I love how The Message renders Phil. 4:4. It really gives us an insight into the proper attitude to possess toward our worship.

> Celebrate God all day, every day. I mean, revel in him!

Just like children, there are many churches in the world, no two of them identical (even "identical twins" have a few differences?). Of course, like family members resembling one another, there are denominational identifiers that are unique to each group. But a Good Father loves all His children. Before some contend I'm making an argument for universalism (the belief that all humans are part of God's elect), let me be quick to say that I'm referring to His *love*, not His *acceptance* of our lost condition. Yes, Jesus died for all (proving God's universal love), but not all accept His sacrifice.

There may be cultural differences between one Christian church and another. One may worship God without instruments, another worships with a full orchestra; one may sprinkle at baptism, another may get the congregant—and all those in attendance—wet from head to toe; one may serve communion elements believing they are transformed into the very body and blood of the Savior, another may view it more symbolically. And they may feel that they are the only ones right...just like each child is convinced he is his father's favorite.

Someday we'll all believe the same (Eph. 4:11–16). Until then,

> Beloved, let us love one another, for love is from God; and everyone who loves is born of God and knows God. The one who does not love does not know God, for God is love. By this the love of God was manifested in us: that God has sent His only begotten Son into the world so that we might live through Him. In this is love, not that we loved God, but that He loved us and sent His Son to be the propitiation for our sins. Beloved, if God so loved us, we also ought to love one another. (1 John 4:7–11, NASU)

Recommended reading list:

- *Perspectives on the World Christian Movement,* Editor: Ralph Winter
- *Church History in Plain Language,* Bruce Shelley
- *Every Good Endeavor: Connecting Your Work to God's Work,* Tim Keller and Katherine Leary Alsdorf

Web sites:

- christianity.about.com/od/churchandcommunity/a/thechurch.html
- www.churchtimeline.com
- www.christianhistoryinstitute.org/magazine

9

Cloning, Eugenics, and the Ethics of What Is Possible

I laughed until I cried, as did most of the crowd when Michael Keaton (of "Mr. Mom" fame) proceeded to act out all four of his "clone" roles in the hit 1996 comedic film *Multiplicity*. As contractor Doug Kinney, he—like many in today's fast-paced world—found there just wasn't enough of him to go around. Surely, anyone who has felt the often counter-posing pressures to be the "all-things-to-all-men" type in our families can identify: community leader, ample provider, consummate spouse, loving parent, loyal friend.

Add to that desire to "be all that we can be," the very real possibility that science and technology may not be that far from making all of that and more possible...well, you get the picture. We may be approaching the *Island of Dr. Moreau* (a 1977—and later re-done in 1996—horror movie in which the DNA of animals and humans were combined) faster than we may be ready. It is possible that our technology may take us where our morality cannot sustain us.

Eugenics was a term created in 1883 by its first proponent, Francis Galton, a cousin of Charles Darwin. He theorized from his study of Darwin's writings that it would be possible to direct the otherwise blind chance of evolution by the careful selection of desirable traits in humans. Although we do this in many species of animals—sheep, cattle, horses, dogs, etc.—by careful breeding programs, the practice in human populations after the 1930s was considered racially motivated. The infamous Nazi doctors of World War II stigmatized the science of eugenics with all of its heinous laboratory experiments, relegating humans to the moral equivalent of lab rats. However, modern advances in genetics and the mapping of the human genome may once again challenge the ethical boundaries of our society.

The 1997 movie *Gattaca*—starring Ethan Hawke, Uma Thurman, and Jude Law—is set in some future time when eugenics is the ruling consideration for eligibility for positions other than menial laborers. It may seem far-fetched to choose eye-color, hair color, or physical traits but in a day and age when celebrities are heralded for deciding to have both of their breasts removed because their family *may have* demonstrated a proclivity toward breast cancer... well, maybe it's not that far-fetched.

The questions are as follows: Should we do something just because we can? Is there some guiding principle we can look to that helps us define the black and the white from the gray? For Christians, these decisions are not as hard as they are for those who have only the boundaries of what is possible. We are moving more and more into the ethics of genetic engineering, life extension, quality-of-life decisions, and the economics of health care...Christians have to know what God thinks about these issues.

Are cloning and eugenics biblical? Is it wrong to want only the best for our future and the future of others? What about the raising of a cloned human...for organs or to multiply our own effectiveness...is it all that wrong? Would a clone have a soul? Where do you draw the line between what is possible and what is ethical? These and other questions are the ones thinking Christians should be asking themselves.

According to a combination of what many dictionaries say, *Cloning* is the process by which an exact genetic duplicate of an organism is made; this process, though it occurs in humans naturally in identical twins, can be induced to occur in simple organisms. It has been induced to occur in as highly complex an organism as a sheep ("Dolly" in 1996, after 276 failures; and in four calves—

two years later in Japan—four of the eight produced died). To date, there is no definitive evidence that a human has been produced, though many have claimed varying degrees of success.

There are different types of cloning:

1. Gene cloning – making copies of genes or segments of strands of DNA.
2. Therapeutic cloning – making copies of tissues for replacement.
3. Reproductive cloning – making copies of whole animals.

Eugenics (from the Greek *eu* which is "good/well" and "genes" meaning "born" or "beginning") is the manipulation of human populations for the purpose of producing more desirable traits.

Answering questions:

1. Are cloning and eugenics biblical?

   Only in the sense that we were created in *His* image (Gen. 1:26); although the Lord does want the best for us (read Deut. 28:1–14), He knows that the good work done in us is to be a work of the Spirit, not of the flesh (Rom. 8:1–14).

   Cloning and eugenics are artificial attempts at an unattainable...perfection if it were possible, it would only deal with the physical realm, not the soulish realm which is where the perfection is really needed.

2. Is it wrong to want only the best for our future and the future of others?

   Of course not; the problem with our desires is not *what* we want, but how we intend to go about getting it. It's a *procurement* problem.

   The Scripture says, "Every good thing given and every perfect gift is from above, coming down from the Father of lights, with whom there is no variation or shifting shadow"

(James 1:17, NASU). Realizing from whence our "good thing" comes helps us procure it. Things from God are not earned or deserved; they are imputed (assigned), as *He* wills. Submission and humility are the requirements.

Besides, the only One who really knows what is best has to be able to know the eventual outcome of an infinite number of possible alternative realities...sounds like God to me.

3. What about the raising of a cloned human...for organs or to multiply our own effectiveness...is it all that wrong?

What made *Multiplicity* so funny was the lack of efficiency of subsequent generation clones...kind of like what a copy of a copy would be like...a faded facsimile of the original. Still, the possibility of accomplishing more or for a longer period of time (life-extension) does have its attractions; but the possibilities become less justifiable if it's at the expense of someone else's life (Phil. 2:3)—which is what making a clone from an embryonic stem would be. Research has been done on DNA strands from other cells that hold some promise.

4. Would a clone have a soul?

Nobody really knows until a human clone is made, but I don't see why not. Identical twins have souls; test tube babies have souls; cloning is just a mechanism and whatever mechanism is used is irrelevant.

David writes in the Psalms that we are "fearfully and wonderfully made" (Ps. 139:14). In fact, if you read all of Psalms 139, you get the definite impression that we are known by a Sovereign God, even before we are made. Sure, we have choices; but He knows which choices we are going to make even before we make them. We were created in his image—that is why we have a soul—the very essence of a soul creature is willfulness.

5. Where do you draw the line between what is possible and what is ethical?

Just because something is possible doesn't mean it is a good idea. God could have made man with nothing restricted—no Forbidden Fruit—but where was obedience with everything lawful? He wanted us to choose wisely and obey. But where was obedience if everything was allowed? Since love is measured in sacrifice, how could Man demonstrate his love unless given a choice…and the Forbidden fruit had to be desirable (Gen. 3:5–6) or it would not have been a temptation. Both trees, the Tree of Life and the Tree of the Knowledge of Good and Evil, were in the midst of the garden (Gen. 2:9). That made the choice clear. Every time Adam and Eve ate of the Tree of Life, the Forbidden Fruit was also available; to turn toward one is to turn your back on the other. To say "yes" to one fruit is to say "no" to the other fruit.

The advances of science may make many things possible—the Scriptures do say that there will come a time when we will marvel when someone dies at the young age of a hundred! (Isaiah 65:20)—but like the Apostle Paul said, "All things are lawful unto me, but not all things are expedient:…" (1 Cor. 6:12, KJV). Although spoken in the context of what was lawful for consumption, it can be applied here. A lot of things *can* be done, but not all things *should* be done…some things have a negative consequence. God could have kept Adam and Eve in the garden (Gen. 3:24); God could have exposed Noah and his family to the same flood as destroyed everything else (Gen. 6:14–19); God could have kept everyone of the same language at the Tower of Babel (Gen. 11:9)…but He didn't.

Parents, in some degree, are responsible for the thoughts and actions of their children. Pastors, in some degree, are responsible for the thoughts and actions of their congregants. Unless we, as Christians, think and act like we should, how are we going to be examples for the rest?

Genetic engineering may indeed offer the answers to many of life's disease challenges…and some ethical considerations, too. We must be informed, open to new ideas, but closed to old traps. "There is a way that seemeth right to a man, but the end thereof are the ways of death" (Prov. 14:12, KJV).

Recommended reading list:

- *The New Genesis: Theology and the Genetic Revolution*, Ronald Cole-Turner
- *Preaching Eugenics: Religious Leaders and the American Eugenics Movement*, Christine Rosen
- *Ethics*, Dietrich Bonhoeffer

Web sites:
- www.gotquestions.org/Christian-ethics.html
- www.comereason.org/sci_bible/sci020.asp
- www.christianitytoday.com/ct/2006/december/15.72.html

10

Cursing (Cussing) and Crude Gestures

"Mary had a little lamb…and a big black dog…" I can't even put in print what our whole squadron shouted at the top of our lungs as we marched to lunch in Arnold Hall at the US Air Force Academy. What is it about being a cadet that was—and I assume is—synonymous with being foul-mouthed? It was as if our toughness was measured in the creative ways we could cuss. It was so bad that we actually had a cadre-wide assembly on how we should clean up our language for the folks when we went home for the holidays… "It's just not cool to say 'pass the %#$%ing potatoes,' even if that's become a part of your normal vernacular," the speaker warned. We may have been in training to be "gentlemen"—at least an act of Congress had declared officers to be so—but the immorality of our language must not have been factored in.

As a senior in high school, I had competed and was offered appointments to the Coast Guard Academy, the Naval Academy, and the Air Force Academy. Selecting the Air Force Academy seemed the shortest route to becoming an astronaut, and I definitely wanted to be "beamed up!" However, in the middle of all that… the forms, physicals, and interviews…I met the Lord. The ensuing contradiction to what had happened in my heart would not manifest itself till I arrived for basic training that summer of 1970. Almost immediately, I fell into the gaping chasm of verbal immorality that was all around me.

I've come a long way since those early days of my Christian walk, feeling more and more that there was a contradiction between my external witness and my internal commitment. As I allowed the Lord to change me from the inside out, I began to identify less with the worldly environment and yearn more and more for the fellowship of those who had committed themselves to a godly morality.

I freely confess that I probably became quite obnoxious in my rejection of all things profane. If my pursuit of piety offended anyone reading this, please forgive me and chalk up my spiritual arrogance to the immaturity of youthful zeal. Although I have endeavored to keep my tongue pure, I am sure that my sinful heart has betrayed me in attitude or actuality. Still, a mentor cannot limit himself to only heralding areas of self-mastery...if I only wrote on subjects where personal mastery had been achieved, this would be a short work indeed!

My father had a saying he used often with the young men he mentored (he was a scoutmaster for twenty-two years). When someone would use the four-letter slang for fecal matter he would say, "You just had in your mouth what I would not have in my hand!" Although cussing is very much a cultural matter—to some "crap" is just as bad—the uttering of an expletive can, for some, act as a release valve for pent-up frustration. To change your speech may be as easy as substituting a more acceptable alternative...easier perhaps than eliminating the source of the frustration.

We were visiting some friends of ours in Atlanta once and heard our two-year-old daughter use "stupid" as a casual adjective. We were appalled and embarrassed to think that our daughter might be using such a judgmental term at her tender years and determined we would search out among her peers the source of such language. Later, that same day, I used the term describing some inanimate malfunctioning part of our car saying, "That *stupid* part needs to be replaced!" Suddenly, embarrassingly, I knew the source of her errant input: ME! We sat her down and re-educated her...I said, "Daddy misspoke. Not *stupid*, but *special*." Ever since, in our household, "special" is code for "stupid." (Gee, I hope I've never told you how special you are to me!)

Is there speech that is more acceptable for a Christian? Shouldn't I express to others how I really feel and not mask it in pretended sincerity or civility when I'm really angry? What about my right of "free speech"? Won't I damage my witness if I pretend to be something I'm not? What part does environment play? What about a slip of the tongue or a reactive crude gesture? These and other questions are the ones thinking Christians should be asking.

According to a combination of what many dictionaries say, *Cursing* is the verbal expression that something hurtful or destructive befell a person or thing. In Christendom, it is also used to describe taking the "Lord's Name in vain." A *crude gesture* may describe any one of a number of culturally unacceptable hand signals that imply that something hurtful, immoral, or destructive befall an individual.

Answering questions:

1. Is there speech that is more acceptable for a Christian?

    Probably the most oft-quoted passage on this topic is the one from Ephesians 4:29:

    > Let no unwholesome word proceed from your mouth, but only such a word as is good for edification according to the need of the moment, so that it will give grace to those who hear. (NASU)

    The Scripture says the mouth will speak out of the abundance of the heart (Matt. 12:34–35). The Christian who fills himself with the Word of God will, from that rich treasure he has deposited within, make timely and abundant withdrawals. The Christian's speech will be an indicator of what he has been feasting on…or what he has been fasting from…or both. Hopefully, he has been feeding his spiritual man and starving his natural man (Rom. 8:5–11).

The Christian has made Jesus the Lord of his tongue (James 3:8–12). Without God's help, taming the tongue is a virtual impossibility. An untamed tongue is as useless to us—and to God—as an untamed horse...power out of control is destructive, not constructive.

The Christian's speech should be instructional, not confusing; bring peace and not chaos; edifying, not critical; optimistic, not pessimistic; and the Christian's words should be few and substantive. How does that saying go? *Make your words sweet; you never know when you'll have to eat them.*

2. Shouldn't I express to others how I really feel and not mask it in pretended sincerity or civility when I'm really angry?

The Scripture says, "Be angry, and yet do not sin" (Eph. 4:26, NASU). Show some self-control (Gal. 5:22–23). Some people are too transparent—everything they think comes out of their mouth! Although God may forgive and forget, others may not. Discretion is the ability to think *before* you speak. I'm not saying to be insincere, but to rehearse in your mind what you are preparing to say. You may realize this is not the time or place for what you have to contribute.

3. What about my right of "free speech"?

If you have truly made Jesus the Lord of all, you have already yielded up that right—along with all others. You are not less free than others, but empowered to do good by that freedom because you have submitted your tongue to Him. These are called "redeemed rights"—rights given back by a God Who's given us His Holy Spirit, too—the right to do something, but with that right comes the power *not to use it* in every circumstance.

4. Won't I damage my witness if I pretend to be something I'm not?

I'm not saying you should "fake it till you make it." This is the world's wisdom. However, there is something to be said for not saying anything until your heart and your head agree. While the head may contain the speech center, the heart contains the wisdom center. The Lord gave you two ears and only one mouth for a reason…maybe we need to listen more…to the voice of the Holy Spirit!

As it says in James, "If anyone thinks himself to be religious, and yet does not bridle his tongue but deceives his own heart, this man's religion is worthless" (James 1:26, NASU).

Our witness is made up as much with what we *do* as with what we *say*. Since doing begins with saying (John 14:10; 3 John 10) and saying begins with thinking (1 Cor. 14:20), we should think before we speak…this will make for less hypocrisy, more integrity, and a better witness.

5. What part does environment play?

Environment is a lot; both the environment you choose and the environment that chooses you. Let me explain. Our ears and eyes go where our feet take us…and often we regret the decision our mind made when it told our feet to take us there! We find ourselves in an unhealthy environment—a movie that is unedifying, a place where others have surrendered their inhibitions and their morality to substances that control them, or simply an environment where the flesh is in control, not the Spirit.

The same feet that took you there can take you away. All that it requires is a *different* decision. Better yet, don't make the wrong decision in the first place. Choose your environment where you are strengthening the spirit-man, not the flesh. God's love forces Him to accompany you wherever you go.

I know that sinners are where sin is; and as soon as you are strong enough to resist the temptation to relapse into a sinful lifestyle, the Lord will send you there. Until then, don't let your empathy for the lost drag you where the Lord has not led you.

As for the environment that chooses you…you may work around many who make cursing an art form. Be the dominant spiritual force there. Set your mind on things above, not on things beneath (Col. 3:2–3). When others see that you don't cuss like them, watch how they change the way they speak when you're around. And don't condemn them. Your godly life will say more to them than any sermon (1 Pet. 2:12).

6. What about a slip of the tongue or a reactive crude gesture?

    Many have hit their thumb with a hammer or have had someone in traffic next to them 'flip them off'—use the middle finger of the hand to recommend fornication under carnal knowledge (or the acronymic version of that)—only to surprisingly respond with a verbal epithet or reactive gesture of their own. Surprise, surprise! I guess you should change your everyday environment. This is when you find out what is abundant in your heart (Matt. 12:34).

    It is forgivable. Just keep short accounts with God—in other words, don't let much time elapse between the offense and the confession. Also, you might just ask those who were the object of your reactive ire to forgive you, too (Prov. 15:1).

    Taking the Lord's name in vain—proclaimed by many to be the condemnation of others on God's behalf (G.D.)—is really calling oneself a Christian without living like it; a sin we are all guilty of from time to time. And don't forget God's admonition through the Apostle Paul: "But now you also, put them all aside: anger, wrath, malice, slander, and abusive speech from your mouth" (Col. 3:8, NASU).

    Cursing may be more than that, though. Since we are called to bless and not curse (Rom. 12:14), cursing may even be more strictly defined as the absence of blessing. When is the last time you failed to be a blessing?

Recommended reading list:

- *The Power of the Tongue*, Kenneth Copeland
- *The Profanity Problem: And What to do About It*, Tom Spence
- *Profanity, What You Don't Know Shows*, Eloise Coker Hunter

Web sites:

- www.christiancourier.com/articles/369-profanity
- www.whatchristianswanttoknow.com/christian-swearing-
- www.patheos.com/blogs/frankviola/swearingchristians

11

Dating and Courtship

You could have knocked me over with a feather! (I wish I could have seen the expression on my face—I'm sure the combination of shock and shame produced a unique expression). I had come downstairs early to find my father in the kitchen getting ready for work. My fiancée was upstairs still sleeping…it was one of those moments that I felt the Holy Spirit had orchestrated. I asked my dad if he had some sage advice for a young man preparing for marriage. His quick response flabbergasted me! He advised, "The first thing I'd suggest is that you start sleeping together to see if you're sexually compatible."

All I could manage in response at the time was, "Excuse me?" I left the room immediately. Didn't he know I was a Bible college student?! That was over forty years ago. I have since realized that I had an unreasonable expectation. What did I think a man who was on his third marriage, to whom fidelity was an impractical and inconvenient concept, would say? He was genuinely giving me what he thought was good advice. At the core of all disappointment is unreasonable expectation. By the way, my fiancée became my only wife (now, over forty years ago) and the mother of my children…although my Christian walk had been marred before by inconsistencies, Lynn and I never had sex before marriage.

Although some see Christian dating and courtship as synonymous, the primary difference is a defined accountability. Few young men or women are wise enough to *seek* accountability. It's one thing to be single and fancy-free and quite another to be a parent; somehow, your perspective changes. What seemed like a good idea before to the single-you is now unthinkable to the parental-you.

Calling

Homes used to have parlors...primarily for courtship. This is where the girl, in the western Christian tradition, would receive her gentlemen callers. One parent or another—usually the mom— would sit and do sewing or needle-point or whatever...you knew you were trusted and accepted if she left the room after a while.

Here's how it was done at the turn of the last century—or so I've been told; it certainly was before my time. The daughter would approach her father and let him know that if someone she approved of—often several beaus had expressed an interest—asked if they could come calling, that he could say "yes." This usually occurred on a Sunday afternoon. When he came calling, he had been given a specific time...sometimes the more popular girls would have the guys lined up...there was a bench—an "on deck" circle, so to speak—on the front porch.

When it was his turn, he would be escorted by an older brother or other sibling into the parlor. There, waiting on the "love seat"— where did you think the term came from?—the daughter would be waiting, the mom on another seat in the room. If it was his first visit, he sat on a chair apart from the love seat. If he was accepted by the daughter *and the family*, she might pat the seat next to her, indicating he could sit there.

All of this family affair had an unspoken accountability to it. The callers could see that pleasing the rest of the family, especially the mom and dad, was a key to their successful courtship. The daughter felt special...and protected.

Over dinner that evening, the whole family would share their impressions of the callers. Those getting a thumbs-up would either get a positive response from her father when future requests were made, or even an approach by a father letting him know he could come calling again if he liked. After several successful visits, he might be asked to a family dinner or invited to join them at church. Later, he might be allowed to go walking with the daughter, a sibling or parent walking behind, but within earshot…the trust was measured in the distance at which the chaperone followed.

Never was the couple actually alone…mom was in the next room or the sibling within eyesight or close enough that an unexpected glance was always possible. The parents seldom had to tell a daughter the rules of the 'calling procedure'; she had been a chaperone herself or seen courtship protocol in her own family already.

But that was then. When the preacher said, "You may kiss the bride," often he was giving permission to a right the groom had *not* already experienced. Today, it is rare that the bride and groom have not already experienced the ultimate in intimacy. Of course the divorce rate is nearly 50 percent, too…*hmmm, I wonder if there's a connection.*

Is courtship or dating a biblical concept? How about "arranged marriages"? Should I look for someone to spend the rest of my life with? How young is too young to begin a romantic relationship? Are there recommended rules for dating or courtship? Doesn't courtship remove most of the choice out of the daughter's hands? What is so bad about dating, anyway? What do you do about someone really cute comes on to you (or, in contemporary terms, "hits on you")? When is a person ready to begin courtship? What about social media—you know, those chat rooms and dating sites? These are the questions thinking Christians must answer.

Courtship, as a historical term concerning certain social interactions in preparation for a life-long commitment in marriage, speaks of a time when gentlemen only sought someone whose chasteness and carriage rendered her a lady. According to a dictionary amalgamation, dating is the method of trying on a relationship by having a series of social interaction experiments that involve candidates for a more long-term commitment. Courtship may involve similar methods but has an added element of accountability.

Answering questions:

1. Is courtship or dating a biblical concept?

    Although courtship and dating are not mentioned specifically in the Bible—both are more recent culturally dictated practices—there does seem to be an endorsement for accountability and family involvement in the mate selection process. Case in point: The selection of a mate for Isaac (all of chapter 24 of Genesis). Read the entire chapter and you can readily see that Rebekah was chosen by God, but she and her family assented, too.

    These two concepts of family involvement and accountability can be combined if the parents—on both sides—are involved, as in the case of Isaac and Rebekah. Whether you meet in a chat room, a dating site (I have two sons; the younger found his mate in a chat room; the elder son found his wife on eHarmony), or were introduced by friends at church, it is what you do *after* meeting them that determines a successful relationship. Both of my sons—and my daughter…ah, but that's another story—got their parents involved in the selection process…they had both families' permission and blessing; we couldn't be happier with their choices *or the grandchildren they have given us.*

2. How about "arranged marriages"?

    I guess it depends on who's doing the arranging. Everybody wants a match "made in heaven." It's kind of like I told my sons: "Everyone wants a 'Proverbs 31 Woman'; no one wants to be a 'Proverbs 1–30 Man.'" To get a "match made in heaven" might require you to be someone the Lord can trust with that.

    Arranged marriages can work. There are a few requirements for success; however,

    A. It needs to be the cultural norm among those who associate together (it's easier to do anything if those around you have given you a successful example to follow).

B. The one doing the 'arranging'—a matchmaker or a parent—must have an extensive knowledge of the candidates (for a parent or a matchmaker, this requires time spent).

C. Priorities for mate selection should be agreed upon by those seeking and by those arranging (agreement here is essential to success...regret is the precursor to divorce)

D. An assessment of compatibility spiritually, mentally, and physically—in that order—must be made.

Do I recommend arranged marriages? For most, this would never work. But if that is the cultural norm, it can.

3. Should I look for someone to spend the rest of my life with? The three most important decisions you make in your life areas follows:

A. With whom are you going to spend eternity?
B. With whom are you going to spend this life on earth?
C. How will you expend the measure of your days?

Since a decision on a spouse is #2 (B) on the list, it needs to be a priority. Mate selection is important, but finding the right person is all about *being* the right person. Whatever it is that you want to attract should give you a clue as to what you must be—flowers attract bees because of their colorfulness; princes marry princesses because...well, they are princesses.

You find princesses in castles not in the projects. Christians find other Christians in church...or in cell groups, community groups or home groups of churches. Many Bible colleges jokingly promise: "A ring by Spring, or your money back." Many Christians have found a mate for life in just such a place...I am one.

4. How young is too young to begin a romantic relationship?

Again, this may be more of a cultural issue than an absolute one. The real considerations are of *maturity*, not age.

When a child is old enough to give proper consideration to the responsibilities—not just the privileges—of a lifelong relationship, that person is ready to begin a romantic one. Young people not having reached an age of emotional maturity have often given their hearts away only to draw back a bloody stub… something that waiting until maturity could have spared them.

There was a time in America when fourteen or fifteen years of age might have been the norm—at least for women; for men the ability to support usually did not come until the early twenties—but today it is often after twenty-five before a lifelong decision by either gender is contemplated.

The things to remember are these:

A. Love is a decision, not an emotion.
B. It is hard to give away anything to someone you do not know well…it is hard to know anyone well until some of their dreams have been realized…*or at least dreamed!*
C. Unless a man is willing to put his money where his mouth is—the ring is paid for, he has secure employment, he has a direction for his life, he has a safe and adequate place to live, and he has dependable transportation—he is only asking some girl to join him in his immature insecurity!
D. It is harder to put out a fire than to get it going…there's no sense in getting a fire going anyway, if you are not ready to be blessed by its heat.
E. The will of God seldom goes against the counsel of the godly.

5. Are there recommended rules for dating or courtship?

Everyone has his own, but the following "Ten Rules for Dating My Daughter" are not entirely tongue-in-cheek. Note that there is accountability involved so courtship may be a more accurate, though less contemporarily acceptable term.

Ten Rules for Dating My Daughter

Although you and my daughter are both adults and, as such, do not need my permission legally to do anything either of you pleases, should you want my support or blessing on your relationship, you will need to comply explicitly with the following:

1. You cannot date anyone else while you are dating her. (This means that you cannot ask anyone else out, spend money on another girl that is not your relative, and you cannot be alone in the company of another girl in the eligible category—"eligible," meaning single, between eighteen and ten years older than you are, and not an "old friend" of at least five years acquaintance.)

2. You will endeavor to have my daughter at her home or mine by midnight of any night you are out with her. In no case will you have her out past 1:00 a.m. in the morning. Permission to be out past midnight is obtained with a phone call and a good reason. (No phone call and no daughter before 1:00 a.m. will result in a search party being sent out—you can ask my daughter...I'm not kidding—made up by members of my family and those whom they recruit. Unless a true emergency exists, we will have to sort this incident out before you spend another moment with my daughter).

3. You will not use the "L" word (love) until you are ready to use the "M" word (marriage).

4. You must profess that Jesus Christ is the Lord of your life and demonstrate by your actions and your lifestyle that that is not an empty profession. (You will demonstrate the reality of your faith by acting Christianly and by attending—that means at least once per week—a Christian church of some evangelical persuasion; otherwise I will consider your profession of faith to be hypocritical and manipulative).

5. When you are with my daughter, you will avoid overt and crude public displays of your affection by refraining from any

physical contact beyond holding hands and short-duration embraces. At all times, you will keep your kisses on her face, your tongue in your mouth and your hands to yourself.

6. You will never put my daughter in a compromising situation or embarrass her or endanger her emotionally or physically in any way.

7. You will not discuss with my daughter the deepening of your relationship, taking things to the "next level," so to speak, unless you've first had that discussion with me.

8. The discussion mentioned in rule #7 will not occur in less than six months time from when you first began to date my daughter.

9. Every time you are on an outing with my daughter, you will spend at least some time with her in prayer (if Christ is not at the heart of your relationship, I will seek to bring your pursuit of my daughter to an end).

10. You will not consume alcohol, any controlled substance, or tobacco in any form *in excess* while in the presence of my daughter or at any other time during your dating relationship.

(NOTE: Nobody's perfect, except Jesus, Himself; there may be a time (or times) when these rules are neglected, forgotten, or even overtly disregarded. Speedy confession and abject humility in the process of repentance and the seeking of my forgiveness may go a long way toward the *possibility* of a restoration of relationship. Should I discover the breach in trust that your violation of these rules indicates from someone other than yourself, the possibility of any future with my daughter will be drastically reduced, so as to be practically non-existent.)

Your signature below indicates that you have read, understand, and agree to abide by these rules. (Your signature below also gives me express permission to run a background check or secure a random drug test at any time during your relationship with my daughter).

_____ **Date:** _____

Yes, I actually used this with a number of potential suitors.

Answering Questions:

6. Doesn't courtship remove most of the choice out of the daughter's hands?

    Not hardly. Both in the 'calling' method above and in the biblical example I enumerated earlier (Genesis 24), the girl actually has more control than the guy.

    Parents, no girl or guy—in this culture—will comply with accountability that removes them from the decision making process. That is the reasonable trade-off; accountability for 'self-determination.' Besides, if you have raised your kids right (Ephesians 6:4), they will have no trouble embracing your counsel and will see the safety of family involvement.

7. What is so bad about dating, anyway?

    If you understand this culture's definition of dating—a series of short, temporary, failed relationships where the participants will build a mental composite of the ideal spousal candidate—you understand what is wrong with dating. (Note: I've already said that Christian dating and courtship may be synonymous terms.) *You cannot build a successful life-long relationship on a series of unsuccessful short-term failed ones.*

8. What does a young person do about some girl or guy that is really cute and comes on to you (or, in contemporary terms, "hits on you")?

    The best response is, "You'll have to talk to my father first." This is usually a sufficient dose of "cold water" to cure all but the most ardent of approaches. Anyone willing to go through the proper protocols may be more than just another pretty face. Character is defined as what someone will do when he thinks no one is watching.

9. When is a person ready to begin courtship?

    Although I really already answered that in #4 above, I want to approach it here from the negative. Let's talk about the consequences of a wrong decision. What if you begin too early...divorce.

More than just a spelled-out line from a country song, divorce separates...maybe that's why divorce falls into a category of those things the Lord hates (read: Malachi 2:16). When one thinks of the economic costs, too—legal fees, child support, alimony, forced sales to split assets, etc.—it's just plain expensive.

Besides, all you have left to give the next relationship is a damaged and needy heart. I'm not saying the Lord cannot save, forgive, heal, and restore, but the price of unity may be maturity. Better to have waited for the right one...*to have become the right one*...than to try and build a future on the shifting sands of a series of unsuccessful false starts.

10. What about social media—you know, those chat rooms and dating sites?

Like I said, how you meet that potential significant other is not nearly as important as what you then do together, but as a wise man once quipped: It's hard to catch bass in a crappie hole. Today's social media can offer a reasonable and effective way to pursue the discovery process if you use common sense and safety protocols.

I've included a list of *Do's and Don'ts of Social Media* to help in this regard:

A. Even if you've seen a picture, they are only telling you what they want you to believe.
B. Never meet someone you don't know alone.
C. If using a dating site, only use a reputable one...and only use one at a time.
D. Always be honest when filling out a profile. The best surprise is no surprise.
E. If you are desperate, you probably aren't ready...any decision you make, you'll probably regret.

F. Differences may be grounds for a good marriage; besides if you are both identical, one of you is unnecessary.

Recommended reading list:

- *Dating vs. Courtship*, Dr. Paul Jehle
- *I Kissed Dating Goodbye*, Joshua Harris
- *Boy Meets Girl: Say Hello to Courtship*, Joshua Harris

Web sites:

- www.ChristianMingle.com
- www.eHarmony.com/Christian-Dating
- www.crosswalk.com/family/singles

12

Death

Perusing the selections in the Men's clothing department in J. C. Penny's, the last call I expected to receive was from my son, Jonathan. "Dad," he said in a serious tone, "grandpa's dead." Immediately my mind raced to a conversation we—my dad and I—had had just three days previous.

"Son," he offered, "the next time you take a mission trip to Belize"—I had been there a couple of dozen times in the past several years—"take me along with you...that is if you think my skills would be useful." You could have knocked me over with a feather.

"Sure, Dad, I'd love to have you with me," was all I could manage at the time. When I got off the phone, I remarked to my wife, "You are not going to believe what my dad just said!"

You have to understand that since 1970, when I turned over my life to the Lordship of Christ, my dad did nothing but mock and ridicule my decision. When I decided to resign my commission and leave the Air Force Academy, he told me I'd regret it the rest of my life. He said, "Who is going to pay your tuition?" When I replied that the Lord would, he laughed.

Once, when I was up on a roof repairing shingles with him, he said, "If you really believe in God, why don't you jump off this roof?" I didn't tell him that test had been tried before.

You have to understand that my dad was one of the greatest dads that a kid could ever have. He played ball with me in the front yard, went to my games, drove my older brother everyday one summer to a private reading tutor (he had hydrocephaly as a child and was brain damaged), volunteered as a scoutmaster for twenty-two years and was always a faithful provider for our family. But as far as being a Christian was concerned, I felt he was as lost as a goose. I had always felt that if anyone had an excuse—and none of us do— he had one...his wife (my mom) had died at age twenty-four of Hodgkin's lymphoma. He had prayed for her healing and even gone to a few faith healing meetings, to no avail. He had to work three jobs to pay off the medical bills.

Though I preached his funeral and comforted those gathered by recapping my mystifying phone conversation with him just a few days earlier, I still don't know for sure where he's spending eternity. Perhaps, before his heart attack—or during—he had enough time to cry out to God. At least he knew what to do; I had made sure of that by my relentless witnessing to him. In the end, that is all we can do. Witness and turn them over to God—the decision, however, is up to the individual.

Whether you are young or old, death is a reality for everyone. And that is the subject of this article.

Is death biblical? What about for Christians—didn't Jesus say, "He who lives and believes in me shall never die" (John 11:26)? Is death the end? What happens to the soul after death? What about purgatory? These, and other questions, are the ones thinking Christians should be asking themselves.

According to a combination of what many dictionaries say, *Death* is the permanent end of what normally sustains a living organism; so death varies in its meaning according to whatever sustains the life of that particular creature. There is brain death—the cessation of brain activity, biological death—which, in the case of those on life support, may not necessarily mean brain death, and spiritual death. According to Christian orthodoxy—from *ortho-doxa* (right belief), spiritual death is separation from God (Gen. 2:17) and the condition of us all (Rom. 3:23, 6:23).

Answering questions:

1. Is death biblical?

    As far as original intent is concerned, no. All creatures were designed to live forever...the angels—which do—Man—who does, in a sense—and all that "creeps" on the earth (Gen. 1:25), "flies" in the air or "swims" in the sea (Ps. 8–8; Rom. 8:19). But, since angels (Ezek. 28:14) and Man (Gen. 1:26) are made in free moral agency—with the right of choice—they are free to choose obedience or disobedience (Gen. 2:17), life or death (Joshua 1:8).

    I said that Man, "in a sense," lives forever. To avoid semantical confusion, before we go any further, let me define our terms.

Eternal – having no beginning or end – Only God falls in this category.

Everlasting – having a beginning, but no end – Angels and Man fall into this category. Since angels have no natural corporeal form (only a soul and spirit)—though they often take on the appearance of material reality (Heb. 13:2)—they live forever; in hell – prepared for demons (fallen angels), or in heaven – prepared for angels. Man, however, has a material body, a soul—reason, will, and emotions—and a spirit (Gen. 2:7). Because his soul and spirit also live forever, the only question is their place of abode—again, hell or heaven—that is what the Judgment is for (Rev. 20:12–15).

Temporal – having a beginning and an end –all creation, having no soul or spirit, falls into this category...sorry, all dogs *don't* go to heaven; although dogs will be in heaven, "Buffy" won't be there...just in a movie and in western cultural theology.

    Did God's plan of creating everything to live forever get foiled? Not at all. Before He created the heavens and the earth, before He even gave Man a choice, He knew he would choose poorly, and His own death would be required to reunite Man (and all creation—Rom. 8:19) with God (Eph. 1:4; 1 Pet. 1:20; Rev. 13:8). This, in fact, was His plan all along. Since love is measured in sacrifice and God is love (1 John 4:8,16), then what greater way for God to demonstrate this truth?

2. What about for Christians—didn't Jesus say, "He who lives and believes in me shall never die" (John 11:26)?

    That is why the Gospel is Good News! As Christians, we have accepted Christ's death on the cross as payment in full for our sins. We never die. Of course, this shell—our body—which houses our soul and spirit, is still under the sentence of death, but the soul and spirit live on. Because of Adam's sin, all die; but because of Christ's—the Second Adam—sacrifice, all can live (2 Cor. 15:45). I said "can" live: you must accept Him (Rom. 10:9–10). It's for "whosoever will" (Rev. 22:17).

3. Is death the end?

    Not for Man…fortunately or unfortunately, as the case may be. I used to give a "good news/bad news" altar call. It went like this:

    > I have good news and bad news. The good news is that at the Judgment you will be given a new body. It can never be killed, it can never be destroyed and it will experience all the five senses to their maximum degree—it lives forever. But I also have some bad news…at least for some of you. The bad news is that at the judgment, you will be given a new body. It can never be killed, it can never be destroyed, and it will experience all the five senses to their maximum degree–it lives forever. Kind of sounds like the good news, doesn't it? It depends on where you are spending eternity…

    We are all going to live forever…it's where that matters?

4. What happens to the soul after death?

For Christians, we go immediately into the presence of the Lord (2 Cor. 5:8). Sure, we have to wait until the final resurrection and the judgment to get our new bodies (1 Thess. 4:16–18), but it is the conscious spirit that is reunited with its body, not an unconscious one.

5. What about purgatory?

Some Roman Catholics still hold to the superstition that they can increase their time in "purgatory" by misdeeds they have done...or decrease their time by acts of penance or service or piety. In fact, it is a part of the Roman Catholic Catechism (CCC 1030 and 1031). By their definition, purgatory is a place between death and our entering into heaven; a place where we are punished or purified until we are worthy of heaven.

Protestant Christians, however, believe that the purification that heaven requires (Rev. 21:27) has been done by Christ on the cross. His is a finished work (John 19:30), and we "come boldly" into His throne (Heb. 4:16) by His righteousness (Rom. 3:25–26), not our own.

The Christian looks at death from a different perspective than the world. For other Christians, he rejoices at their graduation; for those obviously lost, he mourns at the end of their opportunity to respond to Christ and experience an eternity of intimate fellowship with their Maker. For those whose final destination is unknown, he is hopeful. That is not to say that the Christian does not empathize with those left behind, but rather he is reminded that there is still time to witness of God's saving grace.

> The Lord is not slack concerning His promise, as some count slackness, but is longsuffering toward us, not willing that any should perish but that all should come to repentance" (2 Pet. 3:9, NKJV).

Recommended reading list:

- *One Minute After You Die*, Erwin W. Lutzer
- *Afterlife: What You Need to Know About Heaven, the Hereafter and Near-Death Experiences*, Hank Hanegraaff
- *Choosing to SEE: A Journey of Struggle and Hope*, Mary Beth Chapman, Ellen Vaughn

Web sites:

- www. truthaboutdeath.com
- www.bible.org./seriespage/death

13

Debt

Ever been so overwhelmed that you thought about hitting the reset button and you got depressed because you realized there wasn't one? One day I just woke up and realized our credit card debt was over $35,000! It might have well been thirty-five trillion! I couldn't even pay the minimum payments on those debts…and that didn't include the mortgage, car payments, etc. How did we get there? One thing is for certain: we didn't just wake up and owe the money; we had lived outside our means for a long time.

God had bailed our bacon out of the fire a number of times. The things that had gone against us that were not of our doing—the robbing of our apartment in 1976, the failure of the company I worked for in 1984, the accident in 1986, the leaving of a sponge in me during the gall bladder surgery of 2001, the strokes, and the tornado, etc.—God took care of all of those. The things I had brought on myself by my own stupidity…well, that was a different story.

Finally, I had to admit I had a problem. So I called a credit counselor. You know, one of those 800-number programs advertised on TV? At their advice—proof of repentance is changed behavior—I cut up all my credit cards, cancelled all my subscriptions, and ceased all the expenditures that weren't as essential as I had convinced myself that they were. They put me in touch with a foundation that was dedicated to helping people get out of debt. The Foundation contacted my creditors, negotiated with them, and put me on a single payment plan, and five years later, I was out of debt (except for my mortgage…which is soon to pay off)!

Is debt biblical? If lending money is okay, how can borrowing be wrong? Is there a limit to how much interest you should charge somebody? Is bankruptcy biblical? How about the US government's power to print money, tax its citizens, to incur debt? Should Christians have a different perspective than others concerning debt? These and other questions need addressing.

According to the dictionary, *Debt* is an obligation owed by one party (the debtor) to a second party (the creditor); technically, one can be considered bankrupt when his (or her) debts exceed their credits or the amount owed exceeds one's ability to pay according to the terms upon which both parties have agreed.

According to the Bible, sin is a debt we all owe, but can never pay (Romans 3:23, 6:23). We were "born" bankrupt, so to speak, but our debt has been paid by Jesus (I Pet. 1:18)—the only one who never owed the debt (Hebrews 4:15)—on the cross (Colossians 1:20); since we've been bought with a price (1 Corinthians 6:20; 7:23), we are not our own.

Answering questions:

1. Is debt biblical?

    "Owe no one anything except to love one another, for he who loves another has fulfilled the law" (Rom. 13:8, NKJV). Of course it's biblical, in the sense that we are all born in debt. Although your personal share of the national debt may be an ungodly sum, the concept of borrowing and lending is godly and found throughout the Bible.

    Debt must be biblical for the Lord speaks of lending and borrowing, but He also tells us which side of the equation is meant for us. "The Lord will open for you His good storehouse, the heavens, to give rain to your land in its season and to bless all the work of your hand; and you shall lend to many nations, but you shall not borrow." (Deut. 28:12, NASU) Or, as it says in Proverbs, "The rich rules over the poor, and the borrower becomes the lender's slave" (Prov. 22:7, NASU).

2. If lending money is okay, how can borrowing be wrong?

    Borrowing cannot be wrong or we would be encouraging others to sin. But every time we borrow, we place ourselves in voluntary servitude to whomever we borrowed from...not good English AND not good practice.

Two rules to borrow by:

1. Never borrow from anyone whom you cannot obey (Prov. 6:1–5). Other Christians are a good source of capital as they are governed by God.
2. Never borrow on anything depreciable. When something's residual value does not exceed what you owe against it, you didn't put enough down in cash...that is the sin of presumption; you presumed that you would be there to make the next payment.

NOTE: Have I ever bought things depreciable over time? You bet; and although I justified it at the time, I always regretted it. *Remember, regret is where the past meets the present to guide the future.*

There are those that rule and those that are ruled. Which end of that do you want? There is a principle involved here. Although we are all sheep (Isaiah 53:6), God has intended us to be shepherds (John 21:7). We were created for dominion (Gen. 1:26). Rulership is our destiny, but to rule as slaves is oxymoronic.

As Christians, we are to lend. It's all His anyway. He owns the cattle on a thousand hills (Ps. 50:10), how much more the hills (Ex. 29:9)?

3. Is there a limit to how much interest you should charge somebody?

In the Bible, interest is called "usury." As Christians, we are told in no uncertain terms not to lend with usury (Deut. 29:19; Lev. 25:36; Neh. 5:10; etc.). In fact, there have been many times when I have lent to other Christians when it became a burden to our ongoing relationship...I recommend in those cases that you forgive the debt. Better to retain the relationship and lose the money.

As far as official lending practices are concerned, many states have laws concerning "imputed interest." In other words, even if you don't charge someone interest, you may be taxed as if you did (at whatever the statutory rate may be). This is one of those laws I definitely don't agree with, but have to obey...it forces me to pay a tax for the privilege of lending. Check with your state.

4. Is bankruptcy biblical?

Bankruptcy is one of those procedures that makes us different from most of the rest of the world and certainly of history. It is a legal proceeding where the result is the cancellation or reduction of the indebtedness of the person claiming protection under bankruptcy laws. It is predicated on the reality that once hope is removed, productivity is also removed. Once hope is restored—through filing bankruptcy—productivity is restored...and a productive individual is a blessing to society where unproductivity drags on an economy.

We have no debtor's prison in America. All of the onus is definitely on the lender. The lender is where the risk should fall...that is what interest is for. It compensates the lender for his risk in lending to the borrower. When the government forces a lender to take a questionable risk, the failure rate of borrowers increases. When this increased failure causes a lender to go bankrupt, the government steps in to ameliorate. This must be done with taxpayer money. This is the source of part of our national debt.

Our bankruptcy provisions may have their source in the year of jubilee that was established by God in Leviticus 25. Starting in verse 10, the whole chapter sets down the rules regarding the ownership of personal and real property. Basically, the year of jubilee occurred every fiftieth year and was designated to be when all property went back to its original owner. If you loaned out money with land as collateral, you knew how many years it was until jubilee and you only made the loan until then because you knew the collateral was only secure till then. Bankruptcy was then originally a biblical concept.

5. How about the US government's power to print money, tax its citizens, and to incur debt?

The US Constitution grants the exclusive power to print money to the Congress (Article I, Section 8, Clause 5; Article I, Section 10, Clause 1). The power to tax and borrow is granted by the US Constitution to the Congress (Article I, Section 8 and the Sixteenth Amendment).

The problem is not who has the authority or how it got that authority; it is how it exercises that authority; just as in life, it is not what you have, but what you do with what you have that makes the difference. The sources of the government's debt— Export Debt (the debt other governments owe us that they're not paying), Import Debt (the debt we owe to other governments), and Social Debt (the debt we owe ourselves through US Bonds, Entitlement Programs such as Social Security, Disability, Medicare, etc.)—are the ones to whom we are in servitude… absolute truth does not consider whether or not it's believed. In the case of owing the money to ourselves…well you can see why it is imperative why we remain a Christian nation.

6. Should Christians have a different perspective than others concerning debt?

Since, as Christians, we know that the borrower is servant to the lender, we should be careful who we make our masters— both personally and as a state and nation. Since we have a representative form of government where others are going to be making laws by which we must abide, we should carefully elect those leaders.

While we may not like debt, it is a fact of life. We owe so much to a Savior Who has given His very life for us. Therefore, we must labor to free ourselves from competing loyalties…"we will either love the one and hate the other, or hate the one and love the other; we cannot love God and mammon" (Matthew 6:24).

Recommended reading list:

- *Your Finances in Changing Times (Christian Financial concepts Series)*, Larry Burkett
- *The Total Money Makeover: A Proven Plan for Financial Fitness*, Dave Ramsey
- *Inherit the Earth: Biblical Principles for Economics*, Dr. Gary North

Web sites:

- www.christian-debtrelief.com
- www.familylifecredit.org
- www.daveramsey.com

14

Education

Surely, one of the greatest gifts the next generation receives from the previous one is the communication of all their knowledge thus far. To not have to start all over to learn those very expensive lessons our parents paid so dearly for is what makes progress possible. I said possible, not inevitable. The ability to learn from our own past, the self-sacrifice necessary to love our children more than ourselves, the patience and commitment it takes to tell them what they aren't mature enough to listen to…these are a few of the prerequisites to progress.

Not everyone can say that they have had home school, as well as private and public education growing up, but my sons can. And they are better for it. We moved to Hot Springs, Arkansas, in June of 1986 and began a journey in education that would end up involving the whole family.

My wife had a master's degree in education which, granted, made her more qualified than the average homeschool mom to teach, but more than that, she had a higher standard in mind that made teaching a drive rather than an avocation. Until the fifth grade (the third, for my younger son), my two boys were private schooled. Before being asked to join the staff of teachers at the school, my wife was happy to make up what the boys may have lacked in their education with supplemental time spent in the books at home.

Familiarizing herself with the school's chosen curriculum, she soon became aware of its inherent inferiority…that asked teachers to become mere monitors in student-directed courses. These majored in the student's ability to recognize verbatim answers in the text, rather than teaching them critical thinking skills. When the school appeared unwilling to change the curriculum, she opted to homeschool. As the school was a part of the church we attended, it was a difficult decision.

The next year brought changes for both of us; I was promoted to the Dean of Students of the small Christian college where I also instructed. Making the decision to homeschool put my wife on the track for a suitable curriculum, and we ended up selecting from several the one which challenged the boys most.

Then a church split sent my wife to work at the school which had meanwhile adopted a new curriculum and sent my boys back to private school. Later, in one of those moments, the boys regretted and still later were grateful for, they attended a public high school for one semester. Like I said, their unique experiences have made them into the balanced young men that they are.

To end the saga, let me say one of my sons homeschools his four kids (the other's being too young), my wife still aids and tutors at a Christian school and I am retired after teaching twenty-six years at the college level. We are a family of educators.

It should come as no surprise then that I believe in the mandate to educate. The only differences in belief that we might hold is to whom this mandate is given...and by whom? I believe that *God* gives the mandate to educate (Deut. 11:19) to the *Church* (Matt. 28:20) and to *parents* (Eph. 6:1; Co. 3:20). Nowhere do I find a biblical mandate to educate given by God to the government.

Is education biblical? Should Christian parents homeschool, private school, or public school their children? What about a child's need for quality academics? Aren't the best colleges reserved for the best educated? What about the child's need for social skills? What about their emotional needs? What about their spiritual education? These are the questions that the thinking Christian must answer.

Education, according to the dictionary, is the act or process of imparting or acquiring general knowledge, developing the powers of reasoning and judgment, and generally of preparing oneself or others intellectually for mature life. According to the Bible, Abram was uniquely qualified to be trusted by God with great revelation because He knew he would "command his children and his household after him" (Gen. 18:19, ASV).

Answering questions:

1. Is education biblical?

    Of all the creatures on the face of the earth, man appears to be least prepared for life. Ruled by an internal mechanism we call instinct, most creatures are on their own from an early age—some from birth. Man, a reasoning creature, must be taught almost everything. Perhaps this is what God was doing with Adam as he walked with him in the "cool of the day" (Gen. 3:8). One thing is for certain. The teaching by parents has always been an ingredient for success and definitely biblical.

    > Hear my son, the instruction of thy father, and forsake not the teaching of thy mother; (Prov. 1:8, KJV)

    > My son, forget not my teaching, and let thy heart observe my commandments; for length of days, and years of life, and peace shall they add to thee. (Prov. 3:1–2, KJV)

    > My son, observe thy father's commandment, and forsake not the teaching of thy mother; bind them continually upon thy heart, tie them about thy neck: when thou walkest, it shall lead thee; when thou sleepest, it shall keep thee; and [when] thou awakest, it shall talk with thee. (Prov. 6:20–22, KJV)

2. Should Christian parents homeschool, private school, or public school their children?

    We Christian parents have to realize that our first duty (after God and our spouse, of course) is to our children and our first role is that of Teacher. It is a responsibility, not an option. There may be times when each of the educational alternatives are viable, depending on the quality of the education offered, the availability of parental input, financial considerations, etc. The important thing to keep in mind is the aspect of authority vs. responsibility. While you may delegate the authority over your children to a public or private school teacher, you can never delegate the responsibility for their education.

For younger children...say up until the seventh grade... homeschooling may be a quality inexpensive alternative. Certainly, the younger children are the more likely you'll feel qualified as a parent to homeschool. Economically, the cost of the loss of income to the family for the parent who stays home to educate must be calculated into the real expense...as well as curriculum and supplies which may be provided in the public or private arena.

Admittedly, it is hard to pay in taxes (currently calculated on a national average per year to be $9,350 per student) for public school education and then still have to pay for private or homeschooling, but look at it as an investment in a peaceable and progressive society. If you don't like what public school children are getting either in curriculum or teachers, get more involved...that's what school board elections are for.

Other considerations like shared expertise, social interaction, testing, and even sports can be provided by many homeschool associations. You should check for local availability and any state laws that might affect a homeschooler.

3. What about a child's need for quality academics?

Homeschooling can often make up in security and personal time spent in instruction what it may lack in quality of academics. Besides, most adults have no problems educating to the elementary level, anyway. Another advantage of homeschooling is the speed with which children breeze through curriculum. Many homeschoolers find a half-a-day, four days a week is plenty to keep up the pace. Use Fridays for field trips or work projects.

Although private schools often have superior academics, especially without the PC (Political Correctness) so prevalent in public school textbooks, no curriculum can make up for the lazy student who did not learn early those study habits that will make him or her successful. Sometimes a homeschool beginning is the best way to ensure a strong private school finish.

Set your child up for success early. If a child has a successful academic experience in the first grade, he or she will love school…it is much more pleasant to ride the wave than feel like you're spending your time under the wave, always trying to catch up. If everyone else is learning their A-B-C's, you need to be teaching Johnnie how to read at home. Ensuring he's at the top of his class in the early years will make his latter years more successful.

4. Aren't the best colleges reserved for the best educated?

Both my sons got full-ride scholarships to good schools (although their high school graduating classes numbered ten or less), proving that colleges look at extracurricular activities and ACT and SAT scores more than anything.

Besides, character is caught, not taught. Small class size and the quality of the personal lives of the teaching staff were more important to me in their formative years when values were being established. The principle "time is a multiplier" is never more applicable than in education. Or, as the Scripture says, "Train up a child in the way he should go, and when he is old, he will not depart from it" (Prov. 22:6, KJV).

5. What about the child's need for social skills?

Do kids need exposure to the culture for relevance's sake? This is the argument most private and public school parents offer as an objection to homeschooling. First, let me say that Christian parents are only called to *insulate*, not *isolate*. Children

get a lot of social interaction in church and on the playground...
and screen time—both TV and the internet—offers more than
enough exposure to the culture.

Second, every child needs the social interaction of team
sports—although your youngster may not be athletically gifted,
that's what neighborhood 'pick-up' games and intramurals are
all about. Besides, there's nothing like a team sport for teaching
self-sacrifice, diligence, and cooperation...and nothing like an
individual sport for teaching patience, focus, and self-control.

6. What about their emotional needs?

This is an oft-neglected developmental need of young people
today. And no, I'm not talking about a young man's need to be
sensitive enough to cry or a young girl's need to toughen up...
though those are worthy goals; rather, I am pointing out that
often parents are too busy working to take time to help their
children navigate the many emotional challenges they face.

Emotional education—how to handle taunts, bullying,
victories, defeats, fear, encounters with the opposite sex, etc.—
should be taught in casual conversation by caring parents
around the dinner table or over a game. This is as much needed
by kids growing up, as academic or physical education, and the
responsibility falls directly on the parents' shoulders.

7. What about their spiritual education?

I have resisted—to this point—the temptation to delineate
between the private school and the private *Christian* school.
Many private schools claim to be Christian, but that claim
doesn't make them so, any more than sitting in a garage makes
you a car! Christian schools are truly *Christian* when their
academics, sports, social programs, curriculum, extra-curricular
activities, instructors, and staff lift up Jesus as Lord.

English philosopher Edmund Spencer said that, "Education
has for its object the formation of character." Christian
education, then, has for its object the formation of *Christian*

character. A Christian parent will have failed if all he or she graduates is someone academically prepared for college or physically prepared for professional sports. The question is, will they be able to keep a job, or stay married, or keep their faith?

Man is a tri-part being...body, soul, and spirit. To not educate the whole man is to educate incompletely. Failure is inevitable.

Education is the most important job of a parent. It's how we make our arrows fly true. And the only way we can affect the future. "Like arrows in the hand of a warrior are the children of one's youth" (Psalm 127:4, ESV).

Recommended reading list:

- *Teaching the Trivium: Christian Homeschooling in a Classical Style*, Harvey Bluedorn, Laurie Bluedorn, Johannah Bluedorn
- *The Core: Teaching Your Child the Foundations of Classical Education*, Leigh A. Bortins
- *Basic Principles of Effective Teaching*, June Crabtree

Web sites:

- www.HomeschoolChristian.com
- www.christianaction.org.za/...artic_christian_education. htm
- www.ehow.com/how_5839441_teach-children-basics-christian

15

Entitlements

Social Security, Medicare, Food Stamps (and some would argue Unemployment Insurance)…these are the programs that have come to be known collectively as "Entitlements." As our senators and representatives have learned, giving a dog a bone is easier than taking it away. But what do you do when the bones are really from the dog's own limbs? Or her puppies' limbs? Or her puppies' puppies? I think you get the picture. Today's entitlements are no more than a form of forced economic cannibalism.

Don't get me wrong; I think anybody that has paid into the system should be allowed to collect from it. Although my mother-in-law's Alzheimer's caused us to move her into our home for three years—and we made the necessary family adjustments—the need for constant medical attention eventually became so great that nursing home care was essential. We were grateful for the assistance Medicare provided. But the way entitlements are run now, they are no more than a government-sanctioned Ponzi-scheme, current obligations being extracted from future contributors in the form of indebtedness.

My father died just six months before his sixty-fifth birthday; although he paid into the system his whole life, he didn't collect a penny. That's okay, because the system's actuaries depend on a certain number of zero payouts. But when the system had five paying in for every one collecting and people didn't live beyond seventy-five years of age...well, you do the math; today's baby boomers are just too numerous and long-lived.

When I had two brainstem strokes in 2009, it left me paralyzed on one side, speech impaired and enduring the ignobility of my wife driving me everywhere. I had to sell my landscaping business and quit my teaching job. Obviously, this radically changed my income stream, but we were surviving on the rental income I had built up over the years...this was to be our "retirement." When half of our uninsured rentals were blown away in a tornado on April 25th of 2011, I was grateful, however, for the small disability check coming in every month. I do not say this as a way of complaining—God is faithful—but I still look forward to the day when my new writing career takes off and I can send back my check.

I think that I am not the only one with this sentiment. I, like everyone else who receives an entitlement, would prefer not to be in a position to *have* to receive it. Although I cannot imagine having to buy groceries with food stamps, I'm sure that most recipients do look forward to the day when their temporary setback becomes a thing of the past.

Are entitlements biblical? What should my attitude as a Christian be toward those who have fallen on hard times or are not able to help themselves? For that matter, is retirement biblical? Since people are creatures of necessity, don't entitlements make them lazy? What about the confiscatory nature of entitlement funding? These are the questions thinking Christians must answer.

According to a dictionary amalgamation, *entitlements* are laws based on concepts of principle ("rights") which are themselves based in concepts of social equality or enfranchisement; specifically including, but not limited to Social Security, Disability, Medicare, and Food Stamps. According to the Bible (and our Declaration of Independence), our "rights" as humans, as far as inalienable God-given rights are concerned, are limited to life, liberty, and the pursuit of happiness, at least as revealed by "nature and nature's God."

However, we have developed an "entitlement mentality." In other words, we have bought into the McDonald's mantra: "You deserve a break today." Believe me, none of us want what we deserve (Romans 3:23, 6:23).

Answering questions:

1. Are entitlements biblical?

    Of course they are. All promises are delivered to those who meet the requirements (Deut. 28). But, like I said before, you don't want what you deserve. The Scripture is very clear, "All we like sheep have gone astray" (Isaiah 53:6).

    This may be bad news, but the good news is that Christ bore on the cross all that we deserved. Fortunately, we don't get what we deserve. If we apply His blood to the lintels and doorposts of our heart (Ex. 12:7; Heb. 9:14)—if we trust His substitutionary death—all that we deserve, He took. Not that we are *entitled* to it; but because of His great grace, we are the recipients of all *He* deserves.

2. What should my attitude as a Christian be toward those who have fallen on hard times or are not able to help themselves?

    One of the most perpetrated lies in existence is the mistaken concept that "God helps those that help themselves." In fact, people swear that this quote comes from the Bible. Nothing could be further from the truth. Actually, *God helps those who can't help themselves* (Ps. 41:1–2). He makes special provisions for those who humbly acknowledge their helplessness (Matt. 5:3–11).

    They didn't have welfare in the times of Moses, but God gave him an instruction that would help provide for the widows, the orphans, the stranger, and the working poor. "Gleaners' rights" were a sacred provision for those who were landless and without family (Lev. 19:10; Deut. 24:21). All that the harvesters dropped was for them. The workers in the field were actually told that they could not pick up anything they left behind...it belonged to the gleaner.

Individual responsibility was, however, the rule of the day. If people could provide for themselves, they were encouraged to do so. Even those who had taken someone into their household to provide for them had the responsibility for them, in order that the Church, who provided for everyone else, would not be burdened.

> If any man or woman that believeth have widows, let them relieve them, and let not the church be charged; that it may relieve them that are widows indeed. (1 Tim. 5:16, KJV)

3. For that matter, is retirement biblical?

Having reached retirement age, it does appear attractive, but I've yet to find anything biblical that justifies laziness or an end-of-life break (of course there are those scriptures in Number, chapter 4, that limit the service of the priesthood to fifty). Sure, because our bodies are getting less able, perhaps a slow-down is to be expected. But, managing our investments—for those that have been wise, like the ants (Prov. 30:25)—or corralling grandkids…these are jobs, too, and justify the existence of the elder population.

Like one actuarial study done by an insurance company reported: they looked at one hundred randomly selected men who had continued working after age sixty-five (group A) and one hundred men who had retired to play golf or enjoy a relaxed lifestyle (group B). Assessing group A at seventy-five years of age, they found that ninety were still alive and ten had died. Assessing group B at seventy-five, they found the opposite: ten were still alive and ninety were dead! It seems as though God agreed with them. If they thought—and lived—as though they were finished…they were!

4. Since people are creatures of necessity, don't entitlements make them lazy?

People *are* creatures of necessity—necessity is truly the mother of invention—but entitlements don't make people lazy, *their basic natures do.* Besides, entitlements were only intended to be a stop-gap measure (in the cases of Unemployment Insurance and Food Stamps).

The government—the people we have elected—has chosen to withhold from pay we have earned (because it was rightly believed we would never pay if we had to do so directly) something to fund our support in old age, infirmity, and economic mishap. The government, by trying to do the family and Church's job to mitigate economic hardship or unfortunate circumstance, has only succeeded in creating a dependency. Although it might be wise for a parent to make provision for his children, the nanny-state, by means of entitlements, has created a juvenile class of us all. It is difficult to train in a good work ethic when you remove the incentive to maturely plan for an inevitably unpredictable future.

5.   What about the confiscatory nature of entitlement funding?

Everybody knows that the "lock box" (the Social Security and Medicare Trust Fund) is a myth. I don't doubt that the initial motivation was honorable, but the temptation to co-mingle for general fund "necessities" was just too great...especially when you have the power to print!

Anytime the law of sowing and reaping (2 Cor. 9:6) is set aside, whether through taxation or mitigation, the consequence is a dependence that fosters unproductivity. There are even some who want to ensure their re-election by making the promise of increased governmental largesse...on the backs of the job-creating wealthy. Economic downturn is the inevitable, though unintended, result.

The Word of God says the poor are a fact of life (Matt 14:7). Of course, there are those who have just experienced the capricious nature of living in a fallen world...that's what private charity and the Church are for. But what if a man has reaped the folly of his ways—he is poor because he has made an unwise investment, or is lazy, or has a costly habit? Entitlements that ease his consequence may perpetuate his foolishness. God intends for his family (or Church) to help him though this difficulty—with their attendant counsel—solving not just the poverty, but the causes of it. A cure is always better than symptomatic relief.

Recommended reading list:

- *Rich Dad Poor Dad: What the Rich Teach Their Kids About Money that the Poor and Middle Class Do Not!*, Robert T Kiyosaki
- *The Millionaire Next Door: The Surprising Secrets of America's Wealthy*, Thomas J. Stanley and William D. Danko
- *The Richest Man in Babylon*, George S. Clason

Web sites:

- www.heritage.org/federalbudget/entitlements
- www.washingtonpost.com/blogs/wonkblog/wp/2013/04/05
- www.bloomberg.com/entitlements

16

The Environment

Almost ten years laboring as a landscaper has taught me a few things about one of God's greatest and most sacred of trusts: The Environment. From the beginning, when "God planted a garden eastward, in Eden" (Gen. 2:8, ASV), He has been involved and interested in Man's treatment of His world. Although the Scripture is clear about His ownership of this world (Ex. 9:29; Ps. 24:1), it is also clear that He has placed us as stewards over it (Gen. 2:8,15).

I've learned a little about this world in the process of trying to beautify other people's gardens. For instance, weeds are the natural order of things. If left alone, gardens, yards, and planting beds only produce weeds. *In fact, it takes a lot of effort to get anything else to grow.* (I suppose you could learn a lot about the natural *moral* order from looking at the natural physical order...that moral entropy was the default, too, but that's the subject of another piece.)

The environment is more than a sacred trust, though. Our treatment of God's creation tells Him a lot about our handling of many other things with which He has entrusted us—kind like you can tell a lot about how a guy will treat a girl by the way he treats his server at a restaurant. This barometer, of sorts, has many people worried. They look at environmental issues and how we treat this world and wonder if God is all that pleased with us.

Perhaps you think that I must be a "tree-hugger" with an attitude like that. Actually, I'm not...it's just that we Christians have allowed others to hijack our stewardship, to take the moral high-ground concerning the environment. This might be acceptable if their environmental philosophy wasn't so wrongheaded.

Take global warming, for instance. Self-described enviro-nazis would have us taxing ourselves into oblivion by buying carbon credits when polluters like China won't subscribe to the same standards. Besides, anyone who's ever filled an iced tea glass to the brim knows that the glass doesn't overflow because the ice melts... flooding of coastal waterways by floating melting icecaps is a myth, too. (Come on, didn't anyone pay attention in science class growing up? The mass of water displaced by ice equals the mass of the volume of water it displaces!) News flash! The mean temperature of earth fluctuates. It always has...it always will; but six tenths of a degree is nothing to put your knickers in a twist—when I was a kid, the headlines were filled with dire predictions by scientists of the coming Ice Age!

Is environmental stewardship biblical? Is Man so valuable as to consider other animals as "second class"? Shouldn't we be more careful about pesticides, herbicides, and other toxins to which we subject a fragile environment? What about preserving our protective ozone layer? Isn't the very presence of Man an intrusion on the rest of nature? These are the questions thinking Christians must answer.

According to a dictionary amalgamation, the *environment* refers to the sum total of the surroundings of a physical system that may interact with the system by exchanging mass, energy, or other properties; it includes all those organisms that live within that certain habitat. According to the Bible, the environment may be limited to an area that is as small as the Garden of Eden—granted, bordered by the Pison, Gishon, Hiddekel, and Tigris Rivers, it may have been hundreds of thousands of square miles—or as large as the whole earth. But more importantly, the Bible confirms a hierarchy of values for living things: Angels above people (Ps. 8:5), people above animals (Gen. 1:26), animals above plants (Gen. 1:30), and, of course, God above all (Gen. 1:1).

Answering questions:

1. Is environmental stewardship biblical?

    Of course it is! We were created in the image of God (Gen. 1:26), given a home like God's home (Gen. 1:1...the Hebrew word for heavens is *shomayim*—the first heaven is earth and its atmosphere (Gen. 1:6–8); the second heaven is from the edge of our atmosphere and through space (Gen. 1:14–18); the third heaven is the dwelling place of God (2 Chron. 6:33; 2 Cor. 12:2) and given a job like God's job (Gen. 1:28, Col. 1:17).

    As God tends and keeps the universe "in Him all things hold together" (Col. 1:17, NASB), so do we keep this earth.

2. Is Man so valuable as to consider other animals as "second class"?

    How a person treats his or her pet will often indicate how he or she will treat others for which they have some care or responsibility. We Christians should set the example for the world for the ethical treatment of animals. That doesn't mean to put animals' needs above humans, but he who would kick a dog or a cat often has abuse issues in other areas. Here's a definition for abuse that might be apropos here: violently taking out our frustrations concerning those things over which we have no control, on objects over which we do have control... or "negative stewardship."

    Although provisions need to be made for research, Christians should never allow pain or disease to be inflicted on animals for the sake of science. We put a man on the moon; surely we can come up with humane ways to learn what we must.

    By the same token, we must never allow humans to become "second class." Jobs and corporate progress must not be held hostage by an "endangered species." Safely relocating organisms to alternate environments should create more jobs, not cost more jobs by holding up progress. This isn't rocket science, but it is hard work...creativity and cool reasoning heads may be required.

3. Shouldn't we be more careful about pesticides, herbicides, and other toxins to which we subject a fragile environment?

Yes, but the environment is not as fragile as we might think. We need to act responsibly—but malaria is not anyone's idea of a good time, either. Spraying malathion—which kills disease-breeding mosquitoes—needs to be responsibly done, not eliminated; careful application of DDT has more beneficial effects than the long-term negatives that some environmental activists warn.

I'm not for indiscriminate spraying of herbicides or pesticides, but waterways that are affected by runoff can be monitored and protected. We just have to make decisions which are responsible and well-reasoned and take Man's dominion into consideration. That's what good stewardship is all about.

4. What about preserving our protective ozone layer?

Anyone ever seen a polar bear or a penguin with a sunburn? Neither have I. (I have a friend that used to work for NASA and he showed me twenty years of satellite photos of a fluctuating hole in the ozone layer…it's only over the poles folks!)

Yes, the ozone layer does filter out harmful UV light. Yes, there is a hole in it. But it occurs naturally and fluctuates with solar cycles…and appears only over the poles. And it is not destroyed by escaping flourocarbons or chloroflourocarbons (CFCs). The ozone layer is in the stratosphere, several miles above the earth. CFCs found in refrigerants and aerosols are heavier than air and go down toward the ground, and not up toward the ozone. Besides, more CFCs were released in the atmosphere in thirty seconds of Mt. St. Helens' eruption than all the agency of Man.

It is easy to perpetrate a lie on an uneducated public… especially when pseudo-scientists only work on projects funded by those whose ends are furthered by results that support their hypothesis.

5. Isn't the very presence of Man an intrusion on the rest of nature?

This is a mantra that is often repeated. I don't know where it originated...perhaps in the junk-science of people like Dr. Paul Ehrlich, author of the 1961 doomsday best-seller *The Population Bomb*. He predicted famines and pestilence beyond our wildest imagination by the year 2000. According to Dr. Ehrlich, the earth just could not sustain such a burgeoning population. Popular Hollywood writers bought into this myth and gave us "Soylent Green" and other disaster flicks. These films began flooding our culture and contributed to the self-preserving climate that justified Roe v. Wade.

Well, I've done the math and a far greater population than even Ehrlich could have imagined would fit inside the state of Texas...just four to a 2,500-sq.-ft., two-story house on a quarter of an acre!

Without the responsible caring stewardship of Man this earth *is* in trouble.

Recommended reading list:

- *Trashing the Planet: How Science Can Help Us Deal with Acid Rain, Depletion of the Ozone and Nuclear Waste*, Dixie Lee Ray
- *Environmental Overkill: Whatever Happened to Common Sense?*, Dixie Lee Ray
- *Inherit the Earth*, Dr. Gary North

Web sites:

- www.godandscience.org/apologetics/environment
- www.christianecology.org/Stewardship
- www.equip.org/articles/christians-and-the-environment

17

Faith, Fear, and Foolishness

The curling wisp of smoke coming out of the shower-house screening and the tell-tale hiss-splash-flush of a cigarette being extinguished were all I needed to know what David Fawcett must be up to. Twelve going on twenty…or so he thought, David had come to Brookhill Camp with two cartons of contraband and a two-pack-a-day habit helped by parents who thought it was cute that their seven-year-old smoked! I learned all this as I walked David to his first activity; he had not shown up for the wagon ride which prompted my investigation into the bunkhouse area—I was his senior counselor and duly concerned with his health…physical and spiritual.

His second activity was sailing, my field of "assigned expertise." Big Lake may have been a term that lacked some creativity but compared to the other smaller ponds it seemed appropriate and plenty big enough to teach basic sailing technique. The sailfish class boats sported a small lanteen sail and a dagger-board that often doubled for an emergency paddle. Today was like most days on the lake—enough wind to get us to the middle of the lake before the heat of the day brought its calm.

David was my student today—I had planned it that way—a captive audience; undivided attention till "dagger-board time." Of course, I had orchestrated this; we were going over nautical terms… preparing him for his oral test at the end of the week. The other boats were close, but out of earshot, so I saw my opportunity… David," I began, "how many times have you tried to quit smoking?"

Hanging his head, he responded, "So many times I have lost count."

After a long pause, I asked, "Have you ever seen a real miracle?"

"No, not really."

"If you ever saw one, do you think you'd have the faith to believe God could take away your desire for cigarettes?" I asked.

"Yeah…I guess…I mean, if it was really real." His response came slowly and suspiciously.

After a much longer pause, I asked, "Did you ever hear in Sunday school about how Jesus spoke to the wind and waves and calmed a storm?"

"Yeah," he came back slowly and warily.

I said, "I suppose if He could calm the wind, He could cause it to blow." Without waiting for a response, I said, "Then in the Name of Jesus, I command the wind to blow!"

Instantly a steady gust began to blow, our sail filled up, and we surged ahead taking water in at the bow until we could shift our body weight rebalancing to compensate. David's eyes widened, and he said, "Look!" He pointed at the other three boats which still languished motionless in the water.

My eyes had to be huge, too. I had prayed, but I didn't expect anything quite so dramatic! Back at camp that night, David shared at Vespers and seven kids surrendered their hearts to Christ at his testimony…*and* David threw away his cigarettes. Okay, so I was young and didn't know better. Seriously, sometimes God moves to prove Himself strong…but it is always purposeful.

Faith and *Fear* are similar in that both are convinced that something you cannot see now is going to happen…the only difference is that one happens *to* you the other happens *for* you—darkness is what gives fear its power—light is what gives faith its power. Sometimes fear can be healthy…fear of the Lord, for instance. But that's not the kind of fear I'm talking about.

Let me explain. Darkness conceals. We fear to walk confidently ahead in the darkness because we don't know if we'll trip on something we cannot see. Light reveals. Faith has us walking confidently forward...not because the darkness fails to conceal, *but our knowledge of His love reveals we have nothing to fear.*

Then there is *Foolishness.* We are foolish when we order God around like some cosmic bellhop. My pastor, Ricky Jones, put it well: Faith is not magic. Magic is slight-of-hand (in fact, the technical term is presti*digit*ation). Nor is it "wishful thinking"; we simply cannot decide ourselves how God is going to move. *That is the Holy Spirit's job.* He must "lead you and guide you" (John 16:12–13) to the truth of a situation...whether it's the approach of a wind, as in the example above, or the existence of an unseen army (2 Kings 6:17).

Deception is so deceptive because we are led to believe a lie. The falseness of a lie is measured in its nearness to the truth. Just because something sounds good does not mean it is God's will... at least not at this time. Because Jesus was "led up of the Holy Spirit" (Matt. 4:1), He was not deceived by Satan's temptation to throw Himself off the pinnacle of the temple (Matt. 4:5–7). Even though the Devil quoted the Scripture at Him (Matt. 4:6; from Ps. 91:11–12), it was not from the Holy Spirit; Jesus also quoted the Scripture back at him, "It is also written thou shalt not put the Lord to a *foolish* test (Matt. 4:7; from Deut. 6:16)." *Foolishness happens, when inspired by the enemy or some selfish personal motive, we decide how God should act in a certain situation.*

Is faith, fear, or foolishness biblical? How do I know when the Holy Spirit is leading me? If fear can sometimes be healthy, how do I know when to fear and when not to? What is the connection between doubt or unbelief and fear? How many times should I ask God to do something before I give up? These and other questions are the ones that thinking Christians should be asking themselves.

According to a dictionary amalgamation, *Faith* is either the system of beliefs that a certain subscriber of that belief holds (as in a religion) or the actual confidence in a person, thing, or deity not proved empirically. *Fear* is an emotion and a basic survival mechanism where one turns away from impending danger. *Foolishness* is an unwise course of action. For the foolish, reasonable thought almost never comes—that's why those who choose this course are called "fools." According to the Bible, "Faith is the substance of things hoped for, the evidence of things not seen" (Heb. 11:1). I kind of like my own practical definition, too: Faith is the willingness to trust yourself to the consequences of your belief.

Answering questions:

1. Is faith, fear, or foolishness biblical?

    "But without faith it is impossible to please Him, for he who comes to God must believe that He is, and that He is a rewarder of those who diligently seek Him" (Heb. 11:6, NKJV). Of course, faith is in the Bible. It is important that the Christian realizes that faith is also a gift from God—sometimes we get to thinking that the miracle is God's part and faith is ours. Nothing could be further from the truth…even the faith required to believe for God's intervention is provided by God. Otherwise, the prayer for faith would make no sense—"Lord, I believe; help thou my unbelief" (Mk. 9:24).

    There is a story told about the great preacher of healing, Oral Roberts. A woman came up to him early in his ministry and asked him to pray for her son who was born without a hip socket. He told her he did not believe in creative miracles. She said, "That's okay. God has given me the faith; you just pray."

    Fear, on the other hand, is often what makes our faith shaky. Sometimes, it is what keeps us from asking…as if we aren't sure the Lord wants to meet our need. Of course He wants to meet our need (Phil. 4:19); He just might want something more important for us…or we might be the limiting factor. The Scripture teaches that, "Beloved, I wish above all things that thou mayest prosper and be in health, *even as thy soul prospers*" (3 John 2). Prosperity of the soul, then, becomes the limiting factor. In other words, God may be more interested in growing you up, than in giving you your childish demands.

"The fear of the Lord is the beginning of wisdom" (Prov. 9:10). Or as we said in our house, "The fear of Dad..." (Maybe you don't believe in corporal discipline...and maybe I'm wrong...but then I'll never have to visit my kids in jail, either.) In any case, as any good psychologist will teach, "Fear of loss is a greater motivator than hope of gain." As the proverb says, "Foolishness is bound up in the heart of a child; the rod of discipline will remove it far from him" (Prov. 22:15, NASU).

While "the fear of the Lord" might be the "beginning" of wisdom, *love is its end* (1 Cor. 13). A small child will obey for fear of the consequences, but the mature will obey to hear, "Well done thou good and *faith*ful servant..." (Matt. 25:21). Fear may be what initially gets our attention, but it is for love of the Master that the mature Christian labors (John 21:15–17).

As for foolishness, "It is the fool that says in his heart, 'there is no God'" (Ps. 14:1). There is no fear where there is no belief in God. No fear, no wisdom.

Now, there is a fear that is unbiblical. I mean, it's in the Bible, but not as a good thing.

> Do not fear those who kill the body but are unable to kill the soul; but rather fear Him who is able to destroy both soul and body in hell." (Matt. 28:10 NASU)

2. How do I know when the Holy Spirit is leading me?

The Holy Spirit will never go against the counsel of the Word of God, so if it's unbiblical, rest assured, the Holy Spirit is not leading in that direction. The Holy Spirit will also never lead you to do anything outside of the character of God.

Generally, the Holy Spirit will provide you with the confirmation sufficient for the moment. If the Lord is leading you down some difficult path, He will give you the confidence you need sufficient for the challenge you face...almost. It will always require some faith to be obedient. (Abraham's sacrifice of Isaac, Moses with his back against the Red Sea, David facing Goliath...these were difficult paths, but God provided—a substitute ram, a powerful staff, or previous experience with a bear and a lion)

3. If fear can sometimes be healthy, how do I know when to fear and when not to?

    It is wise not to have your kids play with poisonous snakes, but the Apostle Paul could shake off one when he was gathering wood to warm a shipwrecked crew (Acts 28:3–7). It is wise to watch the weather channel and seek shelter from an oncoming storm, but Jesus wasn't stupid to be asleep in the bottom of a boat being tossed by a storm (Mk. 4:36–39). As my friend and very talented artist, Ralph Irwin, once quipped—he was a medic without a rifle in Viet Nam—"The safest place to be is the center of God's will."

4. What is the connection between doubt or unbelief and fear?

    When we have faith, we believe God is on our side (Rom. 8:31). Nothing that happens to us is really detrimental to us in the long run, but even what we perceive as against us will work out for our good (Rom. 8:28).

    If we have fear, it is because we don't really believe that God loves us, because "perfect love casts out fear" (I John 4:18, NKJV).

    Doubt and unbelief come in when we say to ourselves, "If God really loved me, He would not let this—whatever 'this' is—happen to me. The reality is that He loved you so much He couldn't leave you the way you were. Besides He knows just how much you can take (1 Cor. 10:13).

5. How many times should I ask God to do something before I give up?

    If we really want something for our birthday or Christmas don't we become quite obnoxious just making sure our friends and family know about it? Although our Heavenly Father knows our needs even before we ask (Matt. 6:8), it shows him just how sincere our heart is when we ask and keep on asking (Luke 11:5–9).

Paul, asked three times to be delivered from his "thorn in the flesh"—though not specified, presumably some physical ailment—and the Lord chose to not answer his request, so he quit asking (2 Cor. 12:7–9). The reason God gave for not answering his prayer is "...*My strength is made perfect in weakness*" (verse 9). Sometimes the Lord has a better 'good' in mind, but like Paul, you will never know till you ask.

I would love to be healed of the effects of the two brainstem strokes I had in 2009. I have the faith to be healed and I've asked...and will continue to do so...and I'm sure He will heal me when it's in my best interest for Him to do so...and till then I'll trust that *His* timing is perfect.

While we might wish we had less fear and more faith, it doesn't take much to move a mountain (Matt. 17:20). Surely your problem is smaller than that.

Recommended reading list:

- *I Don't Have Enough Faith to be an Atheist*, Norman L. Geisler and Frank Turek
- *The Secret Power of Speaking God's Word*, Dr. Joyce Meyer
- *Fear Not*, Max Lucado

Web sites:

- www.acts17–11.com/faith.html
- www.soulinscriptions.wordpress.com/2013/05/20/ faith-without
- www.gracethrufaith.com/ask-a-bible-teacher/ fear-and-faith

18

Family

Sitting on the couch at sixteen, knowing what my dad was going to say, did not make hearing it any easier. "Okay, kids," my dad said resignedly, "your mom and I have called this family meeting to let you know that we're getting a divorce." There was a long pause…my half-brother, Matthew, ten years of age, started crying. My mentally handicapped brother, three years my elder started crying, too. This was the culmination of years of a bickering, nagging-and-retreat-to-his-workshop verbal estrangement of my mother and father that resulted in more relief than pain on my part.

Family was not meant for fracture; from my perspective, there was something good that resulted from my parents' divorce: it became the seed for my salvation a year later. For that, and the relief it brought from the emotional abuse to which I had been subjected, I was and am grateful.

I have always thought that family was important. Even though my own mother died when I was two, her parents—my grandparents— always embraced the role of grand-parenting and saw to it that we had their input or provision or whatever we needed. On my father's side, my grandparents were appropriately doting, even after my grandfather died early, at age sixty-one. My grandmother Sargent annually hosted the holiday meals. She was a consummate cook and her five children—my four aunts and my dad—and her fourteen grandchildren—my cousins—always ate at her blissfully chaotic Christmas table. Therefore, it was not out-of-character for us to move to Tulsa (a year ago) to be with our children and offer free childcare for our grandchildren.

Is the concept of family biblical? What does family have to do with identity? Is the traditional nuclear family relevant to today's culture? What about divorce, re-marriage, and the single-parent home...what do you do when you find yourself in a family with these challenges? What is the proper flow of authority in the family? These and other questions need addressing.

According to the dictionary, *Family* is a fundamental social group in society typically consisting of one or two parents and their children. This would be an emotionally bereft definition a hundred years ago, but sadly, this basic—and hollow—definition is certainly more apropos to today's families who spend much less time together than their immediate ancestors. The good news is that more families have come to the realization that there is just no substitute for time spent together.

Dr. W. J. Doherty, in a recent book entitled *Putting Family First*, has noted a recent incline of 28 percent of families that have begun eating dinner together around the family table (at least five times per week), with the attendant benefits.

Dr. Doherty states, "For young children, meal time at home is a stronger predictor of academic achievement and psychological adjustment than time spent in any of the following activities: school, studying, sports, church/religious activities, or art activities. For teens, having regular dinners with parents is a strong predictor of academic success, psychological adjustment, and lower rates of alcohol use, drug use, early sexual behavior, eating disorders, and risk for suicide."

I'd say this is pretty strong evidence that screen-time may be giving way to face-time, at least in America. Although the family table can be a site for squabbles and other less-than-calm exchanges which can demean and belittle, that is what parents are for. It can also be where children relate the events of their day, learn the basic manners of social grace and conversation, receive wisdom from older siblings and parents, and express their own frustrations within a non-threatening problem-solving forum. Something neither Facebook nor *World of Warcraft* can accomplish.

Answering questions:

1. Is the concept of family biblical?

    "It is not good that the man should be alone" (Gen. 2:18, KJV). God starts out His assessment of Man's condition of singleness—a clue to the Creator's ultimate plan of marriage for most of us—with a recommendation of close fellowship with someone of the opposite sex (read the context). The family, complete with children (Gen. 4:1,2; 5:4), has been God's plan from the beginning. Of course it is biblical.

    Add to the evidence found in His creation, the first command which He gave to all creation: "Be fruitful and multiply" (Gen 1:22,28). Lest we think this applied only up to the time of the flood, God reiterated this command to Noah and his descendants (Gen. 8:17, 9:1). And, lest you have bought into the propaganda of Stanford University's Paul Ehrlich, who wrote his 1968 book *The Population Bomb*, to warn that the earth would soon (before the turn of the century) not be able to sustain its own population…I've done the math. The entire population of the earth could fit in an area not much larger than the state of Texas…giving everyone a one-fourth-acre lot, a two-story house, and only two children!

2. What does family have to do with identity?

    The two earliest and most universal questions are "Who am I?" and "Why am I here?" In fact, the answers to these two questions are all wrapped up in western civilization's human naming system and our quest for identity. The first or "given name" describes who you are—or who your parents wanted you to be…thus answering the first question. Although the second or "family name" is for the purpose of defining your heritage, in most cases, it derives from the family occupation—

Colliers were coal vendors, Smiths were craftsmen or hand-manufacturers, Coopers were barrel-makers, etc., thus answering the second question.

Even the Name of the Savior follows this pattern. Jesus Christ: "Jesus" is the Greek form of Joshua (which means Savior—think of the other Joshua's role as the leader of Israel who led the people into the Promised Land) and "Christ" comes from the Greek *Christos* (which means Anointed One—think of the purpose for which Christ came).

As Christians, knowing who we are and why we are here will eliminate the possibility of an identity crisis. Those who had played a pivotal role in the direction of history often received their names from God, either being named initially by God—in the cases of Ishmael (Gen. 16:11), Isaac (Gen. 17:19), John (Lk. 1:13), and Jesus (Matt 1:21), or having their names (and direction of their lives) changed—as in the cases of Abram (Gen. 17:5), Sarai (Gen. 17:15), and Jacob (Gen. 32:28).

Have you received a name from God? Ancestry on my mother's side came from the Old World as part of the German emigration of the seventeenth and eighteenth centuries. These "Pennsylvania Dutch" took biblical names and destroyed the old records, believing that since a new life awaited them in the New World, they should have new names. My ancestry chose the name Israel, hence my mother's maiden name is Israel. Whether you have chosen a new name or been given one by God, it is much easier to *claim* a new destiny than to *acquire* one.

3. Is the traditional nuclear family relevant to today's culture?

The days of a *Leave It to Beaver*, *Father Knows Best*, or an *Ozzie and Harriet* role model may be over, but surely the *Partridge Family*, the *Brady Bunch*, and *My Three Sons*, or even the more contemporary *Simpsons*, and *Modern Family* offer us nothing better. As Christians, we have to look back much farther to get a non-fictionalized model worthy of emulation.

One of our Founding Fathers comes to mind. John Adams, a devout but practical man who took seriously his role as a father, had an able wife in Abigail. She knew how to be supportive of her husband's endeavors without losing sight of her chosen calling: mother of five children—two girls and three boys. She knew tragedy, as her last child, Susannah, died in childbirth, and her first child, Abigail, died as a toddler. She also knew triumph, as her eldest boy, John Quincy, became the sixth president of the United States. She oversaw the family farm business and was her husband's chief unofficial adviser; her over 1,100 letters of correspondence with her often-absent mate were filled with her opinions on the political issues of the day. She read all the works of Shakespeare and Milton and was self-educated to a high degree. We would have to look long and hard to find a better role model for family than the Adams.

A family with husband, wife, and children may seem old fashioned or too provincial for modern mores, but not irrelevant. The challenges that face the modern family have not lessened, but increased. Nothing can provide security like a man and woman in a committed life-long relationship. The need for a strong, confident, hard-working, father-figure in the home is needed now, more than ever. Women, who know how pivotal a role they play as "help-mate" (Gen. 2:18), the importance of their role model to the future generation they raise in their home, and the valuable contributions they make to the income, stability, and health of their home, are vital…and relevant.

4. What about divorce, re-marriage, and the single-parent home…what do you do when you find yourself in a family with these challenges?

    God hates divorce (Mal. 2:16), but, in rare cases, makes allowance for it (Matt. 5:31–32). Being married for nearly forty years (never divorced—yet both of us come from homes quite acquainted with divorce) has given me some insight on what it takes to stay married. Here are the ingredients for a successful marriage: forgiveness, unconditional love, forgiveness, accommodation, forgiveness, commitment, forgiveness, humility, forgiveness, self-sacrifice, forgiveness, hard work, forgiveness, friends, forgiveness...oh, and that most-important ingredient...FORGIVENESS.

Divorce may disqualify you from some roles of leadership where example is important, but it is no greater (or lesser) than any sin, as all sin separates us from a Holy God. But that's why Jesus came (Matt. 20:28). Divorce, like any sin, can be forgiven. However, repairing your relationship with God, Who separates you from your sin as far as the east is from the west (Ps. 103:12) and Who has the ability to "remember no more" our sin (Jer. 31:34), may be less difficult than repairing your relationship with your spouse, who, by the way, has the memory of an elephant!

Yes, remarriage is possible, with your former spouse... or someone else, *if* you are forgiven (presuming you are the offending party), but the way you end something is the way you'll start the next thing *unless change occurs*; if the divorce was caused by some flaw of character, the flaw must be fixed first.

Single-parenting is not God's perfect plan...it is kind of like trying to save a marriage when adultery is the problem...not impossible, but as hard as putting the toothpaste back in the tube, I've actually tried this and it is possible, but it requires a lot of patience, hard work, and it is messy.

If you have good extended family or a good church, single-parenting is easier. The male or female role model—whichever one is missing—can be supplied by some other caring and patient individual. The Lord has used many a Sunday school teacher or some grandparent or uncle or aunt to take up the slack.

Divorce and single-parenting also often come with complications...like custody, visitation, and child support. Although most of the time, divorce is like abortion (ultimately an act of selfishness and immaturity...with collateral damage); it can lead to absence of conflict (not to be mistaken for peace). The cessation of hostility can lead to more clear thinking...

though a good counselor might have told you that and saved you some grief.

Legal separation might give you the needed perspective also. Less permanent than divorce, it may give you the time for the reflection and counsel that will save a marriage. Better yet, a long engagement period and the counsel of good friends or a pastor before the fact.

The thing to remember: whatever is best for the kids. Often, they are the innocent victims in the situation. The counsel you get needs to take them into consideration.

5. What is the proper flow of authority in the family?

Anything with two heads is a monster. There are times when the role of Protector, Provider, and Guide may be the delegated position of the husband or the wife, but the ultimate responsibility falls squarely on the shoulders of the man (I Tim. 5:8). My son Jonathan is homeschooling his four adopted kids…his wife Michelle goes to work every day as the primary breadwinner. Just because she has been willing to use her energy and effort to be the provider for their family does not alleviate Jon from his responsibility. While authority may be delegated, responsibility cannot.

The proper flow of authority for the Christian family is simple: God – father – mother – older siblings – younger siblings. I know I will be accused of sexism, misogynism, and male chauvinism, but the Scripture records God as "Our Father…"(Matt. 3:29), not our mother. However, the male authority in the home comes not from God's gender example, but from a passage in the Book of Genesis. "To the woman He said: I will greatly multiply your sorrow and your conception; in pain you shall bring forth children; *your desire shall be for your husband, and he shall rule over you*" (Gen. 3:16, NKJV).

Now, one could get from this some inferior position for woman; nothing could be further from the truth. Women were considered by God as equally worthy vessels of His Holy

Spirit as evidenced by their presence at His outpouring in Acts 1:14–2:5.

As the old—and factual—saying goes, Woman was not taken from man's feet that he should walk over her, nor from his head that she should rule over him, but from his side that they should walk together through life, side by side. Besides, who has more influence, the head or the neck that turns it?

Recommended reading list:

- *Putting Family First: Successful Strategies for Reclaiming Family Life in A Hurry Up World*, Doherty, W. J.
- *The Dr. James Dobson Parenting Collection*, James C. Dobson
- *Restoring the Christian Family: A Biblical Guide to Love, Marriage, and Parenting in a Changing World*, John and Paula Sandford

Web sites:

- www.focusonthefamily.com (Focus on the Family, Dr. James C. Dobson)
- www.frc.org (The Family Research Council)
- www.christian-family.net

19

Foster Care

Having never been a foster parent might seem to disqualify me from writing an article on this subject (or you, not desiring to ever become a foster parent, from reading this); however, if I could only write from my personal experience, this would be a short work indeed! Christians need to have an "ethos"—a worldview or way of thinking—on this subject, especially. Besides, I did consult the laws in various states and my son and daughter-in-law, who reviewed the foster system extensively before adopting their four kids.

Everything we do or think has an impact on someone. As Christians, with a positive outlook on life, the knowledge of God's expectations and the power of His presence in our lives, we have a unique opportunity and *responsibility* to transmit all of this to the next generation. What better way than taking in a captive audience—a foster child? (*Note: Regardless of your faith, foster parents are expected to continue the traditional religious upbringing of the child...Buddhist, Muslim, or whatever—Christian foster parents may want to designate that they will take children only from a Christian religious tradition.*)

One of the Church's earliest ministries to the community was a rescue mission. Many Roman families, seeking a male heir, would throw unwanted female offspring off the bridge over the Tiber to perish in the dark waters of the river that flowed through Rome. Christians would wait on the shore, underneath, in the shadows of the bridge, for the tell-tale splash of a discarded child and jump in to rescue them. Christian families would then raise the child until some more permanent situation presented itself—perhaps a barren couple's prayers were thus answered.

For centuries, this Christian response to the secular practice of infanticide testified to the Church's value of life. Now that medical technology has made abortion safe (*for everyone but the baby in the womb!*)—and political expedience has made it legal—Christians have more than one front for their efforts. Still, until voters come around to the Church's persuasion, quality foster care can offer part of the solution to former Surgeon General (under Clinton) Jocelyn Elder's "every child a wanted child" problem.

The whole debate about what to do with unwanted children needs to change. Children need to be seen as valuable; as an opportunity for influencing the future. They are a blank slate waiting to be written upon. If children are our arrows shot into the future—a reference to a quote from Psalms 127:4—then we should fill our quiver full of them (verse 5). But it doesn't "take a village"—as Hillary Clinton titled her book—but rather a family; and a Christian family at that.

Unfortunately, today's foster system is not run by a spiritually motivated Church seeking the children's role for the future, but a politically motivated government that sees their charges as problems seeking a solution. Kids that enter foster care as innocent children often come out as hardened cynical adults that inflict their worldview on subsequent generations or populate our prisons. They need love, security, and guidance...not lust, fear, and distraction. Although the foster care system may place children with families, because they are representing a secular government, no spiritual consideration can be regarded. This is one third of a child's being.

And then there's the profit motivation. Funds, originally intended to defray the added costs of childcare, have become the bribery money to encourage a continued dependency on the system—by the parents *and* the medical community who prescribe the children's drug-induced sedation. The more labels that can be placed on these kids—ADD, ADHD, hypertension, RAD, ODD, night terrors, Tourette's syndrome, etc.—the larger the subsidy. There is no incentive to remove them from these mind-numbing substances, but rather it is much more profitable to keep them drugged-up. Foster parents convince themselves it makes the children more adoptable because they come with a paycheck.

Christian Foster Care is the answer. Kids raised in the "nurture and admonition of the Lord" (Eph. 6:4) have a potential for making a positive contribution to society. Foster care, which was designed as a *temporary* interim solution, then acts to properly prepare kids for a more permanent situation—either a return to biological parents who have solved the issues that made them temporarily ineligible or to adoption by a qualified family. Kids should be so loved, nurtured, and guided by their foster parents that they look at something more permanent as an opportunity for identity and not an escape from an imprisonment or a slavery.

Is foster care biblical? What causes a child to be placed in the foster care system? How is foster care different from adoption? Should only the family that has both parents consider foster care? Am I too old for foster care? What about the funds available for 'special needs' kids? These are the questions thinking Christians should be asking themselves.

According to a combination of what many dictionaries and encyclopedias say, *Foster Care* is the temporary assignment of children to an institution, a group home or certified private home to receive care until more permanent situations can be found. Sometimes minors have been removed by the circumstances of biological parents or guardians, often quite tragic, but always the foster care system endeavors to lessen the impact of those tragedies to the child.

Answering questions:

1. Is foster care biblical?
    Although they didn't have the foster care system we have come to know today, the children of Israel did have specific

instructions as to how God expected them to treat aliens—Gentiles—in their midst (Deut. 10:19; Num. 15:15). Not only were they to treat them with love and kindness, they were to show no partiality when judging them (Deut. 1:16).

In the New Testament, we are given an even greater mandate as Jesus told us to "do unto others, as we would have them do unto us" (Luke 6:31). Not only that, but the Apostle Paul said—in Philippians 2:13—that we are to esteem others more highly than ourselves.

Inherent in the concept of foster care is fostering. This means that the biblical concept is one that encourages the growth of its subject. This implies the same protection, provision, and guidance that the parent supplies to his biological children must also be applied to those others that may be temporarily within his household. David's care of the needs of his charge—Jonathan's son—Mephibosheth, is a good example (2 Sam. 9:6–13).

2. What causes a child to be placed in the foster care system?

Some children are placed in the foster care system because their biological parents are temporarily unable to parent them. This may be due to debilitating accidents, legal or criminal issues, neglect or abuse. When the parents get out of the hospital, jail, or counseling, provided they have been recertified by the courts as "fit parents," the children may come home. Of course, there are circumstances where that may not be possible or the parents may give up their parental rights. In such cases, the children may become adoptable by the fostering parent or someone who has gone through that state's prequalifying process. It is not uncommon for a child to have several foster parents fill this temporary role while a more permanent provision is sought.

Sometimes, when the biological parents are killed, and no immediate placement can be made to an adopting relative or other adopting family, an interim situation, a foster parent, needs to be used.

3. How is foster care different from adoption?

   Really, the basic difference is time. The fostering of a child is temporary, while the adoption of a child is permanent, the child having all the legal rights of inheritance and the parents having all the legal obligations they have for their biological children.

   Parents contemplating adoption need to consider these obligations soberly *before* making the commitment that adoption requires. The basic roles of provider, protector, and guide will be their legal and moral obligation. I don't know how much Dr. James Dobson had foster parents in mind when he titled his book *Parenting Isn't For Cowards*, but it applies to them 'in spades!'

   Adoption, in all of its repercussions, needs to be carefully reviewed, before offering a child the security it will provide. Not only is a decision 'non-refundable,' but adopted children who experience the regret of parents are at least as hurt as biological children who suffer the same kind of 'buyer's remorse.' Parenting of either kind is a serious and life-altering decision.

4. Should only the family that has both parents consider foster care?

   Of course, there is a value in the division of labor and having a male and a female perspective can be helpful, but many single men and women have made effective foster parents. Remember the key word is *temporary*. Although I would still defer to the family that has a mom and a dad for adoption, what can be added by a foster parent in the special ministry that occurs between him (or her) and a child is very meaningful.

   A willing and caring Christian single parent can make a good foster parent. Remember, the key is that the foster parent is working himself (or herself) out of a job; all input is to prepare the child for something more permanent. For instance, the care a Christian foster parent provides might include praying with the child for the adoptive parents or familiarizing the child with those scriptures that talk about God's adoption of us as His children.

5. Am I too old for foster care?

The foster caring of infants may be best served by an adult who has the strength to pick them up, but from the toddler age and up, love and experience might be the better preparations anyway. Older foster parents may make better recruits for those willing to work hard wanting to "stay young" and make a positive contribution in the life of a foster child.

6. What about the funds available for 'special needs' kids?

This should never be seen as a source of income for the "professional" foster parent, but rather as a helpful reimbursement for the expenses of care. The Christian foster parent will carefully manage these funds to diligently steward over them to make sure that the child fully receives their benefit. The Christian foster parent is always looking for scriptural alternatives (where appropriate) for the meds and the hours of counseling and therapy that are often prescribed for these children, seeking to make them less dependent, not more so.

Recommended reading list:

- *Parenting Isn't For Cowards*, Dr. James Dobson
- *This Means War: Equipping Christian Families for Fostercare or Adoption*, Cheryl Ellicott
- *Orphanology: Awakening to Gospel-Centered Adoption and Orphan Care*, Tony Merida

Web sites:

- www.christianhomes.com/foster-care-for-children
- www.shilohranch.org
- www.allgodschildren.org

20

Gambling

I'll bet you thought I'd never get around to this topic! Oh, I'm sorry: I meant to use the amoral politically correct term: *gaming*. Sounds more innocent and innocuous, doesn't it? Seriously, by any other term it is still *poor stewardship*.

"I'll call and raise you two." I felt so grown-up. Being invited to the family poker table for the annual Christmas holiday bash was awesome! There were cookies, cold drinks, chips, your choice of opened deli-dips and other treats…but, more importantly to a ten-year-old, was getting to play what you had only been able to watch in years gone by, penny-ante poker! Poker chips were a penny each and the most you could lose was a dollar.

By the time I was eleven (scouting age), I had brought the game to our campsite at Boy Scout Camp Fred Darby. I was adept in at least a dozen poker games from five-card stud to "Bull and Heifer"—five card draw, Jacks or better to open-progressive, three-of-a-kind or better to win—and could bluff with the best of them (I had even learned the fine art of telegraphing a fake "tell"). Of course, we were only betting the spent .22 casings from the riflery range, but our troop was the closest to that range and we had a limitless supply of "chips."

When camp was over, it seemed a natural progression to graduate to the "quarter game" at the Harris's grandmother's house on East Side Boulevard—quarters were chips and a guy could lose in one hand hours of lawn-mowing sweat. I played a couple of hands—long enough to realize I was betting what I couldn't afford to lose. That was the beginning and end of my non-recreational gambling—er, "gaming"—career.

And that is where risk becomes a fool's errand...where wishing and faith find their disparate meanings. When you risk what you cannot afford to lose, to gain what someone else sweat to obtain... well, sin is at the door.

Is gambling (or gaming) biblical? When does recreation become more than that? What about lotteries and other games that benefit education or charities? What about games that require some skill? Isn't the stock market just gambling on a higher plane? What about Las Vegas (or Wall Street) where it is legal? These are the questions thinking Christians should be asking themselves.

According to a combination of what many dictionaries say, *Gambling* is the means by which money or something of material value is risked or wagered on something whose outcome is uncertain to gain money or something of material value. *Gaming* is the same, only legal or officially sanctioned by some governmental body.

Answering questions:

1. Is gambling (or gaming) biblical?

If you are referring to the soldiers who wagered over the Messiah's robe (Luke 23:34), yes, but not as a recommended course of action. In fact, the Bible looks askance at any ill-gotten or quick gain.

> Ill-gotten gain gets you nowhere; an honest life is immortal. (Prov. 10:2, The Message)

> A tyrannical ruler lacks judgment. One who hates ill-gotten gain will have long days. (Prov. 28:16, WEB)

> The trustworthy person will get a rich reward, but a person who wants quick riches will get into trouble. (Prov. 28:20, NLT)

The problem with quick or easy gain is that you do not acquire with it the requisite character for its wise or beneficent use. That's where the "easy come, easy go" maxim is derived. Many who gain too quickly lose it in the same manner. Oh, I know you think you would be the exception...wanna bet? That's the problem, isn't it?

2. When does recreation become more than that?

    To answer specifically, when having fun has turned to greed or dread (depending on your fortunes), it is one thing to enjoy the "thrill of victory" or the "agony of defeat" when competitiveness is learning how to temper itself. It is quite another to wonder if you have just won so much that others will do without or lost so much that you or others may do the same.

    The Christian can never risk what is not his, nor can he want someone else to suffer loss at his hands...except when the risk is frivolous. This may make recreational games—frivolous risk—possible, but when someone stands to gain or lose what is of real value, it is no longer frivolous or fun. Some think gaining value at the expense of others is fun, but that doesn't make it right. Risking your stuff (or even your life) for your country or family is one thing, but risking either in frivolity is foolishness.

3. What about lotteries and other games that benefit education or charities?

    Just because someone else is legally the designated beneficiary of gambling (or gaming), even if they are doing a good work, does not legitimize the immorality of the gambling. I know there are millions of dollars raised for education by state-sanctioned lotteries, but that is what taxation is for. Besides there are always those who "administer" the lottery... and they get their percentage (more could go to the schools if those dollars were included).

    Yes, that includes bingo for churches...just a ploy to buy the Christian vote. Look at who pays the advertising budget promoting lottery votes; it'll be pro-gambling lobbies every time.

4. What about games that require some skill?

    My dad said, "Never play another man's game." Good
    advice that means regardless of how skillful you think
    you are…there's a reason you were invited to play pool,
    or poker, or whatever. Something about separating a fool
    from his money.

    Seriously, the only cure for gambling losses in "games of
    skill"…is not more practice! Lick your wounds, count
    yourself blessed it wasn't more…and walk—or better yet,
    run—the other way! *The only sure cure for gambling addic-
    tion* is forgiveness from the Lord followed by cold-turkey
    abstinence from you.

5. Isn't the stock market just gambling on a higher plane?

    I'm not sure it's even a higher plane. When your piddling
    investment doesn't cause the ticker to move, maybe you're just
    playing "the other man's game." Unless you've done your due
    diligence—checking out the company's asset value, contingent
    liabilities, market position and philosophy, history of return,
    management personnel, etc.—you are playing a guessing game
    more subject to chance than you realize.

    Calling a gamble in the stock market an investment does not
    mitigate the losses or justify the gains. If you want to make an
    investment, do your homework first, never risk what you cannot
    afford to lose, never invest borrowed money—use money saved
    for that specific reason, ask all those concerned if they can afford
    to lose it, too…and ask yourself if investing it in the kingdom of
    God would yield better returns (Mk. 10:29–30).

6. What about Las Vegas (or Wall Street) where it is legal?

    Again, like state-sanctioned lotteries, just because it's legal
    doesn't mean it's moral. There are many things that have been
    made lawful that God does not smile at; that's why we must
    be careful whom we elect. A friend of mine is the pastor of a
    church in Los Vegas. He has a real moral dilemma on his hand;

does he accept the tithes of those of his congregation who are dealers in the casinos?

Leadership is not about doing the popular thing, it's about doing the right thing; it's about hearing from God amidst the culture's cacophony of competing voices; it's about valuing the blessing of God more highly than the applause of men.

Recommended reading list:

- *Turning the Tables on Gambling: Hope and Help for Addictive Behavior (e-book)*, Gregory Jantz and Ann McMurray
- *Gambling: Mapping the American Moral Landscape*, Alan Wolfe and Erik C. Owens
- *Gambling: Don't Bet On It*, Rex M. Rogers

Web sites:

- www.ag.org/.../Position_Papers/pp_downloads/pp_4186_gambling.pdf
- www.ezinearticles.com/?Gambling-Addiction---From-a-Christian
- www.efrankking.blogspot.com/2012/04/christian-perspective

21

Giving

There aren't many times in life where one has the ability to truly give "all" to the Lord. I even have to put "all" in quotes because "all" is not really *all*...I mean even if you do give all your money, can you give all your time, energy, creativity, etc.—the things that are less tangible—to the Lord? When I was a student at ORU (in Tulsa, OK...in the 70s), an on-campus singing group—Living Sound— gave a concert. At the end of the concert, they took an offering and I gave "all"...I remember it vividly.

I was with a girl named Carol. It was our first date...she was quite pretty...and, like all guys on a first date, I was trying to make a good impression. I had it all planned out in my mind. After the concert, I was going to take her to the SUB and get her something to eat. Then they took the offering, explaining that they were going to use the money raised to go to Poland on a musical missionary tour set up by the Cardinal of Krakow. I had just finished Oral Roberts' book on "seed faith" giving. It was a new concept for me— give what you need—if you lack time, give time; if you lack wisdom, give what little wisdom you may possess; if you lack money, give the money you *do* have.

The closer the plate got, the more I argued with myself. Part of me wanted to sow money, part of me could hear my father saying, "Leaving the Air Force Academy is a mistake you'll regret for the rest of your life—who do you think is going to pay for your education?"

When I responded, "God is," he just laughed. So I toyed with putting the $10 bill in—my wallet had every penny I owned: a one, a ten, and two twenties—then came the thought, *How big is your need?* I reached for the twenty, but as the plate came down our row, I just dumped my whole wallet in it.

Immediately, panic set in. It was just a moment of indiscretion. *What was I doing?! If my dad could see me now!* I wanted to get up and go to the end of the aisle and make change...and I probably would have, except for Carol. *What must she be thinking about me now... wait till she has to pay at the SUB?* It was just a very brief moment of faith...just a mustard seed—but what God can do with a mustard seed! For the rest of the story, you'll have to read to the end.

Is giving biblical? Shouldn't we be reasonable in our giving? What about the tithe? What about my bills and the other things I owe? What about pledging? What about those emotional appeals those guys on TV make with those emaciated children? These are the questions that the thinking Christian must answer.

Giving, according to the dictionary, means to bestow or present voluntarily without thought of compensation. According to the Bible, giving is measured in sacrifice, God giving us His Son as the gift that truly "keeps on giving"—setting a standard by which all giving can be measured.

Should we expect less of God? Imagine giving up what is most precious to you. "God so loved the world that He *gave* His only begotten Son, that whosoever believes on Him should not perish, but have everlasting life" (John 3:16). Compared with that standard of giving, most of us don't qualify, myself certainly included. I think if love *is* measured in sacrifice, we also have to give up to His control that which is most precious to us...for some of us that means family; to others it is career, or prestige, or material possessions...to all of us it is the right to choose our own paths, to be the master of our own destinies, to be the lord of our lives.

Answering questions:

1. Is giving biblical?

   Of course it is. We've already established that God set the bar in the gift of His Son, but it goes much deeper than this. Jesus—the member of the Godhead of Father, Son, and Spirit, Who was the active agent of creation (read John 1:1–14)— creates Man *knowing* he would choose to do the one thing he was restricted from doing: eat of the Tree of Life (Gen. 2:16–17)...knowing it would cost Him His life.

   > Knowing that you were not redeemed with perishable things like silver or gold from your futile way of life inherited from your forefathers, but with precious blood, as of a lamb unblemished and spotless, the blood of Christ. For He was foreknown before the foundation of the world, but has appeared in these last times for the sake of you who through Him are believers in God, who raised Him from the dead and gave Him glory, so that your faith and hope are in God. (I Pet. 1:18–21, NASU)

   That is why Jesus uses the widow and her two mites—we would say pennies today—to say that her gift was more highly regarded than the rich who gave much larger gifts (Mark 12:41–44). She gave out of her need, they gave out of their abundance. A principle of giving is revealed here. It is not equal giving the Lord requires; it is equal sacrifice.

2. Shouldn't we be reasonable in our giving?

   Of course we can't give what belongs to someone else— the utility company, mortgage company, etc.—however, the question should not be, "How much of what is mine am I going to give to God?", but "How much of what is *His* am I going to keep for myself?" This puts the emphasis where it belongs. As a steward, the Christian carefully and *reasonably* gets the most out of his Master's possessions.

3. What about the tithe?

   I love the way my pastor puts it: "Let's respond to the Lord by giving Him *His* tithes and *our* offerings." We cannot *give* an offering until we've *paid* our tithe. The offering is a freely given amount, whereas the tithe is what we owe. Call it "God's use tax" on the earth…call it what you will, it's not that God—or the church, for that matter—won't be able to pay the light bill if we don't tithe, but maybe *we* can't pay the light bill unless we tithe.

   How much is a tithe? Read the context. It is always a tenth unless it mentions specifically some other amount. The first incidence of a tithe being paid was Abram in Genesis 14:18–20 when he paid Melchizedek a "tithe of all." The Hebrew word there is *ma'ser* (tithe or tenth). Many translations actually translate this word "tenth."

   To whom is the tithe paid? The Scripture says to "bring ye all the tithes into the storehouse" (Malachi 3:10, KJV). That command ought to be enough for us to pay the Church tithes, but just so we can see how it is tied to our own ability to pay *our* utility bills, He adds this promise: "and prove me now herewith, saith the Lord of hosts, if I will not open you the windows of heaven, and pour you out a blessing, that there shall not be room enough to receive it" (Mal. 3:10, KJV).

4. What about my bills and the other things I owe?

   Christians, I'm sad to say, do not have a good reputation in this regard. Quite some time ago, when I was paying off a loan to the bank and sitting at the VP's desk, he said to me, "I see you have a fish on your check."

   Thinking he was getting ready to reveal an undisclosed spiritual kinship, I eagerly replied, "Yes, I'm a Christian. Does that symbol mean anything to you?"

   He quite matter-of-factly replied, "Just that I've given all my tellers instructions to check the balances of anyone presenting a check with a fish or a dove on it." I didn't even know what to say, so I said nothing.

If we obligate ourselves above our ability to repay, it's a bad witness before the world. We'll never have the money to give if we don't budget...and the first item on our budget should be our tithe. It's not a matter of amount; it's a matter of priority.

5. What about pledging?

There's nothing wrong with pledging. To commit to God, the church, or even some body doing a good work is okay. Just remember it is a promise and your word is at stake. God takes a dim view of promises made and not kept, but will do good for those that keep their word.

> You will pray to Him, and He will hear you; and you will *pay your vows.* "You will also decree a thing, and it will be established for you; and light will shine on your ways. (Job 22:27–28, NASU)

> Offer to God a sacrifice of thanksgiving and *pay your vows* to the Most High; call upon Me in the day of trouble; I shall rescue you, and you will honor Me. But to the wicked God says, "What right have you to tell of My statutes and to take My covenant in your mouth? "For you hate discipline, and you cast My words behind you. When you see a thief, you are pleased...you associate with adulterers...you let your mouth loose in evil...I will reprove you and state the case in order before your eyes... Now consider this, you who forget God, or I will tear you in pieces, and there will be none to deliver. (Ps. 50:14–22, NASU)

6. What about those emotional appeals those guys on TV make with those emaciated children?

It is said that after giving the heart, giving money doesn't hurt, but many have been manipulated by those who are master purveyors of guilt. To give out of a motivation of guilt, or fear, or pride is not a good thing. The Scripture says, "Each one must do just as he has purposed in his heart, not grudgingly or under compulsion, for God loves a cheerful giver" (2 Cor. 9:7–8, NASU).

Those who are fed by the televangelists should give to them (which has nothing to do with the tithe). And they can reasonably expect to receive some support (I Tim 5:18; I Cor. 9:9). But they are also, obligated to honestly spend what is given to them, not "consuming it on their own lusts" (James 4:3).

Here is the rest of the story:

In the Spring of 1981, almost ten years after that embarrassing evening with Carol, I was back in Tulsa. This time I was manning a booth at the Tulsa Christian Business Show. My "business" was Butterfield Trail Camp, a ministry to camp-aged children I had started a couple of years earlier. Looking for some place to send his two older kids, Terry Law wandered up and started talking about my camp. In the course of the conversation, it came up that we had been at ORU at the same time. When he introduced himself and mentioned he had founded Living Sound, I excitedly told him about my 'mustard seed' gift...and what had happened.

The night had played out pretty much like I thought it would, except I preempted what I figured was going to be an embarrassing moment later with Carol. I told her I wasn't feeling well—which was sort of true—I mean, losing all my money did kind of make me sick to my stomach—anyway, I took Carol back to her dorms early.

Then, checking my on-campus mailbox the next day, I got a letter from my summer employer, Camp Takatoka, informing me they had over-withheld taxes from my pay and refunding me a check for $27.50. The next day, I got an unexpected reimbursement for my school insurance in the mail from my dad—which flabbergasted me—I mean, *from my dad*—for $23.50. (Now, if you're keeping track—and I certainly was—that's exactly the $51.00 back!)

Needless to say, I began checking the mail three or four times a day! About a week elapsed and I said to God, "Now where's the 'good measure pressed down, shaken together and running over?'" (Luke 6:38). It was then I realized maybe I was looking to the mailbox as my source and not God.

Going back to my dorm appropriately upbraided, whom should I bump into but my old junior high chum Frank Sullivan. He asked, "Hey, Sarge, how's it going?"

"Well, aside from the fact that I can't pay next month's tuition installment, great."

He replied, "They are hiring waiters at La Fiesta Cantina at Fifty-first and Harvard. Why don't you check them out? In fact, I'm getting ready to go to work right now. I'll put in a good word for you."

Suddenly, I felt surely this was how the Lord was going to meet my need. (I was working at a Pizza Hut twenty hours per week and making a whopping $1.40 per hour, minimum wage at the time.)

To make a long story shorter, I took the job and never made less than $7.00 per hour in tips—a fortune in those days. Of course they made me buy a uniform...guess how much it cost? That's right: $51.00!

When I finished this story, Terry turned to me and excitedly said, "Now let me tell you what happened to your gift!"

"That night, we had the largest offering we'd ever received. It allowed us to go behind the Iron Curtain for the first time and really catapulted our campus ministry into what it is today!"

I could go on and tell you of the commitments his kids, Scottie and Misty, made to the Lord that summer. Or how I went to work for his ministry, met Pope John Paul II, or about the cars that were given to me...or any one of the many other blessings that came from that 'moment of indiscretion.' But that's another story.

Recommended reading list:

- *Productive Christians in an Age of Guilt Manipulators*, David Chilton
- *The Latent Power of the Soul*, Watchman Nee
- *The Treasure Principle*, Randy Alcorn

Web sites:

- www.DaveRamsey.com
- www.tithing.com
- www.philanthropy.com

22

Gluttony, Obesity, and Self-Control

"I've lost three hundred pounds...fifteen pounds, twenty times!" If we were all honest about our weight loss, this—or some similar version—would be heard often, no doubt. Although I boxed at 152 at the Air Force Academy, marriage has added its forty pounds... one-fourth pound per month for about twenty-five years (in case you're doing the math, that's really about 225 pounds; which makes sense—it was about fifteen years ago that I realized my problem was not going away by itself—I had to be more pro-active—I began a chronic dieting plan and have wandered my way back to about 180).

The real problem is gluttony, which I define as *the inability to say no to food*. It's not that I can't say no, it's really that I don't want to bad enough...guess my mouth is too full, and it is so impolite to talk with food in your mouth!

Seriously, why is America so obese? Yes, it is lack of exercise—my lifestyle has become quite sedentary; blame it on technology—I mean, it's not my fault that it's easier to change the channel from the couch by remote than it is to get up and physically turn the knob, is it? (TV's don't even have knobs anymore!)

Yes, it is commercialism—making me want things I never knew existed before—sweet potato fries, lemon-berry cream slushes, and 'death-by-chocolate'—all of which can be super-sized (almost makes me wish I lived in New York City)!

Yes, it is the nearness of the refrigerator, delivery pizza, the tastiness and convenience of fast food, shopping when I'm hungry, and a myriad of other things...but mostly, it's gluttony. Until I'm honest with myself, there's little hope of applying any cure that is more than a temporary fix—which is why the diet industry is thriving.

Maybe I'm not the only one out there that struggles with this; maybe America's collective gluttony is just a product of a culture of gluttony...and maybe it's not just food we can't say no to. I'm just saying...

Gluttony is one of the "deadly sins" listed in Roman Catholic catechisms—though Roman Catholics seem to struggle with obesity as much as the rest of us. Still, Christians have—or *should have*—less excuse. We Christians have the Holy Spirit available to us and He is the Source of self-control (Gal. 5:22).

Gluttony is deadly, not just in the sense of atherosclerosis and high blood pressure, but it is spiritually dangerous as well. Gluttony, the very nature of self-indulgence, can make us just as *spiritually* lethargic as obesity makes us physically lazy. Who wants to pray—a spiritual labor—when it requires so much spiritual energy? Even to "kneel" in your heart requires you to "get off the couch."

Is gluttony biblical? How about dieting...is it any different from fasting? What about those whose "temples" are gargantuan; are they any less anointed just because they struggle with their weight? I can see where Mother Teresa might need to be thin, but I don't have a ministry to the starving in India...why must I be thin? Can't self-control get 'out-of-control' (anorexia/bulimia)? These, and other questions, are the ones thinking Christians should ask.

According to a combination of what many dictionaries say, *Gluttony* is the act of being over-indulgent in the area of food; in Roman times, these were called Epicureans; today we would say they are "pigs" (I wonder if the police's infamous affinity for Twinkies and donuts has rightfully earned them this moniker). *Obesity* is the accumulation of body fat beyond usefulness to the point of general health endangerment. *Self-control* is the ability to say no...in this context, saying no to food.

Answering questions:

1. Is gluttony biblical?

   No, in the sense it is not a recommended motivation. There are many verses on this. (For a semi-complete list go to the Web sites at the end of this article.) The Bible takes a pretty dim view of gluttony:

   > And put a knife to your throat if you are given to appetite. (Prov. 23:2, ESV)

   Perhaps it's not just the overeating but the self-indulgence that leads to it. Call it a lust for food. Anything you can't say no to is a god before Him, isn't it? (Ex. 20:3)

   There are many motivations common to the natural man. In Roy Garn's book, *The Magic Power of Emotional Appeal*, he identifies *romance*, *self-preservation*, *money*, and *recognition* as the four most basic motivations. I add a fifth for Christians: *God's Will*. For the natural un-regenerated man, he is not able to experience anything not directed to self. For the regenerated spiritual man, he is able to access the power of the Holy Spirit and say no to these baser self-centered drives…and say yes to the others-centered will of God (Rom. 8:4–9).

2. How about dieting…is it any different than fasting?

   When it comes to food, all fasting is dieting, but not all dieting is fasting. Both may have to do with self-denial, but fasting has a spiritual purpose that may have a physical benefit, but with dieting, both the purpose and the benefit are physical. In other words, to refuse to eat *in fasting* is to deny one's body the physical sustenance one gets from food in preference of the spiritual sustenance one's spirit gets from the denial of the flesh's desires. As Jesus said, "I have food to eat that you do not know about" (John 4:32, NASU).

   Fasting sharpens the focus of one's spirit, making prayer more effectual. As Jesus said, "But this kind does not go out except by prayer and fasting" (Matt. 17:21, NASU). He was referring to a particularly tenacious demon whom His disciples could not cast out. Apparently, the desires of one's flesh provide sufficient distraction to diffuse the power of prayer such that spiritual force is diminished. It is not that God's power is any less, but our ability to move the hands of God in prayer is.

3. What about those whose "temples" are gargantuan; are they any less anointed just because they struggle with their weight?

In a word, no. Although there are many preachers who are over-weight, their problem—or problems—may not necessarily be spiritual. It could be stress, hormonal, hereditary, or any one of a number of physical or psychological challenges that result in the body's inability to properly process nutrition.

It is easy to judge by appearance, but such judgments are unreliable. We usually just don't have enough information. As Christians, we should just pray for them...let's leave the judgment to He Who can see the heart (Jer. 20:12).

4. I can see where Mother Teresa might need to be thin, but I don't have a ministry to the starving in India...why must I be thin?

Who said you have to be thin? The culture does not pressure the God's-will-directed Christian. Do not be pressured by the opinions of others.

On the other hand, there is the proper witness—the positive image of a man or a woman submitted to God, not ruled by his/her flesh—that we, as Christians, are supposed to maintain. It's hard to say you're not ruled by your flesh when you are constantly struggling with your weight.

If you struggle with gluttony, you probably struggle with your weight. Perhaps you might make this an object of prayer... and fasting! Sometimes the best way to take authority over the demon of overeating is to starve it!

The best saying I've ever read concerning overeating was appropriately on a refrigerator magnet. "Nothing tastes as good as being thin feels!" Still, using a smaller plate, not eating after 7:00 p.m., never having seconds, never having dessert, and weighing yourself daily only goes so far. Self-control—a fruit of the Spirit (Gal. 5:22)—is only available to the submitted Christian. When something inside of you is saying no, it is easier to say no yourself.

5.   Can't self-control get 'out-of-control' (anorexia/bulimia)?

Of course. Many who diet are trying to reach their weight-loss goals through methods that are only trading one addiction for another. Anorexia—seeing yourself "fat" regardless of evidence to the contrary—and bulimia—the act of chronically throwing up your food to avoid calorie consumption—are two of the conditions people end up with when they try to substitute self-denial—often an act of soulish determination—for self-control.

Gluttony, giving into the lust for food, only leads to other problems. Saying yes to any lust is always saying no to God. Our pursuit of God is a pursuit of His control...which is, after all, what Lordship is all about.

Recommended reading list:

- *Gluttony (The Seven Deadly Sins)*, Francine Prose
- *Glittering Vices: A New Look at the Seven Deadly Sins and Their Remedies*, Rebecca Konyndyk DeYoung
- *Fatal Distractions: Conquering Destructive Temptations*, Kay Arthur, David Lawson, BJ Lawson

Web sites:

- www.christianitytoday.com/ct/2000/september4/3.62.html
- www.christianity.com/christian-life/...gluttony
- www.weightlossforchristianwomen.com

23

Gossip and Flattery

Maybe it was because she had never met anyone who could quote so many scriptures—Johnnie (not his real name) certainly wasn't that good looking—but when he offered her a ride home for the holidays, she decided to trust him. After all, didn't he work security at the Bible college she attended? Her fears seemed to be unfounded as he dropped off first this student and that one along the way. He had always acted like a perfect gentleman...at least until he had dropped off everybody but her.

When he could no longer drive for weariness, he rented a room at a motel explaining the rate was too high to get more than one room...but it would be okay, he had said, because he would sleep in the car; she could have the motel room all to herself. She should have suspected something when he had hauled in her luggage, but failed to remember to give her the key when he left.

Tired herself, she lay down exhausted from nearly twenty straight hours of travel. She had barely turned out the lights when someone quietly slipped in bed beside her. Startled, she screamed and jumped out of the bed and turned on the lights to find Johnnie naked and offering what she was not prepared to accept. She chased him from the room. Needless to say, she didn't get much sleep that night.

The next morning, Johnnie knocked on her door and asked if she was ready to go. Apparently, she thought, he was going to treat the episode as if it never happened. She surely never brought it up. Traveling the last few hours hugging the door handle and finding another way back to school after the holidays, she thought it was just one of those unfortunate incidents one has when one is too trusting.

Suddenly, back on campus, she could feel the accusing eyes of some of her classmates. When she'd had enough, she went to her best friend and asked what was wrong. Her friend explained that Johnnie was spreading the rumor that he had been intimate with her on vacation...that *she* had seduced *him*!

A year later, while Lynn and I were getting to know one another, she shared this story with me. I asked her what had happened when she reported him. What she told me would teach me a valuable lesson.

She said the Lord had told her not to defend herself. That if she did, it would be the only defense she had; that He would be her Defender. So, she never contacted his employer and never defended herself among the students.

Johnnie lost his job over another unrelated issue and Lynn's friends defended her against what soon became obvious lies. Her honor was restored...the Lord had done His part. I'd like to say I would have been so noble, but I'm afraid if I had been able to get my hands on him, I'd have gone to jail. "Truthful words stand the test of time, but lies are soon exposed" (Prov. 12:19 NLT). Gossip is like a boomerang; the one most injured seems to be the one who let go the lie in the first place.

We humans have been given a wonderful gift: speech; but we neglect, abuse and mangle it. "From the same mouth come both blessing and cursing. My brethren, these things ought not to be this way" (James 3:10, NASU).

Gossip does a lot of damage, but flattery may do more in the long run. Gossip is based on the expansion of truth over time and people; flattery is a lie intended to deceive while giving an advantage to the one selling it over the one who just bought into it.

According to a combination of what many dictionaries say, *Gossip* is idle talk or rumor about someone's private life; often someone shares this information so they can be recognized as having an "inside track" or be known as the source of some "hidden truth" that most don't know. *Flattery* is false or insincere praise intending to ingratiate the subject of the flattery. According to the Bible, gossip is also called back-biting, especially when something false is spread to gain an advantage (2 Cor. 12:20). The Bible decries a flattering tongue as deceptive (Prov. 28:23).

Is gossip or flattery biblical? If what you say is truthful, why is it gossip? If I don't tell others, how will they know how to pray? If praise is sincere and honest, is it flattery? What's wrong with sharing the truth about others? Why do women have more trouble with gossip and flattery than men? These are the questions thinking Christians should be asking themselves.

Answering questions:

1. Is gossip or flattery biblical?

    No, not in the sense it has biblical endorsement; but as long as man has been speaking, there has been a tendency to abuse the ability to communicate. The serpent in the garden challenged what God had told Adam and Eve about the fruit of the Tree of the Knowledge of Good and Evil. He is a liar and the father of all liars (John 8:44).

    In the Bible, gossip is called tale bearing (Prov. 11:13) and backbiting (Prov. 25:23), and none of the references recommend this activity, but speak of such in the most negative terms. Rather discretion—the ability to conceal a matter—is heralded as noble and as Falstaff said "the better part of valor." (Shakespeare—*Henry the Fourth*—Part 1, Act 5, Scene 4) Not that hiding the truth is good, but "there is a time for everything" (Eccl. 3:1), or more specifically, "A time to be silent and a time to speak" (Ecl. 3:7, NASU).

    Flattery is spoken of as seducing (Prov. 7:21), it is spoken of as being double-hearted (Prov. 12:2) and proud (Prov. 12:3). In fact, in Job it says, "For if I tried flattery, my Creator would soon destroy me" (Job 32:22, NLT).

2. If what you say is truthful, why is it gossip?

    Although speaking the truth is always recommended, the Christian lives by an over-arching principle, commonly called the "Golden Rule" (Matt. 7:12). Because you would never want someone to even speak what is true about you without being there to bring a defense from your perspective, you will not speak about another person outside of his presence.

    Always remember the warning of Scripture:

    > But there is nothing covered up that will not be revealed, and hidden that will not be known. Accordingly, whatever you have said in the dark will be heard in the light, and what you have whispered in the inner rooms will be proclaimed upon the housetops. (Luke 12:2–3, NASU)

3. If I don't tell others, how will they know how to pray?

    This is a common excuse given by the gossiper. The rule is, *Go to God about people and go to people about God.* The only ones who have the power to make change are that person and God. Confronting them about what you have heard may help them, but it will certainly help you to understand and to pray. Going to someone else only perpetuates the problem. Time is a multiplier; the longer a person is in sin, the farther from God he will stray. Besides, next time it is likely to be you. Make your words sweet; you may find yourself eating them!

4. If praise is sincere and honest, is it flattery?

    Timing is everything...so is motive. As the proverb says, "A word fitly spoken is like apples of gold in settings of silver. Like an earring of gold and an ornament of fine gold is a wise rebuker to an obedient ear" (Prov. 11:24–25, NKJV). Indeed, praise to be valid, must have no private selfish agenda...otherwise it is just flattery and ultimately hypocritical—like the person who always puts himself down to elicit an oblique word of praise.

5. What's wrong with sharing the truth about others?

Again, what is your motive? To make yourself look good by comparison? To disqualify them from something for which you think you are more qualified? These are self-serving motivations.

There is what is true and then there is the truth. Did you speak in love? Then be kind, merciful, humble, and forgiving (I Cor. 13). The truth, spoken in love, is very powerful (Eph. 4:15). What is true, spoken in jealousy, envy, vengeance, or avarice leads to somebody getting hacked up or hacked off. If it is the truth, it's a scalpel; if it is merely true, it's a machete—it's hard to do delicate work with a big swing.

6. Why do women have more trouble with gossip and flattery than men?

Because God made men and women differently. Men are, in general, are poor communicators...they don't express themselves well or often and they are poor listeners. That Adam was with Eve while she was being tempted only underscores my point...he should have spoken up (read Gen. 3).

Women, in general, on the other hand, are compulsive communicators. These two opposites need each other. The randomness of a woman's mind together with the more linear thinking of a man's mind leads to productive creativity. Alone, men cannot think outside the box—and women need the constraining influence of the male sides of the box to maximize the productivity of their creativity.

Recommended reading list:

- *The Problem of Gossip: Guidelines for Christian Speech*, B. Franklin Wise
- *Me and my Big Mouth*, Joyce Meyer
- *Words That Hurt, Words That Heal*, Rabbi Joseph Telushkin

Web sites:

- www.joyfulheart.com/maturity/gossip.html
- www.encouragementforwomen.com/page7.htm
- www.everydaychristian.com/blogs/post/7092

24

Greed and Envy

You'd think that envy would be the predominant area of the "Have-nots" and that greed would be the exclusive territory of the "Haves"... and you'd be mostly right. *Greed* is most often experienced by those fearing loss, while *Envy* is usually the prevailing sentiment of those seeking gain...just not willing to work for it.

Collectively called covetousness, greed and envy affect all of us, if we are honest with ourselves; excepting you, of course. Seriously, there is a difficult balance we are to maintain between being happy with our present circumstances—contentment—and wishing our situation would improve—discontentment. The whole reason we set goals is because we want things better than they are. How can this be wrong?

All "progress" is not forward. In other words, some change which we call "progress" is actually "regress" because it takes us in a backward direction. Let me explain. There is an *absolute* forward and an *absolute* backward. We may think that because in space there is no up or down, everything is relative; but every Christian knows that the good go up toward God and heaven and the bad go... well, we know where they go. Just as there is an absolute right and wrong—congruence with God's will is right—so also there is a forward toward that right and a backward away from that right... and toward the wrong. Or, in mathematical terms, change is *not* an absolute value.

To avoid greed and envy is easy; just want what God wants. It may sound easy or simple, but it's not; for to want what God wants, one has to have *His* motives; much easier said than done.

David was called a "man after God's own heart" (I Sam. 13:14). His pursuit of the things of this world, with a few notable exceptions, was with *godly* motives. When it says in Psalm 37:4—a Psalm of David, by the way—and "He will grant you the desires of your heart," He *does* make this caveat: if we "delight yourself also in the Lord." We are exhorted by the Lord, Himself, to "seek first His Kingdom" (Matt. 6:33), then all the things we need will come, too. It is not the wanting of the thing that is evil; it is *why* we want it that the Lord weighs. Greed and envy are only present when we want something for the wrong reason. Remember, it is the *love* of money that is the root of evil, not the money itself (1 Tim. 6:10).

The Scripture says that "Godliness with contentment is great gain" (1 Tim. 6:6). Perhaps this godliness comes from wanting what God wants...*and why He wants it*. Is it possible to submit ourselves to His motivations even when we don't understand them? I certainly hope so, because it is hard enough just saying "I want what He wants"...let alone *knowing* why it must be so!

Are greed and envy biblical? Is it possible for a "fallen" Man to have pure motives? Are greed and envy made pure by the end they accomplish? (Or by recognition or by any selfish motive?) Surely God wants me blessed, so it must not be greedy to want what He wants in that case, right? Is it wrong to "covet someone's prayers"? These, and others, are the questions thinking Christians should be asking.

According to a combination of what many dictionaries say, *Envy* is the insatiable desire to possess what someone else has, while *Greed* is the inordinate desire to acquire possessions or wealth for the purpose of self-consumption. The Bible speaks of these desires as covetousness.

Answering questions:

1. Are greed and envy biblical?

   Yes, but in the sense that they are condemned (Exodus 20:17). They are in no place recommended to the Christian as an emotion or a desire to be cultivated. Rather, they are to be avoided; the Christian recognizes this as his natural default, but seeks to be generous, treating others as better than himself (Phil. 2:3).

2. Is it possible for a "fallen" Man to have pure motives?

   No (Isaiah 53:6; Romans 6:23); that is why all of us must be saved. Most of what we call "pure" motives come from an "over-active justifier," you know, that organ of the soul that makes everything look right in your own eyes.

3. Are greed and envy made pure by the end they accomplish? (Or by recognition or by any selfish motive?)

   The end never justifies the means. We live in a world of situational ethics where everything is gray…nothing is absolutely right or wrong, given the correct circumstances. The Christian realizes he or she may have to take unpopular stands that the rest of the world justifies, but recognizes his or her witness comes from this very distinction.

   The Christian also recognizes the error of past generations without judging. Slavery, the breaking of treaties with Native Americans, unjust wars, etc.—while making reparations where reasonable and possible, the Christian also tries to keep himself from making similar errors. He realizes no present generation can pay enough to correct the grievances of the past, nor is guilt, once forgiven, still held against the sinner.

4. Surely God wants me blessed, so it must not be greedy to want what He wants in that case, right?

   Yes, but as Christians, we are blessed to be a blessing (Gen. 12:2), not to consume it on our own lusts (James 1:14). In medieval times, there was an understanding. It was a principle called *noblesse oblige*. It meant that those born with much had an obligation to help those less fortunate. Surely, we have been blessed for the purpose of sharing. To want what God wants is always righteous; to justify what we want by saying that God wants it too may not be.

A friend of mine used to live in a house trailer. When those attending his living room Bible study became too numerous to be comfortably accommodated, it should not have surprised them that a large house was given to him...he was just being rewarded by a good God, Who recognized his sacrifice. However, some criticized him, being envious of his blessing. Perhaps that is why persecution often accompanies reward (Mark 10:29–30).

5. Is it wrong to "covet someone's prayers"?

No, but it is probably wrong to use this confusing phrase. Christians are often mocked by a confused world for good reason. We should avoid using a word like "covet" except in the negative context it is usually rendered.

The world around us is constantly judging us...usually wanting to justify their shortcomings by ours. Christians should never resent this, but use such pressure to drive them to better and more careful behavior.

Greed and envy are never to be the motivations of Christians. Wanting to please a generous God, Christians should emulate Him, helping others wherever possible with a selfless heart of sacrifice.

Recommended reading list:

- *Jealousy-The Sin No One Talks About: How to Overcome Evil and Live a Life of Freedom - eBook*, R. T. Kendall
- *Envy: The Enemy Within – Overcoming The Hidden Emotion that Hold God's Plan Hostage*, Bob Sorge
- *The Ground for Christian Ethics*, T. M. Moore

Web sites:

- www. plato.stanford.edu/entries/envy
- www. www.deadlysins.com/sins/greed
- www. www.eternallifeministries.org/lrs_covetous.htm

25

Gun Control

This is more than having a cabinet that locks—a designated and safe place for your firearms and all their respective ammunition. I remember learning from my dad and from Boy Scouts respect for the awesome killing power a gun had. From hunting trips with my father, from watching super-8 movies of my uncle Raymond's safaris in Africa—he was a high-up in the NRA—from taking the mandatory gun safety course for the Riflery merit badge…all these taught me the basics of how to cross a fence safely with a loaded weapon, to never point a gun at anything you didn't want to kill, and to always treat a gun as if it were loaded.

When I was a kid growing up in small-town Oklahoma, every kid had a Red Rider BB-gun…even those who were not school age had cork-guns or water-pistols or hand-made rubber band guns… my grandson (three years of age) makes guns of every Lego he can. Yet, it is not the "gun culture" our kids grow up in that causes the periodic gun control debate in our lawmakers' halls; rather, it is the tragic result of the helplessness we feel every time someone innocent dies at the hands of a gun-wielding maniac.

Is gun control biblical? (For that matter, does a God who has told us "thou shalt not kill" even want Christians to own killing equipment?) Were our Founders crazy to put the Second Amendment in the Bill of Rights and to call themselves Christians? If we argue that magazine size is a problem because of the number that can be killed, why not outlaw all guns…is it less tragic to the parent who has only lost one child? If we are against "weapons of mass destruction," isn't it hypocritical to own them ourselves? These are the questions that the thinking Christian must answer.

Gun Control, according to *Wikipedia*, is any law, policy, practice, or proposal designed to restrict or limit the possession, production, importation, shipment, sale, and/or use of guns or other firearms by private citizens. The legislation that is proposed is usually the emotional knee-jerk reaction of a Congress that wants desperately to raise their approval ratings, not the thoughtful response of elected representative leadership that operates according to unwavering principle—could this be the reason they have engendered such a lack of confidence in the first place?

Christians should seize the opportunity that public debate affords. To have an opinion and to be able to support that opinion in the marketplace of ideas: logically, respectfully, calmly—this is our calling—Christians at the fore of every cultural forum, establishing the biblical principles upon which our nation and all Christendom should be founded.

Answering questions:

1. Is gun control biblical? (For that matter, does a God who has told us "thou shalt not kill" even want Christians to own killing equipment?)

   Obviously, guns were not even invented then. But "weapons control" was a common practice—usually those recently subjugated were forced to surrender their weapons as an act of submission...and to make future uprisings less practical (Ezekiel 39:-12). In fact, the Lord wants the wicked to be deprived of weapons and only the righteous to have them (Psalm 75:1–10). The reason for this is that it has never been an issue of "gun control," "sword control" or even "hands control" (the legend that martial arts folks have their hands registered as weapons is a myth); it is an issue of *self-control.*

Self-control is a fruit of the Spirit (Galatians 5:22). People with self-control don't need gun control. The question should not be whether people should be allowed only certain guns, but whether certain people ought to be allowed to carry them at all...which goes to the whole debate on background checks and the mentally incompetent.

As to the commandment, "thou shalt not kill" (Ex. 20:13—the sixth commandment), the word kill in Hebrew is better translated "murder": the shedding of innocent blood. Matthew Henry, in his famous commentary, said it best: "It does not forbid killing in lawful war, or in our own necessary defense, nor the magistrate's putting offenders to death, for those things tend to the preserving of life; but it forbids all malice and hatred to the person of any (for he that hateth his brother is a murderer), and all personal revenge arising therefrom; also all rash anger upon sudden provocations, and hurt said or done, or aimed to be done, in passion: of this our Saviour expounds this commandment, (Matt 5:22)." (From *Matthew Henry's Commentary on the Whole Bible*, PC Study Bible Formatted Electronic Database Copyright © 2006 by Biblesoft, Inc. All Rights reserved.)

2. Were our Founders crazy to put the Second Amendment in the Bill of Rights and to call themselves Christians?

As the above passage from *Matthew Henry's Commentary* states, exceptions to the sixth commandment, lawful war and self-defense, are to be allowed. Our Founders had this in mind when they crafted this amendment. Many of their countrymen lived on the edge of the frontier and they depended on hunting for food and protection from wild beasts and wild Native Americans. They felt as if provision and protection were Christian mandates (I Timothy 5:8).

They also were including the responsibility for protection from an encroaching government. The Second Amendment reads, "*A well regulated Militia, being necessary to the security of a free State*, the right of the people to keep and bear Arms, shall not be infringed." Our Founders believed that the best way to keep a government doing the right thing was to keep it knowing that the people would settle for no less.

3. If we argue that magazine size is a problem because of the number that can be killed, why not outlaw all guns...is it less tragic to the parent who has only lost one child?

    The experiences of Columbine, the theatre in Colorado and Sandy Hook Elementary are still fresh in the minds of America...and in the hearts of those our beloved departed left behind. But the solution is not to restrict guns...the type of gun or the size of the magazine that holds the bullets is not the problem. *People* kill, not bullets or guns. Tragedy cannot become less tragic by the laws made after the fact. We have plenty of laws, if we'd just enforce them. Besides, the decadence of our culture is a sin problem, not a law problem.

    Do we have too much violence in our culture? Sure...and not enough parenting, mentoring and discipline; but those require time and a shift in our value system. Meanwhile, we need to protect the vulnerable and enforce existing laws that punish the offender...not make more laws which restrict the freedom of the law-abiding.

4. If we are against "weapons of mass destruction," isn't it hypocritical to own them ourselves?

    We as Americans and Christians (not all Christians are American, nor are all Americans Christian—one is often a matter of birth, the other *always* a matter of re-birth) should act responsibly...I hate to quote a comic super-hero but "with great power comes great responsibility." We cannot undo what the Manhattan project accomplished, anymore than we can put toothpaste back in the tube. Now that we have the power to wipe out mankind, we have to show the world by our example that this force must be a deterrent to the unthinkable, not a threat to the weak.

To surrender such a power now would only insure that those with less noble intents would take up that power to gain an advantage over the disadvantaged.

Recommended reading list:

- *More Guns, Less Crime: Understanding Crime and Gun Control Laws*, John R. Lott, Jr.
- *Gun Fight: The Battle over the Right to Bear Arms in America*, Adam Winkler
- *The Seven Myths of Gun Control: Reclaiming the Truth About Guns, Crime, and the Second Amendment*, Richard Poe

Web sites:

War on the Second Amendment
- http://www.waronthesecond.com/

Gun Control – Just Facts
- http://www.justfacts.com/guncontrol.asp

26

Holidays (and Other Celebrations)

You could say my wife is the 'Celebrater-in-Chief,' at least in our house. She has a door-wreath for every occasion, a tree-decorations bag for all holidays and miscellaneous wall-mantle-and-hearth-hangings to match…not to mention the musical and video accoutrements that accompany Thanksgiving and Christmas and other really special holidays. There is no occasion too trivial for us… and I think that's how it's supposed to be!

Christians were meant to celebrate life (the picture my mind conjures up is that of King David—much to his wife's chagrin—dancing wildly and joyously down the streets of Jerusalem as the Ark of the Covenant was being brought home in 2 Samuel 6:12–16). In fact, every time they turned around, the Children of Israel were celebrating something—the Feast of Tabernacles, the Feast of First Fruits, the Feast of Passover, the Feast of Lights… unless you've looked at a concentration camp photo, I'll venture you haven't seen many thin Jews; besides, being fat in most countries of the world is a sign of certain prosperity.

But we're too busy condemning folks for giving the politically correct greeting at Christmas to celebrate the coming of our Savior (forget that "Happy Holidays"—holy days—is a spiritual greeting itself)! Correcting a well-meaning checker or sales associate is just so much "Bah, humbug" coming from a Christian; oh, it was zealous of us, but not very well-received.

Christians should celebrate birthdays—we are happy the day someone arrives (Prov. 23:24–25). We should celebrate national holidays—happy that our history has yielded advancement (Nahum 1:15). And we should celebrate anything that commemorates an event that brings us closer to God—like my marriage—or the anniversary of anyone's "graduation" from this world to the next, especially if his or her life impacted ours significantly. Actually, that is what All Saints Day was for—so many Christians had been martyred on every day of the year that celebrating them all on one day made more sense; All Hallows' Eve—Hallow E'en, or Halloween, as we know it today—was the evening feast time before that celebration.

Holy Communion is one of those celebrations that Christians celebrate often (1 Cor. 11:25) to commemorate the sacrifice of Jesus, God's Son, as payment in full for our sins (Rom. 3:23; 6:23). Perhaps the "celebration" aspect gets lost in the repetition, but it shouldn't. Christ's substitutionary death is the *only* reason a Holy God could have fellowship with an unholy Man.

To "celebrate" anything means to *openly demonstrate happiness at the memory of an event.* Although there is certainly a place for mourning, we need to celebrate more, commemorate more, praise more…and mourn less.

Are holidays biblical? Should we celebrate something we don't understand? What if my family and friends have never been big on celebration? What about our national holidays…aren't they really just an excuse for a long-weekend? Isn't Christmas really on the wrong date? Isn't it wrong to pretend to our kids that Santa Claus delivered the gifts under the tree…I mean, why do we continue traditions that are obviously based on lies? These are the questions that thinking Christians should be asking.

According to a combination of what many dictionaries say, a *Holiday* is a special day in which something—often a historical event—is commemorated and results in the regular activities of that day being set aside for more preferred traditions or celebrations. Governments have created a list of "legal holidays" in which workers get time off, or are paid higher pay rates for those willing or mandated to work during that time. In America, there are national holidays and religious holidays…an increasingly secular state is attempting the replacement of religious holidays with their secular equivalents so as to be more inclusive. The introduction of Fall Break—in replacement of Thanksgiving—Winter Break—in replacement of Christmas—and Spring Break—in replacement of Easter—makes it easier for Jews, Muslims, adherents to other religions, and atheists to palatably celebrate these traditionally Christian holidays.

Answering questions:

1. Are holidays biblical?
    Of course they are; I've already named four feasts or holidays above and I didn't include Yom Kippur (the "holiest" holiday—to the Jewish people) or Rosh Hashanah (the Jewish New Year). The Festival of Purim was named by Mordecai even when the Jews were in captivity (Esther 9:19–22)…then there is Sukkot, Shavuot, etc.…the list is almost endless.
    The general attitude of the New Testament, however, is to make every day a celebration (Luke 9:23). In fact, the whole gist of the ban on the celebration of days is that Christ has come, the Reality for which the feasts were mere shadows, making every day worthy of celebration.

    > So don't let anyone condemn you for what you eat or drink, or for not celebrating certain holy days or new moon ceremonies or Sabbaths. For these rules are only shadows of the reality yet to come. And Christ himself is that reality. (Col. 2:16–18, NLT)

2. Should we celebrate something we don't understand?
    Let's not make our ignorance the rule. Besides, most of the edicts the Jews put on festivals included celebrating them as a means of educating each generation on the reasons for the

holiday. The Passover was to be eaten standing up, with their shoes on and their staff in hand.

> And you shall observe this event as an ordinance for you and your children forever. When you enter the land which the Lord will give you, as He has promised, you shall observe this rite. And, when your children say to you, 'What does this rite mean to you?' You shall say, 'It is a Passover sacrifice to the Lord, Who passed over the houses of the sons of Israel in Egypt when He smote the Egyptians, but spared our homes.' And the people bowed low and worshiped. (Ex. 12:24–27, NASU)

In the interest of educating at least the Americans in my readership, let me list the current federal holidays (and the reasons we celebrate them).

Federal Holidays

(At least those when the banks and the post offices are closed)

New Year's Day Celebrating the beginning of the Gregorian calendar—Jan 1 (and football—the college bowl games begin)

Birthday of Martin Luther King, Jr. Celebrating the birth of the civil rights champion
(Celebrated the third Monday of Jan—actually January 15, 1929)

Inauguration Day Celebrating the inauguration of a president (this only happens every four years on the 20th of January)

Washington's Birthday Celebrating the birth of America's first president—actually on the 22nd (also called President's Day to include Lincoln's birthday on Feb. 12th—celebrated on the third Monday of February)

Memorial Day   Celebrating the death of all soldiers, it was originally established to commemorate the soldiers of the American Civil War (Celebrated the last Monday of May)

Independence Day   Celebrating the adoption of America's Declaration of Independence—July 4, 1776 (Celebrated on the 4th of July)

Labor Day   Celebrating the achievements of laborers (Celebrated on the first Monday of September)

Columbus Day   Celebrating the landing of Christopher Columbus in the western hemisphere—in the present day Bahamas (Celebrated on the 12th of October)

Veterans Day   Celebrating the contributions of all American soldiers, this holiday was originally called Armistice Day and celebrated the signing of the armistice of World War I (Celebrated on the 11th of November)

Thanksgiving Day   Celebrating the survival of the Pilgrims with a turkey dinner—sometimes called Turkey Day—with Native Americans who helped them—though they probably ate venison, corn, and beans. (Celebrated the fourth Thursday in November—"Black Friday," so called because merchants sometimes only then reach operating-in-the-black margins, follows because many shoppers are also given time off the Friday after Thanksgiving)

Christmas Day   Celebrating globally the birth of Jesus Christ (Celebrated on the 25th of December)

3. What if my family and friends have never been big on celebration?

Although I'm reluctant to recommend that anyone do differently than their own family's traditions, there are some people who have reached adulthood with no sense of celebration at all. Setting your own family's traditions is even more important for those who have never celebrated much of anything growing up. The need for establishing and commemorating important dates can help mark the passage of time, remember the sacrifices of our ancestors, and give a measure of importance and self-worth (birthdays).

I have some friends of mine that didn't celebrate Christmas (they exchanged gifts on Thanksgiving) or other holidays and wouldn't let their daughter date till she was sixteen. Although they had religious reasons for their restrictions, their repressiveness caused their daughter to rebel, and the boy she invited to her sixteenth birthday got her pregnant (instead of working themselves out of a job, too much release of authority all at once resulted in tragedy and regret).

4. What about our national holidays…aren't they really just an excuse for a long weekend?

It may seem that way…and I'm not saying that we shouldn't take a long weekend when it's a gift. But let's not forget why we are celebrating, either. If you're a parent or grandparent, it is important for you to set the example for others. Independence Day has to be more than another trip to a lake or a reason for a picnic. Let's not make birthdays an inconvenient obligation.

Christmas needs to celebrate the arrival of our Savior, not the departure of our savings.

5. Isn't Christmas really on the wrong date?

Probably. Early Christians may have chosen the date because, under persecution, it may have been important to celebrate when everyone was celebrating anyway. Christmas' coincidence with the pagan holiday, the Feast of Saturnalia, may not have been as accidental as first thought.

There are some indications that biblically recorded celestial phenomenon—the star of Bethlehem—occurred at the approximate time of year of the current celebration, but no one knows for sure. The mystery surrounding His miraculous appearance should not dampen our enthusiasm at celebrating what He came to do or lessen our recognition of what He willingly gave up to leave His heavenly home.

6. Isn't it wrong to pretend to our kids that Santa Claus delivered the gifts under the tree...I mean, why do we continue traditions that are obviously based on lies?

Perhaps in our attempts to venerate the generosity of the Bishop of Myra—in present day Turkey—we have gone overboard making the giving of gifts an obligatory expression of our materialist culture of hedonism. The real Saint Nicholas would find little resemblance between his random acts of kindness and the combined lore the cultural march over the centuries has produced—the Santa Claus of North Pole legend.

As Christians, we need to emphasize the *eternal* nature of salvation—symbolized by the *ever*green Christmas Tree of Life (Gen. 2:9); the ornaments of good works and a meek and quiet spirit (1 Tim. 2:14; 1 Pet. 3:4)—symbolized by the tree's ornaments; the shining star of Bethlehem (Matt. 2:2)—symbolized by the star atop the tree.

The "lies" of our traditions are based on truths that have stood the test of time.

Do we celebrate the holidays at our house? Absolutely! Sometimes, the financial realities of our personal economic condition have caused us to try to make a big deal out of a meager gift—sorry Jon. Sometimes, we have been tardy with our expressions—sorry Caleb. But always we have reaped the benefits of kids and grandkids that know they are loved and appreciated.

Recommended reading list:

- *Christ's Time for the Church Calendar*, Laurence Hull Stookey
- *Jewish Holidays: A Brief Introduction for Christians*, Rabbi Kerry M. Olitzki and Rabbi Daniel Judson
- *The Adventure of Christmas: Helping Children Find Jesus in Our Holiday Traditions*, Lisa Whelchel and Jeannie Mooney

Web sites:

- www.publicholiday.org/tag/christian-holidays
- www.christianity.about.com/od/holidaytips/qt/seasonsoffaith.htm
- www.holidays.christiansunite.com

27

Homosexuality (and Other LGBT Issues)

When Keith became Kimberley, I was shocked. What would his wife and kids say? Had we not spent time with my wife's cousin just recently? He seemed perfectly "normal" back then. His (her) letter to the family was unmistakable, though. You could have knocked me over with a feather. However, heterosexuality is no longer a "given" in our culture. I could just as easily have shared my shock at my own cousin's sexual orientation decision made back in the 60s. Lesbians, Gays, Bisexuals, and Transgenders (LGBT) are militantly and rapidly changing our value-neutral culture in the name of tolerance and diversity. This is the hotbed issue (no pun intended) of our day.

There are many who would like to redefine the family. But God, Who created us, had a different idea in mind when he created us male and female (Genesis 1:27) and the Creator generally has the say over His creation.

However, He made Man unique, not just giving him a flesh and blood body, but also giving him a soul…and in so doing made him a rational and willful creature, giving him the ability to weigh options and choose the course he would take. Having choices does not change our created nature, though. It may seem cheaper to run a car on water, but it was made with gasoline in mind.

Is homosexuality biblical? Are people born with a proclivity for a certain sexual orientation? What part does environment have to play? What should the Christian attitude be toward those who have a different sexual orientation? Should homosexuals have positions of leadership in the church, Boy Scout troop, or the sports team? What about gays in the military? These and other questions need to be addressed.

According to the dictionary, *Homosexuality* is romantic attraction, sexual attraction, or sexual activity between members of the same sex or gender. Between males, it is called being *Gay*; between females, it is called being *Lesbian*; *Bisexuality* is defined as a person who is sexually attracted to and engages in sensual or sexual relationships with people of either sex. A *Transgender* is someone who believes they are not identified by one of the more traditional sexual roles. They may identify themselves as asexual, polysexual, pansexual, heterosexual, or homosexual.

According to the Bible, anyone that is "without natural affection" (Greek *astorgos*—Rom. 1:31; 2 Tim 3:3) is an abomination—detestable—to the Lord. Since He is Creator, He has the right—in fact, *the exclusive right*—to determine what is and what is not "natural." He defines this in the Scripture: "...*women exchanged the natural function for that which is unnatural, and in the same way also the men abandoned the natural function of the woman and burned in their desire toward one another, men with men committing indecent acts and receiving in their own persons the due penalty of their error*" (Rom. 1:26–27, NASU).

Answering questions:

1. Is homosexuality biblical?

    Only in a negative connotation. Nowhere does the Bible present homosexuality in any other than a negative light. In fact, it is the only sin that evoked total destruction of cities—Sodom and Gomorrah (Gen 19:24). Sodom is where the term "sodomy" comes from and refers to anal or oral copulation and sex with an animal (more commonly known as "bestiality.")

    Although California's Proposition 8 and the Defense of Marriage Act have been passed by their duly elected legislatures, the courts have held up the enforcement of these laws which uphold the traditional view of marriage. As a result, those who have held that marriage should be reserved for the union of a man and a woman can now have joining their sacrosanct ranks homosexuals and, arguably, polygamists. In an attempt to overcome legal challenges, there have been over thirty states that have written the traditional definition of marriage into their state constitutions.

Although you cannot legislate morality, all laws are written to notify the electorate what is and is not acceptable behavior. When a law is passed, Christians are obligated to obey it (Heb. 13:17,) but only if the law of God—a higher law—is not violated (Acts 5:29).

2. Are people born with a proclivity for a certain sexual orientation?

The whole topic of genetic predisposition could come up for discussion here. Are we genetically predisposed to certain behaviors...or do we use this explanation as a crutch for explaining why certain of our habits are not our fault? The truth is that all of us have a predisposition to sin. It's called a "fallen nature." The root of the problem is the sin nature all of us have inherited from Adam. Of course there are many who would point to this study or that. Whether or not it is genetic or environmental may be up for debate, but it would be wise to ask who funded the study before you quote its statistics.

Those who try to numb the will with drugs or try to manage behavior with discipline or counseling or a change in environment (or a combination) are only masking the symptoms, not dealing with the root cause.

3. What part does environment have to play?

Although I do not have a degree in psychology nor have I ever held myself out to be an expert in the field, I have had, over the years as a youth pastor, as a scoutmaster, and as the dean of Students for a Christian college, the responsibility and privilege of counseling with many young men and women. Occasionally, they would reveal some tendency they had toward feeling some affection toward the same gender. Inevitably further discovery would reveal some environmental influence—molestation as a child by some parent, relative, sitter, or authority figure; exposure to deviant pornography (there is no non-deviant pornography); the normalization of questionable sexual behavior, etc. Usually some strategic forgiveness, counsel, or change in environment would set them on a road to a right perception of themselves and others.

4. What should the Christian attitude be toward those who have a different sexual orientation?

What follows is a posting on the internet from someone who obviously has a different perspective than mine AND my response. I think my response is the best way to answer this question.

Ten Things I Wish the Church Knew about Homosexuality

1. If Jesus did not mention a subject, it cannot be essential to his teachings.
2. You are not being persecuted when prevented from persecuting others.
3. Truth isn't like wine that gets better with age. It's more like manna, you must recognize wherever you are and whoever you are with.
4. You cannot call it "special rights" when someone asks for the same rights you have.
5. It is no longer your personal religious view if you're bothering someone else.
6. Marriage is a civil ceremony, which means it's a civil right.
7. If how someone stimulates the pubic nerve has become the needle to your moral compass, you are the one who is lost.

8. To condemn homosexuality, you must use parts of the Bible you don't yourself obey. Anyone who obeyed every part of Leviticus would rightly be put in prison.
9. If we do not do the right thing in our day, our grandchildren will look at us with the same embarrassment we look at racist grandparents.
10. When Jesus forbade judging, that included you.

By Jim Rigby, a Presbyterian Minister in Austin, TX (reprinted from a May 16, 2012 posting in *Good Feed Blog*)

MY RESPONSE:

TEN THINGS I WISH HOMOSEXUALS KNEW ABOUT THE CHURCH

1. The Church believes that while Jesus makes no direct mention of homosexuality (He makes no mention of abortion either), He does say that marriage is between a man and a woman (Mark 10:6–9)
2. The Church loves homosexuals...not their homosexuality (Prov. 29:27).
3. Disapproval of a lifestyle does not mean persecution. Anyone persecuting the homosexual is wrong. The Church does not and should not persecute anyone for any behavior...but pray for them (Luke 6:28; I Thess. 5:17; James 5:16).
4. Rights that are "inalienable" are given by God, acknowledged in the Declaration of Independence, and the Church believes there are no "rights" for the creature outside those given by the Creator.
5. The Church believes personal religious views are irrelevant. Sincerity is only the test of truth in a world where might makes right, not in the Church where the truth is a Person...Jesus...and absolute.

6. The Church believes that marriage is not a civil ceremony, but a spiritual union. If anyone wants to call it something else...well that, too, is irrelevant (see #1 and #5).

7. The Church believes that the "How to's" and the "What's" are important to the well-being of the creature and are outlined specifically in the Owner's Manual (read Bible) of the Creator. Water in the gas tank may be cheaper, but the owner's manual doesn't recommend it.

8. Fortunately, the Church believes that Jesus's death on the cross covered our shortcomings (which cover our numerous indiscretions about the rules in Leviticus and the other sixty-five books of the Bible).

9. The Church agrees that the next generation is highly influenced by the example of this generation...which is why the absolute truth of the Bible and the Person of Jesus Christ should be our guide. Things are not godly because they are moral, but moral because they are Godly.

10. Jesus never forbade judging, just judging by a standard that you wouldn't apply to yourself (read the context of Matthew 7:1–2). In fact, we (the Church) shall judge angels (read I Corinthians 6:3).

5. Should homosexuals have positions of leadership in the church, school, Boy Scout troop, or the sports team?

The best form of leadership is by example. As the old saying goes, "Character is not taught, it's caught." If we hold our leaders up as examples worthy of emulation, then we need to be very careful of the examples they will make. General Petraeus recently resigned his CIA Directorship because of a marital affair. He knew his example had been tainted by his behavior... and I respect him for the decision he made.

The Boy Scouts of America is debating this very topic. The Head Coach of Notre Dame, Joe Paterno, lost his job because he knew his assistant was engaged in molestation and he did not inform authorities. The list could go on...from sports heroes to Olympians to Congressmen to church leaders...to paraphrase the superhero's motto, "With great influence comes great responsibility." That's why the Bible says, "Let not many of you become teachers, my brethren, knowing that as such we will incur a stricter judgment" (James 3:1–2, NASU).

6.   What about gays in the military?

Although I think it is wrong to have an official policy of "non-transparency," that is exactly what the stupid PC term "Don't Ask, Don't Tell" was. I'm glad the military did away with that policy...but not for the same reason the Obama administration stated.

The only example many foreigners have of America or Americans is our US Military personnel. Therefore, they must be of unimpeachable character. For any soldier to have questionable behavior is a bad reflection on his or her country. Any personal behavior that must be hidden to be acceptable must not be good. I know that there are those who say that there should be a separation between the personal life and the public, but they are wrong. Character should be defined as *what someone does who thinks no one is looking*.

This topic is not going away. As our culture becomes less Christian, the stance I have taken will become less popular. But it's time Christians came out of the closet, too...everyone else is!

Recommended reading list:

- *Coming Out of Homosexuality: New Freedom for Men and Women*, Bob Davies and Lori Rentzel
- *What Do I Say to a Friend That is Gay*, Emily Park Chase
- *Homosexuality and the Politics of Truth*, Dr. Jeffrey Satinover

Web sites:

- www.exodusinternational.org
- www.focusonthefamily.org
- www.regenerationministries.org

28

Humanism

Raised in public school in the mid-fifties and sixties, I was in that transition generation where I went from reciting the pledge of allegiance to the American flag and praying a morning prayer over the intercom to being a member of the evolutionist-dominated Oklahoma Academy of Sciences in my junior year. Maybe the juxtaposition is not obvious, but it is difficult to pray to a Creator and believe in evolution at the same time.

To say that public education has gone through a metamorphosis over the last fifty years would be an understatement of great proportion; from daily prayer in school to having it virtually outlawed by the US Supreme Court in 1962 (Engel v. Vitale); from creation not needing to be taught—it was everyone's commonly held belief—to evolution being taught as fact (not theory); from chewing gum as the number one problem to drugs raids on lockers—I guess that beats the metal detectors so prevalent today. To quote Loretta Lynn's 1978 hit song, "We've come a long way baby." However, it is not necessarily in a positive direction.

Although "separation of church and state" was the stated objection to state-sponsored prayer, the quote cannot be found in the Constitution (rather it is taken out of its context in a personal letter from Thomas Jefferson to the Danbury Baptist Church). Today, the religion of Secular Humanism—and its atheistic philosophy of evolution—has replaced Christianity in many of our culture's most influential institutions, including the public school, its house of worship.

Don't believe that Secular Humanism is really a religion? Read what celebrated humanist Charles F. Potter said in 1930: "Education is thus a most powerful ally of humanism, and every American school is a school of humanism. What can a theistic Sunday school's meeting for an hour once a week and teaching only a fraction of the children do to stem the tide of the five-day program of humanistic teaching?"

One quote; big deal! Really? How about this one taken from an article in 1983 in The Humanist by John J. Dunphy: "The battle for humankind's future must be waged and won in the public school classroom by teachers who correctly perceive their role as the proselytizers of a new faith: A religion of humanity -- utilizing a classroom instead of a pulpit to carry humanist values into wherever they teach. The classroom must and will become an arena of conflict between the old and the new -- the rotting corpse of Christianity, together with its adjacent evils and misery, and the new faith of humanism."

After my folks got a divorce—I was sixteen—my father, older brother, and I moved into a rent house across from the First United Methodist Church. I remember coming home from church and my dad asking me, "How was crutch?" This was our pet name for those who felt the necessity of keeping up appearances. My dad and I shared a Secular Humanist belief in the superiority of self. Nothing came to anyone except by the sweat of the brow. If there was a God, and we doubted there was, surely He didn't care about man.

How did someone like me go from Consensus Christianity— that's what I call most Americans' belief systems back then—to Secular Humanism; to a saving faith in the Lord Jesus Christ? It was an interesting journey—probably the subject of a book-length tome someday. Suffice it to say, like John Wesley at Aldersgate: "I felt my heart grow strangely warm."

The two most dangerous and seriously misled philosophies of today are Darwinian Evolution and Secular Humanism...

and they are connected. Until Charles Darwin gave the scientific community a theory that postulated a godless alternative to special creation, Secular Humanism was just a powerless, wheel-less mode of transportation—you could ride, but you weren't going very far. Evolution provided an alternative "scientific" explanation that made humanism, relativism, and atheism possible.

Our culture has been in decline since the rise of Secular Humanism. The Church is not entirely faultless in this trajectory, either. Christians—with a few notable exceptions—C. S. Lewis, Francis Schaeffer, and the like—have allowed these nonsensical philosophies to go unchallenged. If we are to be relevant to our culture, we have to articulate intelligent answers for the serious questions that are surfacing...enquiring minds want to know!

Is humanism biblical? Why can't Man be the measure of all things? Can one be a Christian and still believe in some form of evolution? What about absolutes...doesn't a close examination of most circumstances in life lead to the inescapable conclusion: "It depends"? How do we know whether special creation or evolution is the real truth about the origin of life? These, and other questions, are the ones thinking Christians should be asking themselves.

According to a combination of what many dictionaries say, *Humanism*—also called Secular Humanism—is that belief system that puts man at the fore, his ethical considerations as the standard. As an ideology, it is atheistic, relativistic, and, from a Christian perspective, immoral.

Answering questions:

1. Is humanism biblical?

     Yes, and no; examples of those who held humanistic philosophies can surely be found in the pages of the Bible, but nowhere is it endorsed by God. If you start with Adam and his firstborn Cain, both thought they had ideas better than God— Adam was convinced that God was holding out on him (Gen. 3); Cain thought it would be better to offer his produce than the blood sacrifice God had required (Gen. 4:3–16).

But the best example of someone having a humanistic philosophy is probably King Saul, especially if you contrast his ideology with that of his successor, King David. Although he was told by God to utterly destroy his enemies and their animals, he was confronted by the prophet Nathan, who said, "What then is this bleating of the sheep in my ears, and the lowing of the oxen which I hear? (1 Sam. 15:14, NKJV).

2. Why can't Man be the measure of all things?

    Although we were made last and the epitome of God's re-creation (Gen. 1:26)—He made the angels first (Job 38) and we, in fact, were made a little lower than them (Ps. 8:5)—we did not make ourselves. Like the old saying goes, "There are two immutable truths in the universe; there is a God and you are not He!"

    Besides, we are flawed, and, if flawed, then no standard worthy of emulation. There was a perfect man; the God/man, Jesus. Patterning our lives after His is not only a good idea, it is commanded (Mk. 10:21; 1 Cor. 4:17). We are told to follow only the example of those following *His* example (1 Cor. 11:1).

3. Can one be a Christian and still believe in some form of evolution?

    Of course you can; if Jesus is Lord, that is all that's required (Rom. 10:9–10); you'll just be misinformed...and helping to support one of the major tenets of Secular Humanism...*and* not a very good thinker. Oh, I know that many with more letters after their names than are in the alphabet espouse some form of evolution. But I have one question for them: "Were you there?"

    Let me give you **Three Reasons Why the Theory of Evolution is Bad Science**:

    •   **By themselves, things don't evolve, they *de*volve; things don't go from chaos to order; things fall apart, not together.** (Since Austrian monk Gregor Mendel, the "father of genetics," published his now-famous paper in 1866, *Experiments on Plant Hybridization*, we have known that desirable traits lose their incidence rate over time.) No matter how many times you pour out a box of watch parts, it will never fall together into a functioning watch.

- **There has not been enough elapsed time since the beginning** (the Theory of Evolution states that time plus chance [through the mechanisms of mutation and the survival of the fittest] results in what we see today in nature; that through a gradual process over eons of time, a single primitive cell climbed out of a primordial sea and became the man we now see). If you take the incidence rate of mutations (1 in 1,000); and multiply that by the incidence rate of beneficial mutations (1 in 1,000); and then multiply that by the incidence rate of dominant traits, as opposed to recessive (1 in 1,000); and then multiply that by all the differences between a single cell animal and *Homo sapiens* (a number too large to fit on this line)…well, there just hasn't been enough time for that to have occurred…the oldest estimated age of the universe is only about fifteen billion years old.

- **There is not one single example alive (or in the fossil record) of a transitional species** (and Darwin's *The Origin of the Species* said the fossil record should be full of them).

Besides, Darwin himself was suspicious of his own theory: "To suppose that the eye with all its inimitable contrivances for adjusting the focus to different distances, for admitting different amounts of light, and for the correction of spherical and chromatic aberration, could have been formed by natural selection, seems, I freely confess, absurd in the highest degree." (from *The Origin of the Species*, J. M. Dent & Sons Ltd, London, 1971, p. 167.)

4. What about absolutes…doesn't a close examination of most circumstances in life lead to the inescapable conclusion: "It depends"?

    Situations may change, but the Word of God never changes. The next time a college professor (or anyone for that matter) tells you confidently that there are no absolutes. ask him if he's *absolutely* certain?

    Imagine trying to navigate without a fixed reference point! Early explorers were plagued until they realized that the North Star—Polaris—was a point in the heaven that did not move (it is a point in space to which the axis of the earth points; perhaps because there is only a star in that place above the Earth's north axis—no such star exists above the Earth's south axis—is why all your explorers were from the *Northern* Hemisphere—Vasco de Gama, Ferdinand Magellan, Christopher Columbus… jump in anywhere and name me one from the Southern Hemisphere…Vasco Nunez de Balboa, John Cabot, Hernando de Soto, Amerigo Vespucci…really, jump in…Jacques Cartier, Sir Francis Drake, Samuel de Champlain…I think I've made my point!)

    Only by navigating by something unchangeable, does forward progress toward a certain destination become possible—replace the Word for the North Star and your life for the ship and you'll see the analogy.

5. How do we know whether special creation or evolution is the real truth about the origin of life?

    Since none of us were there, and since it takes more faith to believe in evolution, I choose the Bible's account: special creation. Evolution promises nothingness, the other promises eternal life from a God who loved us enough (John 3:16) to send a Substitute to take the death I deserved (Rom. 3:23 and 6:23) and give me His life in exchange. Where's the decision?

    It was Dr. Francis Schaeffer who said, "All roads from Humanism lead to chaos." No word can better describe our culture than "chaos." Violent crime is worse, teenage pregnancy is higher, abortion is much higher, church attendance is lower, drug and alcohol abuse is rampant, public education is in disrepair—I could go on—since "Man" has been the measure; since evolution and secular humanism have replaced God in the public discourse.

Why? Two reasons. (1) Nobody knows the answers to the hard questions anymore. (2) Political correctness and pluralism have silenced the Church.

It's time for Christians to stand up and be educated...and then to speak to a culture going down a wayward path.

Recommended reading list:

- *Understanding the Times*, Dr. David Noebel
- *How Should We Then Live*, Francis A. Schaeffer
- *Exploring Christian Ethics: Biblical Foundations for Morality*, Kyle D. Fedler

Web sites:

- www.secularhumanism.com
- www.christiananswers.net/q-sum/sum-r002.html
- www.biblicalworldview21.org

29

Human Trafficking

Slavery and kidnapping have been illegal in most countries since the middle of the nineteenth century, but human trafficking is no more about the methods of delivery than drug dealers are about drug problems. Our efforts at the drug war by controlling the supply are noble but wrongheaded. Both societal plagues have to do with consumers not suppliers. As long as there is a market for drugs, there will be dealers and cartels—and the attendant violent crimes. Similarly, as long as there is a perverted desire willing to pay for illicit behavior, there will be human trafficking.

As marijuana is a gateway drug—often the entrance to other harder-to-break addictions—so also pornography is a gateway sin… and the lustful passions that are fueled by this pornography have made human trafficking the most common result. With the advent of the internet, delivery capability has made pernicious pornography even more available and abundant. The demand for new objects of these lustful passions has been fueled by this pornography, and human trafficking has profitably provided the supply of innocents. It is a malady that attacks hardest the family—the very foundation of a civil society.

So stop the pornography and you attack the supply line for the lustful passions that create the sexual addictions. This, in turn, should lessen the demand for human trafficking. Let me give you a historical example. During the great Welsh revival of the nineteenth century, pubs shut down by the thousands…not because of some new law enacted to outlaw alcohol consumption, but pubs shut down for lack of consumers. The demand for alcohol declined because of the new wave of morality that revival brought. The same will happen if a new awakening hits America. When the desire for illicit sex declines because of an increase of morality, the demand for human trafficking will dry up. This is the war we must be fighting.

This may require legislation limiting internet pornography; it may require interdiction efforts at the borders and other places where law enforcement has choke points on kidnappers; it may require the Church to preach morality and holiness from the pulpit; but it *will certainly require* a far-reaching and long-lasting revival—an awakening—for *revival* becomes *reformation* only when society is so pervasively changed that men *and* laws are affected.

Is human trafficking biblical? Weren't the children of Israel led away captive as slaves by nations raised up by God to do so? Aren't there scriptures that instruct slave owners how to treat their slaves…how then can God be against slavery? Is sex wrong? How about the wife who says, "I don't care where you get your appetite as long as you come home for dinner?" These and other questions are being asked by thinking Christians.

According to a combination of what many dictionaries say, *Human Trafficking* is the forced abduction of people, mostly women or young girls, for the purposes of sexual slavery, organ harvesting, or forced labor. This is not indentured servitude, which historically has been mostly voluntary, but often kidnapping is involved.

Answering questions:

1. Is human trafficking biblical?

    Not in the sense that it is acceptable or normative behavior, but it has been used by God as a judgment on both heathen nations and the children of Israel—God often uses heathen practices to act as a judgment on those whose acts have earned His displeasure.

Examples of this can be seen in 2 Chron. 12:8 (under King Rehoboam) and when God allowed the children of Israel to be sent as slaves to Babylon (Jer. 2:20, 28:14). God, in His longsuffering mercy, postponed His judgment until He could ignore their idolatry no longer—they were sacrificing their children to heathen gods (Is. 57:5).

But aside from using the enemies of Israel to judge His children for their apostasy, God does not promote or endorse this kind of behavior from anyone. Rather, He judges those who practice human trafficking (Ex. 6:6).

2. Weren't the children of Israel led away captive as slaves by nations raised up by God to do so?

Yes, but like was said before, that was God's judgment. In His efficiency, He even uses the heathen to serve His purposes. And, though the children of Israel went into a forced captivity for seventy years, He restored them to their land and their possessions under the leadership of Ezra and Nehemiah (see the books of the Bible by their names).

3. Aren't there scriptures that instruct slave owners how to treat their slaves...how then can God be against slavery?

Slavery goes against the whole concept of "free will." But, like the example of the Hivites in Joshua 9:7–26, voluntary slavery—the act of knowingly accepting a bondage—is also an act of free will. That doesn't make the one doing the binding less wrong, it just makes the ones being bound easy targets... and unwittingly complicit. Sometimes we choose poorly and we default to a familiar slavery rather than shoulder the responsibilities that come with freedom.

As far as the Bible giving advice to slaves and slave owners is concerned, it is important to take the rather all-encompassing term of "slavery" and break it down to its various expressions in historical context. There was the "indentured servant," who, for economic reasons, sold himself, so to speak, to someone to whom he owed more than the sum total of his possessions for a specific period of time or until his debt was paid off. This practice was continued in colonial times with many people selling themselves for a year in exchange for their passage to the New World. (There are even some today who feel "enslaved" by their employers.)

Then there was the "apprentice"—someone who had signed a contract of service for a number of years in exchange for learning a trade or marketable skill.

And, of course, there was the traditional slave—who might have been made so by a conqueror, subjugating the more able-bodied of his defeated foes and selling them into slavery—he might have been born a slave (the offspring of a slave)—or he might have been a political slave, made so by an enemy, either foreign or domestic.

As the concept of illicit sexual behavior is not new, neither is human trafficking or sexual slavery. Historically, slavery was generally for the purpose of hard labor; however, modern sexual promiscuity, fueled by the prevalence of non-traditional morality and the availability of internet pornography, has made the modern concern of human trafficking mostly sexual.

Biblical advice to slaves and masters alike can be found throughout the New Testament, but most famously from the passage in Ephesians:

> Fathers, do not provoke your children to anger, but bring them up in the discipline and instruction of the Lord. Slaves, be obedient to those who are your masters according to the flesh, with fear and trembling, in the sincerity of your heart, as to Christ; not by way of eyeservice, as men-pleasers, but as slaves of Christ, doing the will of God from the heart. With good will render service, as to the Lord, and not to men, knowing that whatever good thing each one does, this he will receive back from the Lord, whether slave or free. And masters, do the same things to them, and give up threatening,

knowing that both their Master and yours is in heaven, and there is no partiality with Him. (Eph. 6:4–9, NASU)

This is not an endorsement of the practice of slavery, but a wise and conscious decision by the apostle to sideline the issue; dealing rather with the concept of submission, not the cultural realities of the day.

4. Is sex wrong?

    To me, "sex"—or sexual intercourse—is too clinical a term to be used as a moniker for the ultimate experience of oneness between a husband and wife. Surely, we are not talking about the instinctive animal act of two individuals seeking an endorphin release and the satisfaction of biological drives…I much prefer the Act of Marriage or Love-Making! If asked in the marriage context (between a man and a woman), no, it is not wrong!

    It is sad that we had to go through a promiscuous era— some would say we're still in it—called "the sexual revolution" for Christians to come to the conclusion that love-making was designed to be more than a means of procreating. Some Christians have even felt guilt for experiencing the pleasure God intended for this reflection of our oneness with Him. Man, like God, is a spirit. This spirit is expressed through a soul and lives in a body—the ultimate sexual experience involves all three and, in marriage, is holy, a celebration of unity and pleasurably guiltless.

5. How about the wife who says, "I don't care where he gets his appetite, as long as he comes home for dinner?"

    This is the wife who has resigned herself to her husband's lustful behavior or addiction to pornography. I have counseled with many couples who have had problems with their "sex" lives. Often, their intimacy has devolved rather than improved over time. One couple had come frustratingly to obtuse and weird role-playing behavior to entice one another to satisfaction;

another couple's sexual habits had them performing intimately eleven or twelve times per week...when I asked each couple for an average length of time for their bedroom experience, they both related, "About five minutes!" Obviously, their intimacy had devolved to an animal level.

Human trafficking may be a twenty-first century problem, but its solution is as old as the Garden of Eden. The tree of life is a cross and its fruit is love. Satisfy yourself with that fruit and the desire for the fruit of other trees will fade.

Recommended reading list:

- *The Act of Marriage*, Tim and Beverly LaHaye
- *The Slave Across the Street: A True Story of How an American Teen Survived the World of Human Trafficking*, Theresa Flores
- *This Immoral Trade: Slavery in the 21st Century*, Baroness Caroline Cox, John Marks

Web sites:

- www.redeemedministries.com/you-are-the-answer-to-human
- www.apu.edu/articles/16871
- www.cbn.com/.../our-ministries/project-humanTrafficking.aspx

30

Judaism, Islam, and Other Religions

Although I can only recollect two Jews I've led to the Lord—Loren and Kris—my record on Muslims is even worse. Perhaps it is lack of exposure...which is my fault, ultimately. I think we Christians have a tendency to turn insulation (2 Cor. 6:17) to isolation. I'm as guilty as the rest. It is easier to live my life surrounding myself with those who believe as I do. Although the Lord does not want us to be like the world (1 John 2:15), He *did* choose to leave us in the world (John 17:15).

Most religions have the same problem. Adherents to one belief system or another have a tendency to surround themselves with the like-minded; so much so that they soon develop what I call the "we/they syndrome." There are Jews...all others are Gentiles. There are Muslims...all others are infidels. There are Christians...and heathens. But there are those who call themselves Jews, Muslims, or Christians...or Buddhists, or Shinto, or Mormons...you name it...who are so in name only, or by culture only. But what we label ourselves is not nearly as important as what God calls us. As far as He is concerned, there is only "the lost" and "the found."

In the final analysis, only God's judgment is relevant. All other opinions are just that. (For the atheist, perhaps all of this seems irrelevant...have you read Psalms 14:1 lately?)

Christianity is different from all other religions. Oh, I know everyone thinks their take on the Truth is the only *real* one, but hear me out. Three primary things separate Christianity from the rest of the pack:

1) All religions have the adherent being rewarded by their God by virtue of their obedience to a set of rules...either the Ten Commandments or the Quran or the Upanishads or whatever...except Christianity. Oh, Christians have a set of rules they have to abide by...it's just that in Christianity, there's the recognition that it can't be done...in fact, by accepting Jesus as our Lord and Savior, we acknowledge that knowing the law only made us universally guilty; that Jesus was the only one capable of keeping the law, and by His substitutionary death on the cross He, Who knew no sin, died for our sins, restoring our relationship with a Holy God; that we have been set free from the bonds of *religion*, having been freed by a *relationship*.

2) I can show you where Muhammad's body lies...I can show you where Abraham's body lies...I can even show you where Joseph Smith's body, or Gautama Buddha's body or Confucius' body is buried...but Jesus is the only Founder of a religion Who was (or even claims to be) resurrected.

3) Name me one other religion that has as its central event the death of its God!

Is Islam the religion of peace that it claims to be? Is Judaism still looking for a messiah to come? Isn't there truth to be found in the writings of Confucius, Joseph Smith, Gautama Buddha, the Upanishads, and other sacred texts? What categorizes a belief system as a cult? What about Atheism? Wasn't America founded on secularism? These and other questions are the ones thinking Christians should be asking themselves.

According to a dictionary amalgamation, Islam is composed of those who "submit"—Muslim means "submitted"—to Allah. Judaism is the belief that the descendants of Abraham, Isaac, and

Jacob—who had twelve sons—are God's chosen people and have, since Moses, been peculiarly led by a written revelation that makes them, according to Muslims, the "people of the Book." According to the Bible—the Old and New Testaments (or Covenants)—Arabs are the descendants of Ishmael, who also had twelve sons (Gen. 25:12)...and arguably of Abraham and Keturah, Abraham's wife after Sarah died of old age (Gen. 25:1–4). Christianity, Islam, and Judaism are the world's three major religions, in order here of number of adherents; they are also unique in that each claim a monotheistic belief.

In order to help the reader learn the basic vernacular of these three groups, I have provided a brief glossary of a few of the most rudimentary terms:

"Judaism-ese" Glossary

Yahweh: The name of God, the Creator, given to Moses (Gen. 2:4); originally the unpronounceable "YHWH" (too holy to be pronounced), but later changed to include the vowels sounds to make it pronounceable.

Jew: The descendants of Abraham—through Isaac and Jacob; the covenant having been ratified by circumcision; God's chosen people (Gen 12:1–4).

Hebrew: Literally, the descendants of Eber (Gen 10:1), the son of Shem, the son of Noah.

Semite: Literally, the descendants of Shem (Gen 10:1). (Note: these three terms are used interchangeably, usually as adjectives (Jewish, Hebraic, or Semitic) but sometimes as nouns.

Menorah: a seven-branched candlestick (Ex. 25:31–37) representing the presence of Jehovah; often used in Jewish ceremonies.

Yamaka or **Kippah**: in some sects of the more orthodox Jewish community, this round headgear or hat is to be worn at all times, especially in public, usually by men; in less orthodox circles, it is only worn during times of prayer and symbolizes the covering of or submission to God.

Torah: the sacred writings of Judaism; although in its most basic term, it refers to the first five books of the Tanakh—communicated to Moses by God at Sinai and at the Tabernacle, it can also refer to the totality of the written and oral interpretations (found primarily in the Talmud and the Midrash) on the word of God.

"Islam-ese" Glossary

Allah: the name of the god of Islam: believed by Muslims to be the Yahweh of the Jews or the Jehovah of the Christians.

Muhammad: The last in a long line of prophets sent by Allah.

Muslim: Those who follow the teachings of Mohammad; literally, the "submitted."

Islam: Literally, "submission."

Quran or **Koran**: the sacred writings of Islam (written in "Surahs" or verses).

Jihad: "Holy war;" declared to effect the will of Allah.

Fatwa: an edict pronouncement of judgment by any qualified jurist—Mufti—against any violator of Islamic law. In Sunni Islam, these can be issued by anyone and are non-binding; in Shia Islam, they are only issued by a Mufti and are binding.

Hadith: a teaching of Muhammad.

Kufis and **Hijabs**: Islamic headgear for men and women, respectively.

"Christian-ese" Glossary

Jehovah: the transliterated Greek name for the Jewish Yahweh; the Christian name for God.

Jesus: again, from the Greek, the Christian name for the Son of God; in Hebrew pronounced "Yeshua"—the same as Joshua; believed by Christians to be the active agent of the "Godhead"—all who qualify as God—in creation (John 1:1–14), has been crucified on the cross for the salvation of the world (Acts 4:10); and to be the final Judge (Rom. 2:16; 2 Tim 4:1).

Trinity: or "Tri-unity"; the Christian concept of God being a Tri-une Being, Father/Son/Holy Spirit; created in the image of God, man is a good example for understanding of this: While I am a father (I have children), I am a son (I have a mother and father), and also a husband (I have a wife), I am not three persons; I am only one, but I operate in three different roles—it just depends on the relationship in which you want to consider me.

Holy Bible: the sacred writings of Christianity comprised of the twenty-seven "Books" of the Old Testament (corresponding to the written revelation of Judaism) plus the thirty-nine "Books" of the New Testament.

Sin: literally, "falling short," an archery term which refers to "missing the mark."

Justification: what happens when by faith a believer trusts Jesus's death on the cross as payment in full for sins past, present, and future.

Sanctification: the ongoing process that a believer begins by salvation, through the action of the Holy Spirit and the reprogramming of his worldly thinking by the Word of God.

Faith: the substance of things hoped for; the evidence of things not seen; the willingness to trust yourself to the consequences of your belief.

Answering questions:

1. Is Islam the religion of peace that it claims to be?

    First of all, we Christians must not paint with a broad brush and swiftly condemn all Islam for the acts of terrorism perpetrated by the radical elements of this religion. Christians don't want to be reminded of the excesses of the Crusades, nor the Jews of the forcible circumcisions under Antipater. Conversions brought about by the coercion or force of zealots seldom result in permanent change. Christians should never fear the logical, peaceable comparison of the "truth" claimed by others. The American Constitution wisely protects a person's right to the "free exercise" of his religion. My Bible says that, "Truthful words stand the test of time; lies are soon exposed" (Prov. 12:1, NLT).

    While we must not condemn the peaceful acts of those who try to persuade by the power of their beliefs, we must unequivocally, universally, and loudly denounce the violent acts of terrorism like happened at the World Trade Center, at Ft. Hood, and at the Boston Marathon. Moderate Islam might have more credibility if it was more vociferous in its condemnation of Islam's radical elements. Those that attempt, or incite others to attempt, acts of terrorism are cowards whose vengeful acts only underscore that their message is not true enough to stand by its own merits.

    The Christian believes that true peace is not the absence of conflict, and that there will never be peace on earth until the Prince of Peace rules in the heart of every man.

2. Is Judaism still looking for a messiah to come?

Gamaliel was right (Acts 5:34–42). As a leader of the Jews in Jerusalem at the time of Jesus, he counseled the Sanhedrin not to oppose the preaching of the early disciples. He reasoned impeccably that if it was like other religious movements, it would soon die away; if not, they might just find themselves opposing God Himself. The end result is that he probably saved their lives. They were beaten and ordered to "no more speak in that Name." Of course, they continued to preach!

The Jews of that time—and the Romans, who carried out the execution—had to come up with a plausible explanation for the empty tomb. They paid off the soldiers who had guarded the tomb and told them to lie about the disciples of Jesus coming to steal away the body (Matt. 28:10–15). Since there were many witnesses to the resurrection (I Cor. 15:6), the Jewish leaders had to stick with their lie till that generation—that had seen Jesus with their own eyes *after the resurrection*—died off.

Today, there are still many Jews that have bought into the lie. Sure, some have received Jesus as their Messiah—completed Jews, many call them—but many still "look for another" (Luke 7:19).

Interestingly enough, the Jewish Seder (Passover) service which was modified in the second century and canonized along with the Torah, Midrash, and the Talmud (circa, 110 AD) has in it the customary hiding of the broken part of the third Matzah (loaf of unleavened bread)—the same loaf Jesus broke when He said, "This is my body which is broken for you" (Matt. 26:26). This hidden part is called the "Afikoman"—the only Greek derived word in the Seder service—and literally translated means "He came."

The Good News is that Jesus Himself said, "Seek, and ye shall find" (Matt. 7:7).

3. Isn't there truth to be found in the writings of Confucius, Joseph Smith, Gautama Buddha, the Upanishads, and other sacred texts?

Yes, the sacred writings of other religions are filled with the collected wisdom of the ages. Confucius, Smith, the Quran, and Buddha may have much of value to say, but, in the words of the Apostle Peter, "Lord, to whom shall we go? *Thou hast the words of eternal life*" (John 6:68, KJV).

4. What categorizes a belief system as a cult?

Interesting word: "cult." We get the word "occult" from it. To astronomers, this means something entirely unexpected to us. It means "to block the light of." An "occultation" is a celestial event which occurs when one heavenly body passes in front of—and therefore "blocks the light of"—another heavenly body. Astronomers use these rare events to learn about the composition of the atmosphere of the "occluding" body.

Cults are much the same. Anything that blocks or changes the nature of the light—read "understanding"—of the True Light (John 1:9; 1 John 2:8) is a cult.

What is the witness of the True Light? Read the context (the entire first chapter of John's Gospel) and you find a few things that all Truth confesses. Before I get to a list of truths, let me make a delineation between what may be true and what is the *Truth*. Although some may say I'm parsing words, the further you get afield from the Truth, the more in trouble you become. Let me give you two principles that may help you.

1. All truth, real Truth, is parallel and co-destinational.
2. The falseness of a lie is measured in its nearness to the truth.

These principles may help you to distinguish between some private—and questionable—revelation you receive, and the in-breathed revelation of the Holy Spirit. Fortunately, we do have leaders to guide us (Eph. 4–10), but ultimately God charges us to be like the noble Bereans who "searched the Scriptures daily, whether those things were so" (Acts 17:11).

Tests for Cults of Christianity

To not be judged as a cult, the following uncompromisable truths must be embraced:

A. The divinity of Christ (That Jesus, by the power of the Holy Spirit and the plan of the Father, is the Creator and not a created being himself)

B. The universal depravity of Man (That Man is at his core sinful and in need of a Savior)

C. Salvation by grace through faith (That Jesus's death and resurrection reconciles Man to God; that at His crucifixion the Father laid on Him the iniquity of all men, past-present-future; and that by making Him Lord and trusting in His resurrection we are saved)

Sure, there are other important issues, but most of those are for denominational consideration. There are churches...and then there is *the Church*.

5. What about Atheism?

The quote from Psalms 14:1 might be appropriate here, but the atheist might think I'm being dismissive. As the famous French philosopher Rene' Descartes put it, "Cogito ergo sum,"—I think, therefore I am—from "Discourse on Method," there are some who find that their pursuit of truth is circular.

Indeed, for the atheist, self-awareness of his own existence is somehow his proof that nothing else is necessary...but he makes a religion of his atheism—and this is not the testimony of Descartes! (Read *all* of his "Discourse.")

The ultimate test of truth lies on the other side of this reality...but it will be too late for the atheist to arrive at a different conclusion. Then he will know the truth of,

Therefore God also has highly exalted Him and given Him the name which is above every name, that at the name of Jesus every knee should bow, of those in heaven, and of those on earth, and of those under the earth, and that every tongue should confess that Jesus Christ is Lord, to the glory of God the Father. (Phil. 2:9–11, NKJV)

6. Wasn't America founded on secularism?

In the first place, America's founding document was the Declaration of Independence—which clearly attests of a mutual belief in God (not the Constitution, though secularists are quick to point out has no mention of God in it...*haven't they read the very date it was signed...AD 1787?—in the year of our Lord, 1787?!*)

In the second place, it could be argued that the real founding document was the Mayflower Compact of 1620—which the secularists never mention, as it's an even more blatant argument against a bedrock secularism.

In the third place, though the Signers may have included a few deists, their devoutness makes Christians of today seem impious by comparison.

I could go on and establish for you the concreteness of the truth that America's foundation was not only religious, but specifically Christian...however, there are those who have catalogued the facts more completely than I. I will give you an incomplete listing of the books I have read on the subject, for further reading.

Recommended reading list:

- *Separation of Church and State: What the Founders Meant*, David Barton
- *Teaching and Learning America's Christian History*, Verna Hall
- *The Light and the Glory*, David Manuel and Peter Marshall
- *America's Dates with Destiny*, Pat Robertson

- *Kingdom of the Cults*, Walter Martin

Web sites:

- www.answering-islam.org/Intro/comparison.html
- www.christianity-islam.com
- www.allaboutreligion.org/islam-vs-christianity-faq.htm

31

Knowing God's Will

Every day he walked by Benjamin Franklin's farm. Every day he gazed up at the weather vane attached at the highest point of the barn. Every day he wondered at the deceptive message that old weather vane broadcast to hapless passers-by: "God is love." When one day he noticed the aging orator precariously perched installing pointed metal objects near the gable peaks, he had to speak up.

"Good day to you, sir," he called up to him. "What new deception are you about today?"

Looking over his horn-rimmed glasses at his neighbor, one bushy eyebrow raised, he remarked, "Deception? I'm quite sure I have no idea what you mean. These are meant to re-direct the force of the lightning that burned my last barn to the ground."

"I see. Another one of your hair-brained contrivances, I'm sure. I just hope it works better than your weather vane. Everyone knows that God's love is unchanging. Putting that message atop a weather vane sends the wrong message."

Smiling wryly, Mr. Franklin replied, "You've got me all wrong, neighbor. The weather vane's message is that no matter which way the wind blows, *God is* still *love*."

Although I heard that story a long time ago—and probably got some of the details wrong—the moral of the story is true. The will of God is like the love of God…*unchanging*…not because it is always to our liking, but because *it always has our best interests at heart*. Contrary to Doc's concluding remark to Marty and his girlfriend in the last installment of the *Back to the Future* trilogy, as Christians, our future is not what we make of it, but what *He* makes of it. When we make Jesus Lord, we submit to His will for our lives. We trust that His will is beneficial, efficient, and immutable.

Knowing that will is the number one concern of most Christians...or, at least it should be; for *the only thing worse than working against God and failing is working against God and succeeding.*

The Scripture says, "Can two walk together, unless they are agreed?" (Amos 3:3, NKJV). Although this is most often quoted in a marriage context, our union with God is certainly apropos here. Do you have His best interests at heart? If you're in a covenantal relationship with Him, you are supposed to.

The other attribute of God's will (other than beneficial, efficient and immutable) is that it is *singular*. I left this to be considered separately because it is, for us as time creatures, so difficult to understand. To be God; to know the end from the beginning; to know all the possible alternate realities—the directions our lives could take, if we chose a certain way—means *that there is no "Plan B."* That is a difficult concept to grasp, but it goes right to the heart of the immutability—the unchanging nature—of God's will.

There is only "Plan A." And that is good news! It means that whatever stupid decision you've made did not ever take Him by surprise. He never elbowed the Holy Spirit and said, "*Now* what are We going to do?" Before you ever contemplated that foolhardy course of action, He knew what your decision was going to be...and what He would have to do to work it out for your good (Rom. 8:28).

Is knowing God's will biblical...is it even possible? If it is beneficial, efficient, immutable, and singular, is it inevitable? What good will it do me to know God's will? How does free will work when God already knows the choice you're going to make? Is prayer frivolous; I mean if He already knows what's going to happen, why pray? These are the questions thinking Christians should be asking themselves.

According to an amalgamation of dictionaries and commentaries, *God's will* is the concept of God having a plan and a purpose for mankind and individually for each human and seeing that plan fulfilled. Much has been written about knowing and doing God's will; arguably, seeking and knowing His will is the prime pursuit of every human being.

Answering questions:

1. Is knowing God's will biblical…is it even possible?

    It seems that knowing His will is at least possible or seeking to know His will or wisdom would never be encouraged; and it obviously is. Hear what James says,

    > But if any of you lacks wisdom, let him ask of God, who gives to all generously and without reproach, and it will be given to him. But he must ask in faith without any doubting, for the one who doubts, is like the surf of the sea, driven and tossed by the wind. For that man ought not to expect that he will receive anything from the Lord, being a double-minded man, unstable in all his ways. (James 1:5–8, NASU)

    The only requirement seems to be pure, unadulterated faith. That is not as easy to do as it is to say. An undoubting faith is one where your own desires don't get in the way. Is it possible to have your own desires not get in the way? Of course it is. All we have to do is die. What desires do dead men have? As one of my pastors put it, "I've never seen a hearse pulling a U-Haul!"

    What kind of death am I talking about? A death to self. Jesus spoke of this death when he said, "If anyone desires to come after Me, let him deny himself, and take up his cross, and follow Me. For whoever desires to save his life will lose it, but whoever loses his life for My sake will find it" (Matt. 16:24–25, NKJV).

    In other words, the only time your desires don't get in the way is for His desires to *become* your desires. What kind of commitment does that require? Total. He requires unconditional surrender…nothing less will do.

> Delight yourself also in the Lord, and He shall give you the desires of your heart. (Ps. 37:4, NKJV)

Part of the problem is realizing that our desires—that is, in our flesh—are contradictory to His desires. Listen to what the Apostle Peter has to say,

> Christ therefore having suffered in the flesh, be you also armed with the same thought: for he that hath suffered in the flesh, hath ceased from sins: That now he may live the rest of his time in the flesh, *not after the desires of men, but according to the will of God.* (I Pet. 4:1–2, Douay-Rheims)

2. If it is beneficial, efficient, immutable, and singular, is it inevitable?

Of course not, but let me back up and show you how it is beneficial, efficient, and immutable.

A. The will of God is *beneficial.*

As Oral Roberts simplistically said, "Something good is going to happen to you." This is not a spiritual 'pipe-dream.' It is sound theology. Read what the prophet Jeremiah, under the inspiration of the Holy Spirit said, "'For I know the plans that I have for you,' declares the Lord, 'plans for welfare and not for calamity to give you a future and a hope'" (Jer. 29:11, NASU).

B. The will of God is *efficient.*

The best way to prove this is to show first, that man's way never ends well.

"There is a way which seems right to a man, but its end is the way of death" (Prov. 14:12, NASU). Then, to contrast that with God's way: "I don't think the way you think. The way you work isn't the way I work. For as the sky soars high above earth, so the way I work surpasses the way you work, and the way I think is beyond the way you think (Is. 55:8–9, The Message).

C. The will of God is *immutable*.

The word *immutable*, unfortunately, has passed out of common usage. It simply means "unchangeable." To say God's will is immutable is self-evident. If God is omniscient—all-knowing—He must not be capable of error. He will not, therefore, *re*consider any plan because He thought of a better one. Maybe that's one of the reason's it says in Hebrews 13:8, "Jesus Christ, the same yesterday, today and forever."

D. The will of God is *singular*.

There is no ambiguity or uncertainty in God's will. Generally, it is always forward; particularly, it is always progressive. That means that God is never surprised and that He effects His purpose sequentially, in order, each emanation following the other as it should.

But the will of God is not *inevitable*. When God placed Adam and Eve in the Garden of Eden and tasked them with tending and keeping it (Gen. 1:28; 2:8,15), He gave them a choice and told them which way to choose (Gen 2:16–17). It was God's plan that man would live forever, but it was not *inevitably* so.

The Scripture says that Christ was slain before the foundation of the world (Rv. 13:8). That means that *in the purposes of God*, Jesus made man, knowing He would not choose wisely and that His ultimate sacrifice would be required. Knowing what our choice is does not remove our free will. His foreknowledge is not His fore-control.

The fact that none of us choose the right path (Rom. 3:23) does not mean we had no choice, or that He does not tell us what that choice should be (Josh. 1:8). In fact, I'm quite sure the greatest pain of hell will not be the eternal burning without being consumed in the lake of fire...*rather it will be seeing the tear in God's eye* at having to cast us there. Although He is "not willing that any should perish" (2 Pet. 3:9), it only accounts for the delay of His return, not for the acceptance of those who refuse Him (2 Pet. 3:10).

3. What good will it do me to know God's will?

    Knowing God's will makes it easier to choose to work with Him, not against Him (Amos 3:3). We make goals in our lives... five-year plans, ten-year plans...even "bucket lists"—things we're determined to do before we "kick the bucket"—but do we consider that God may have an agenda? Knowing that agenda and making His agenda ours are what divine appointments are all about.

    If you haven't felt His Holy Spirit speaking through you a word in season (Prov. 25:11) or felt virtue flowing out of you as His healing power coursed through you (Lk. 6:19), then you may not know this *divine cooperation*. But it is the reason He left us here (Eph. 2:10).

4. How does free will work when God already knows the choice you're going to make?

    Like I said, His fore-knowledge is not His fore-control. Our free will is also known as free moral agency—the right to choose a path of evil or a path of righteousness. Although the law gave the Jews the upper hand—it's great to know what God's expectations are—it only served to condemn man because he didn't have the power to live up to them (read Romans 7).

    When Jesus left His Holy Spirit with man (Luke 24:49, Acts 2), He gave them the power within to obey (Phil. 2:13). Not only did he pay the price on the cross for our sins (small "s," plural), but He gave us the power over Sin (capital "S," singular).

5. Is prayer frivolous; I mean, if He already knows what's going to happen, why pray?

Prayer doesn't change God, it changes us. When we pray about a situation, it's to get God's mind on the matter. Jesus said He never did anything He didn't see the Father dc (John 5:19). No wonder Jesus had His prayers answered; they were always in concert with God's will.

There is an old phrase called "praying through." This simply means praying until you know the will of God and then praying the will of God. (Fasting just helps take away the voices of distraction...the voices of those around you; your flesh; the Devil.)

Prayer is our way of telling God that His will reigns supreme; that our will is submitted to His...and that is powerful (James 5:16), not frivolous!

Closing with one more story: There was a port on the coast of Africa that was every sea captain's choice for winter harborage. The only problem was its popularity...and the narrowness of its passageway. To get a berth, you had to be early and skilled. When harborage became scarce, the last ships had to anchor close to the mouth of the passageway. Each additional ship became an obstacle to the arrival of the next one. Some ships, over the years had failed to make it safely and their submerged hulks only made navigation more treacherous.

Finally, somebody got a bright idea to build a series of three torch towers on the hills behind the port. Any captain who lined up his entering ship on their fires was assured safe passage. The will of God is like those three alignment towers. If the Word seems to confirm it, the circumstances are lining up, and you have the confirmation of God's inner voice [remember, His sheep know His voice (Jn. 10:27)]—a witness with your spirit (Rom. 8:16)—then you can confidently proceed.

Recommended reading list:

- *Knowing God*, J. I. Packer
- *The Will of God*, Leslie Weatherhead
- *Wild Goose Chase*, Mark Batterson

Web sites:

- www.goodoilonbooks.com/2013/06/14/gods-will-for-your-life
- www.easyspeak.hubpages.com/hub/How-To-Find-The-Will-Of-God
- www.allaboutfollowingjesus.org/knowing-gods-will.html

32

Legislating Morality

"You're out of here!" The silence that followed was deafening. Then my daughter began to whimper. "Fix him his favorite meal, Mom," I said, "while he gets packed." This was my eldest son, but in open rebellion to the rules of the house. The ensuing scene—my wife and daughter crying their way through a final meal preparation, my son packing his things noisily, his brother helping him…quite willingly, and me taking a long walk and asking God where I had failed and what should I then do—was like something out of a day-time drama…surreal.

His offense? Playing *Dungeons & Dragons*, though not a spiritually healthy exercise in and of itself, was not the point; abject rebellion against my family's rule of behavior, lying about it, and putting the rest of his family in danger *was*.

I had no idea how to handle this situation. As far as my own experience as a parent was concerned, it was totally uncharted territory. I won't go into the next six weeks of pain and bewilderment that followed (his mom was one of his teachers in a Christian school); suffice it to say, it was the most difficult thing I've ever done…and to this day, I wonder if I did everything right. Still, my son is happily married, has given me a wonderful daughter-in-law and two beautiful grandchildren, is serving the Lord faithfully, and successful in his career. Of course, this may be in spite of me…

Can you legislate morality? Can anyone, by sheer edict cause others to act in a morally upright way? On the one hand, you have to say, "No, of course not." God tried that already, didn't He? As I recall, Moses, who delivered that law (Ex. 24:12), was not even allowed to enter the Promised Land himself (Num. 20:11–12). And all of us, though we may try to be obedient, have lawlessness bound up in our hearts (Is. 53:6; Rom. 3:23). On the other hand, all law is based on morality!

The real question is, whose morality? For the Christian, there is only One Who is qualified to be the source of all standards: God. Some will ask, then, Who is God? For the Christian, it is Jehovah, the Triune God of the Bible: the Father Who sent the Son, Who sent the Holy Spirit. It makes abundant logical sense that the Creator would make the rules for His creation...just like every manufacturer knows best how his product should operate. For this reason, the Bible has been called: The Operator's Manual for Man. Water may be cheaper, but a car runs best on gasoline.

It doesn't take much study of this (or any) Operator's Manual to realize it is full of laws—instructions on how to get the best performance out of the equipment. Laws on how to worship (John 4:23–24), laws on Whom to worship (Matt. 4:10), laws on paying taxes (Luke 20:22–25), laws on vengeance (Rom. 12:19), laws on murder, rape, incest, homosexuality, stealing, slander, gossip, gluttony, envy, greed, poverty, wealth, marriage, singleness, anger...you name it. The Bible is full of rules...which we cannot obey (not that trying is bad—just destined to failure). There was only one perfect man... and they killed Him. In fact, it was His death (and resurrection) that made it possible for a Holy God to once again have fellowship with an unholy man (Eph. 4:22–24). And it is His Holy Spirit in us that makes it possible for us to please God (Phil. 2:13).

Our nation is a nation of laws based on the Declaration of Independence and the Constitution. The Constitution was put in place to replace the Articles of Confederation which, among other weaknesses, lacked the strength of a centralized authority. But it is the Declaration of Independence that is our *founding document*. It is the document that relates back to God's Ultimate Authority. It is what makes our Constitution legitimate. The second paragraph begins, "We hold these truths to be self-evident, that all men are created equal; that they are endowed by their Creator with certain inalienable Rights..." Laws passed to protect these rights makes our government a legitimate agent of God (Rom. 13:3–7; Heb. 13:17).

Christianity, however, is an acknowledgement that no government can write laws fast enough (or voluminous enough, or detailed enough), nor can they train and arm enough police, or build enough prisons or create enough incentives...to make an unruly heart submissive; you cannot legislate morality. But we can and do submit our unruly hearts to the transforming power of our Creator. He has promised to give us hearts of flesh for our hearts of stone (Ezek. 11:19).

Is legislating morality biblical? Wouldn't getting rid of rules eliminate guilt? How about those laws that violate my faith...am I supposed to obey them, too? Isn't morality a heart issue...can't I do anything as long as I don't feel condemned? What about those things that are *legal*, but in a Christian context, *immoral?* These, and other questions, are the ones thinking Christians should be asking themselves.

According to a combination of what many dictionaries say: *Legislating morality* is the making of laws to live by. In a sense, all laws are rules to live by, and a governing body's attempt—whether municipal, county, state, or federal—to create an acceptable standard of behavior...in one sense, to legislate morality. Choosing the standard, at least in America, is what elections are all about...at least they're supposed to be (many elections, however, have become popularity contests with the winner being someone who out-spent his opponent rather than a referendum on character).

Answering questions:

1. Is legislating morality biblical?
    The whole Bible is a book of laws and their application... what happens when you obey them...and when you disobey. So, in that sense, of course it's biblical. But you can't make a

person good by telling him what's bad…or even by making disobedience costly.

All laws have an enforcement provision, consequences for disobedience; from a fine or incarceration to the death penalty; the greater the offense, the greater the punishment. This takes into account collateral damage—all sins may be the same to God (Matt 5:21–22; 27–28), but the damage done to innocent bystanders and the unintended consequences cause law-makers to consider different offenses differently.

By the way, parents not wanting to spend their time in visiting their kids in prison would do well to visit them more growing up. Doing your disciplining while they're young keeps them from the government trying to do your job after the fact by punishing them. Discipline is hopeful—looking forward to future correct behavior; punishment is hope*less*—looking backward to past wrongs.

2. Wouldn't getting rid of rules eliminate guilt?

This school of thought is Sigmund Freud's dubious contribution to modernism. His philosophy—of eliminating guilt by making everything lawful—may work on paper but the human heart is not so easily convinced. The Creator's law is written on our hearts (Eccl. 3:11; 2 Cor. 3:2), and so we are without excuse (Rom. 1:20). You may tell someone something is right, but that does not change the guilt he feels. Lies never defeat the truth.

3. How about those laws that violate my faith…am I supposed to obey them, too?

The American colonists were perplexed by this too. There was a Christian consensus in America, and many were looking for some biblical basis for their participation in the American War for Independence. Was it rebellion to authority—as the sin of witchcraft (I Sam. 15:23)—or was it obedience to God (Acts 4:19)?

Junius Brutus, a sixteenth century author well-read by the common patriot, wrote *A Defense of Liberty Against Tyrants*, which deals with this subject. He reasoned it was better to obey Someone Who ruled in eternity than someone who only ruled in this realm. Sounds like impeccable logic to me. The passing in California of the Consenting Adults Sex Bill (AB489) in 1975—legalizing fornication, adultery, and homosexuality—led me to leave that state and seek a more sane abode in Arkansas.

4.   Isn't morality a heart issue…can't I do anything as long as I don't feel condemned?

Yes, morality is a heart issue, though I usually like the less-confusing word *soul* rather than confusing the temporal organ for pumping blood with the brain, the organ that houses the eternal soul. Condemnation usually means you are trying to do the Holy Spirit's job of convicting. The sinner's proper response to the Holy Spirit's conviction—confession and repentance—produces much more change than the condemnation of the self-righteous. Condemnation only produces self-justification, rebellion, and blame-shifting—seldom leading to any change that is real.

Self-condemnation is another thing. Some would say ignorance is bliss, and you *are* only held accountable for doing things you *know* are wrong; the context of the passage in the Bible that talks about that—I Cor. 9—says that we are not to abuse our inside knowledge of God's grace as an excuse to demonstrate our freedom. Causing others to stumble doesn't make our walk any less wobbly.

Condemnation is prejudicial; it assumes guilt; it is accusation, judgment, and sentencing all wrapped up in one act. You and others will appreciate the opportunity that conviction brings… it is much better to turn yourself in than to be apprehended running away.

5. What about those things that are *legal*, but in a Christian context, *immoral*?

Paul says, "All things are lawful for me, but not all things are profitable. All things are lawful for me, but I will not be mastered by anything" (I Cor. 6:12, NASU). Unprofitability and slavery, these are to be our reasons why, though we may have the right to live our lives according to the letter, our heart constrains us otherwise.

There was a legendary kingdom called Shangri La where there was only one law: be kind. They had no crime, for one could not want something that belonged to another because it would be…unkind. The law of love is that way. When we demonstrate the fruit of the Spirit (Gal. 5:22), we will find ourselves obeying every other law.

My eldest son? He went to the house of a friend of his…and to his surprise, found they had rules there, too. When he came back home, he had to individually ask everyone's forgiveness and permission to move back home. Everything went fine till he asked his younger brother…who had humorously moved his bed and taken up the preferred location in the closet.

Recommended reading list:

- *This Independent Republic*, R. J. Rushdoony
- *Democracy in America*, Alexis de Tocqueville
- *Legislating Morality: Is It Wise? Is It Legal? Is It Possible?*, Norman Geisler

Web sites:

- www.equip.org/…/is-legislating-morality
- www.midwestoutreach.org/journals/legislating.html
- www.vision.org/visionmedia/article.aspx?id=732

33

Medications and the "Healing" Arts

Hypochondria, the conviction that one is sick from things imaginary, may torment others, but I have been free of sickness for most of my life. To swallow my little morning cup—and little evening cup of pills (seven different medications)—is quite out of character for me. I am grateful for the healing properties that researchers have found in nature and in the various chemical compounds they have synthesized, but I am a little suspicious when some formerly trusted medication makes the list of those against whom a class action suit has been filed.

You see them every day: so-and-so wants you to know that if you've taken some unpronounceable medication and suffered from it, all you have to do is call 1-800-*reprehensible* and a fund has been set up to compensate you for your trouble…seriously? No wonder tort reform is needed. Forget that it costs millions to do all the research and then years for all the trials and FDA hoops to jump through…forget the caveats required now that cause every TV commercial to be sixty seconds long just to list all the possible side effects (which always include "death")…no wonder the latest wonder drug costs a fortune and always arrives one month too late for grandma!

However, medical professionals have come a long way from the quack physicians that killed President Washington by bleeding him to death. Read the account of how they treated the elder statesman—and the founder of this country—for probably what was flu-like symptoms and you'll probably agree it was inexcusably barbaric by today's standards. That is the point. Medications and treatment considered accepted practice or protocol today very likely will be discarded for something far more effective tomorrow. The practice of the "healing arts" is, after all, a continuum.

What is the Christian perspective on medications? If it works, swallow it (or breathe it or IV-it) (Eph. 1:11)! Really, why is there so much controversy over the healing arts? Do you think God's reputation is at risk or He is threatened by our use of medical doctors, hospitals, and medicines? God's miracle working power is not so easily challenged. Besides, how do you know God didn't bring healing *through* those medical doctors, hospitals, and medications? Everything man knows he learned from observing the world God made (Rom. 1:19). Every medication is from a plant God created or a synthesis of compounds mimicking the effect of some naturally occurring chemical He originated (Gen. 1:30).

A surgeon only knows what he has learned from the study of something God created first. The anesthetist uses compounds made from elements God placed here. Nurses may get their skill from practice, but their caring comes from God's heart through theirs. Medical techniques come from anatomical research of how God made our systems to work and medical professionals' skills are only more evidence of a divine calling…whether they admit it or not.

Are medications and the healing arts biblical? Can a Christian take medication or see a doctor or go to a hospital without making a negative faith statement? How about prevention…isn't it better to prevent than to treat? What about natural cures or living a healthy lifestyle? What part does prayer play? These and other questions are the ones thinking Christians will ask.

According to a combination of what many dictionaries say, *Medications* are any compounds used medicinally to diagnose, treat, or cure a disease or alleviate the suffering of an affected person or animal. The "Healing Arts," always used in this article in quotes— for as a Christian, man treats, but God alone heals—refer to all those practices that attempt, in combination or separately, to alleviate the physical or mental suffering of individuals.

Answering questions:

1. Are medications and the "Healing Arts" biblical?

    Of course they are. Luke was a physician. The serpent on the pole—which Jesus Himself referred to (John 3:14)—is today the "healing arts" symbol.

    The best scripture on the proper Christian attitude toward the body follows:

    > Or do you not know that your body is a temple of the Holy Spirit who is in you, whom you have from God, and that you are not your own? 20 For you have been bought with a price: therefore glorify God in your body. (I Cor. 6:19–20, NASU)

    Note that the temple is not to be worshipped; it is a *place* of worship. Reverence and respect to its Designer is appropriate—even adornment—but to give it more regard than it is due is to ignore What it houses and the fact that it will one day be discarded in favor of something more eternal (1 Cor. 15:44).

    The only thing Christians need to keep in mind is that man, created in the image of a Tri-une God, is also a trinity… spirit, soul, and body. Treating only part(s) of the problem(s) yields only a partial solution. Medical professionals that deal only with the physical or mental should not be surprised when their results are only temporary. Disease and decay are mostly a direct or indirect result of sin.

2. Can a Christian take medication or see a doctor or go to a hospital without making a negative faith statement?

    Of course he can. However, he (or she) must keep in mind that "faith" in medications or doctors or hospitals only go as far as they can go. All doctors will tell you that they have come to a place where they have done what they can…beyond which only God can move. As far as modern technology and medicines can take one, nothing can contradict this principle: Doctors treat, but only God heals.

One must also remember, that sometimes a person is sick because of lifestyle choices he has made. Although one day AIDS may be curable, the underlying irresponsible behavior (for some) must come to an end or the problem will only reassert itself.

Some ailments can be spiritual, as well—although there may be physical consequences. Some say that cancer may well be connected to ongoing unforgiveness.

3. How about prevention…isn't it better to prevent than to treat?

It was Benjamin Franklin who said, "A ounce of prevention is worth a pound of cure." Or as an old English proverb states: "A stitch in time saves nine." Although this saying might be wisdom for the surgeon, it speaks of action taken earlier to forestall greater action later. Often a dietary or lifestyle change prevents the need for surgery…like a gall bladder removal and ant-acids the rest of your life or having a lung removed. Both may have been perhaps prevented by more vegetables or fewer cigarettes.

4. What about natural cures or living a healthy lifestyle?

Here are some basic rules to live by:
- Don't eat after 7:00 p.m.
- It's the hours of sleep before midnight that count the most.
- You may "burn the candle at both ends," and you will get twice as much light…but only for half as long.
- Think clean, speak clean, live clean.
- Optimism always outlives pessimism.
- You are what you eat.
- When you quit on life, life quits on you.

As far as natural cures are concerned, the Native Americans' medicine man (or the African witch doctor) and alchemy practices used a mixture of spiritism (encouraging the activity of demons), superstition, tradition, and potions made from plant parts and compounds. Most of their knowledge of plants came from trial and error or watching other animals. Not until Leeuwenhoek's invention of the microscope in about 1590 did we really begin to learn why certain natural cures worked.

Most towns have health food stores and some grocery stores have whole aisles dedicated to foods that have fewer preservatives or were raised free of pesticides. Since it costs more to raise foods this way—and no preservatives means greater spoilage—it may be much more expensive to eat this way. One has to balance the upfront increased food costs with the medical savings…pay now to save later.

5. What part does prayer play?

Huge. Some say that nothing happens apart from someone's prayer. Sometimes prayer is answered just as you pray…it's as if God was just waiting for us to ask (James 4:3); sometimes we ask for things God knows we shouldn't have (2 Cor. 12:7–9). But the word promises that "if we ask anything according to His will, He heareth us:" (1 John 5:14, ASV).

I think that's what is called "praying through"…praying until you get God's mind on the matter. The only thing worse than praying against God's will unsuccessfully, is praying against God's will successfully.

I don't believe that God helps those who help themselves… in fact, God helps those who *can't* help themselves. However, it makes no sense to pray for God to act when He's waiting for *you* to act.

Medications and the "Healing Arts" are not the enemies of the faithful, but our friends. Doctors, surgeon, nurses, and other medical professionals know the limitations of their craft and need to access the Source of true power as much as we. They will turn to Him just like we do…when their skills or efforts are not enough.

Recommended reading list:

- *Reclaiming the Body: Christians and the Faithful Use of Modern Medicine*, Joel Shuman, Brian Volck, M.D.
- *Medicine and Christian Morality*, Thomas Joseph O'Donnell
- *Alternative Medicine: The Christian Handbook, Updated and Expanded*, Donal O' Mathuna and Walt Larimore

Web sites:

- *www.Medi-Share.org*
- www.mybodyhistemple.com
- www.bible-knowledge.com/christian-diets-and-nutrition

34

Money

We, my family, as far back as it has been recorded, have come from the middle class—some would say the "muddle" class—not much progress, especially when you consider inflation. But how you see yourself is more a product of value and relative comparison than of financial net worth.

Money is a strange thing. At least since 1965 in America, it has had no intrinsic value—except for pennies; since 1982, though, even they have been mostly zinc. Therefore, since money's value is mostly perception, a dollar is only worth what someone is willing to exchange for it. Did you know that there was a time in America when you could buy a loaf of bread for a penny?!

Of course, money, having no intrinsic value, is good only where it's valued…American money used to be valued in lots of places… outside of America! (In fact, in the former Soviet Union, there were stores where Russian rubles were *not* accepted…in these stores where you could buy car batteries, tires, stainless steel tools, etc., they only took US dollars—dollar stores was what they were called!) I've been in some places in Central America where they actually preferred US cash over their own currency…and they loved checks written on US banks…but not anymore!

Today, most countries require all purchases made within that country to be in its own printed currency. In Europe, it's the euro; in China, the yuan; in Japan, the yen; in South Africa, the rand…and each currency has an official exchange rate posted for that day. If you are a tourist, you estimate the amount you'll spend in that country and exchange only that much currency because the buy-back rate is always lower. (Now, anyone that's done much international traveling already knows that, but I'm going somewhere with this.)

What did Jesus have to say about money? Plenty! (Although I'm going to share only one verse here, He actually talked more about economic issues than any other subject!) He said to look at a denarius—our equivalent of a dollar coin. He asked whose image was pictured? When someone responded that Caesar's image was there, He said to render unto Caesar what was Caesar's, and unto God what was God's (Mark 12:17).

He was saying much. Not only was He endorsing the power of government over us physically, but He was also reminding us of the ultimate superiority of God, Who made us. Since both pronouncements revealed physical realities, we have to delineate them by their time factors—temporal and eternal. Although governments may tax, enforce law, conscript, etc.—all physical realities—they are subject to God's *authority priori.* The government may *appear* to exercise sway on this side of eternity, but on the other side, God openly and alone rules in the affairs of men. While the temporal realities only exist at His allowance—and He uses them to bring about His will—the eternal realities of heaven and hell are exclusively His realms, spiritually and physically.

One may use US dollars or euros, etc. to effect economic transactions in the temporal realm (depending on country); in the eternal realm, however, this currency is not recognized. Only the currency recognized by the ruling authority—God—is accepted. What is the currency of the eternal? Love. "For God so *loved* the world that He gave His only Son that whosoever believes on Him should not perish, but has *eternal* life" (John 3:16). The currency is love; the denomination is sacrifice.

It isn't so much a money issue as a *value* issue. To know we were considered by God more valuable than silver or gold—of sufficient value to be bought with the precious blood of Christ (1

Pet. 1:18–19)—should give us such self-esteem that depression becomes impossible.

Is money biblical? Don't we have to have money to buy things? I've heard it said that "the lack of money" is the *real* "root of all evil"...isn't that a greater reality? Is God so hard up that He needs my money or are all these televangelists off base? These, and other questions, are the ones thinking Christians should be asking themselves.

According to a combination of what many dictionaries say, *Money* is anything of value that is used and recognized by the governing authority of a subject region as payment for goods and services. What makes a good medium of exchange? Its portability, storability, and universal acceptance as an object of value.

Answering questions:

1. Is money biblical?

    Of course it is; even Jesus used money...to pay taxes (Matt. 17:27); in His parables (Matt. 10:29; Mk. 12:42–44); and in his teaching (Mk. 12:17).

    Christians know we live in a world where money is a reality, but they also know that God is aware of our physical needs (Luke 12:30) and will provide them for us (Phil. 4:19). It was King David who said that in all his life he had "never seen the righteous forsaken, nor His seed begging bread" (Ps. 35:27).

    Christians know that those who don't work should not eat (2 Thess. 3:10) and that hunger in the present comes by lack of diligent effort in the past (Prov. 6:6–11). And Christians know they must ask God (Matt. 7:7)—and keep on asking—ask specifically (James 4:3), and be generous (Luke 6:38).

    So Christians know that lack of provision may come from laziness, lack of dependence on God, failure to ask, asking amiss, or stinginess. It is a question of ownership. The question for Christians is not how much of what is ours shall we give to God, but how much of what is His should we keep for ourselves?

2. Don't we have to have money to buy things?

Yes, of course we do; but He knows we have needs for these things and says we are "more valuable" than the lilies of the field, which He gloriously clothes, or the birds of the air, which He amply feeds (Matt. 6:26–30). For Him *and for us*, it is a matter of priority (Matt. 6:33). If we'll keep Him and the things He loves first place, then He'll keep our needs met (note: He is obligated to meet our need, *not our greed!*).

3. I've heard it said that "the lack of money" is the *real* "root of all evil"…isn't that a greater reality?

No, the Scripture is plain. It is the "love of money" that is the root of all evil (I Tim. 6:10). Now, an argument can be made that those who "lack money" are the ones who rob, cheat, or covet. But the question remains: why do they lack money in the first place? Is it because they are lazy, rebellious, or stingy? There is a biblical cure for them (see #1, above).

Those who love money will find themselves cheating on their taxes, comparing themselves with the proverbial "Joneses" and always coming up short, seeking to get rich by some "easy" means (which is what gambling is all about), or constantly justifying some evil deed to get what they "deserve." The funny thing is…they'll get what they deserve, alright!

4. Is God so hard up that He needs my money or are all these televangelists off base?

No, He owns the cattle on a thousand hills (Ps. 50:10) and, with the price of beef what it is, He would make the wealthiest rancher seem like a pauper by comparison. Besides, He owns the hills, too (Ps. 23:1)! Seriously, any televangelist who preaches that he's going off the air if you don't give is not very sure of his calling. He's more dependent on people than the Lord.

God is not hard up. That is not why we give. And we don't give in order to receive, either. Sure, the Word promises that whatever we give up for His sake or the Kingdom's, will be multiplied back (Mark 10. 29–30), but we give because we are following His example (John 3:16). That we receive anything is entirely beyond the point.

Money is not a necessary evil. It is not an evil at all. It is the means by which a lot of good works are done, and we are to be given to good works (Matt. 5:16; 1 Tim 6:18; 1 Pet. 2:12). Money is a tool, and without an excess of it, we would be hard pressed to meet the needs of others. The trick is not to hold on to it too tightly, or it will get a hold on you!

Recommended reading list:

- *Frontline Christians in a Bottom Line World*, Brook Lind Rios
- *Your Money God's Way: Overcoming the 7 Myths that Keep Christians Broke*
- *Your Finances In Changing Times*, Larry Burkett

Web sites:

- www.christianmoneymanagement.org
- www.finance.christiansunite.com/Money-
- www.daveramsey.com

35

News Media

I'm still waiting for my fifteen minutes of fame…that somebody, somewhere promised me the news media would one-day give— like it was my due or something. Probably as close as I came was the occasional photo and story where my name was usually spelled wrong in the local paper. In fact, no one I know in my or my wife's family ever achieved the icon status so easily afforded to many… we've never run for public office, or played professional sports, or been filmed in anything. I don't think anything I've said or written has gone "viral" or even influenced too many people (yet—I'm always hoping…I'm a half-full kind of guy).

Christians, along with most in our culture, have a tendency to give special credence to a story they see on the screen or read in print. It was Ben Franklin who said, "Believe nothing of what you hear, and only half of what you see." Because of the sensationalism of our media, perhaps we should assign what we see or read the same credibility as he gave rumor. In any case, we should be a little more reluctant to believe what some are peddling, knowing that they only make money if the news is bad enough.

The issue, of course, is *truth*. The Scripture says that "truth stands the test of time" (Prov. 12:19). If what the press is telling us is true, then it should have its due influence. However, just because something made the news, does not make it so. During the old Soviet era, the government controlled press service was ironically labeled "Pravda"…*Truth* in Russian.

Thinking Christians need to be wary of the timing of news events. Some news items receive little or no attention because they are released when other less important items are given center stage—"pay no attention to the man behind the curtain" the imposter warned Dorothy and her trio of unlikely friends in the Wizard of Oz. Many news items of great significance are released on Friday evening, when unsuspecting viewers are getting ready for a welcome weekend after a week of hard work.

Also, the thinking Christian always asks the pertinent question: Is the event congruent with the ideology of the reporting agency? If not, was their treatment balanced with opposing viewpoints? Sometimes, a light treatment of a news item may help the news executives to sleep at night, but one must ask himself if it was covered in enough detail. Sometimes, the best conclusion is drawn from a number of renderings; the truth lying somewhere between the positions taken.

One of the best recommendations for truth-detecting is every investigator's number one rule: *follow the money!* Ask yourself who stands to gain from this revelation? Are they selling a book or a product? Is there a vote about to be taken? Sometimes it is not who will gain but who will lose? Remember the worldly philosophy, *the enemy of my enemy is my friend.*

There is a healthy skepticism that must be brought to bear if we, as Christians, are going to avoid the manipulation we have been so subject to in the past. Those with political agendas that are anti-Christian seek to influence us because their dark deeds only thrive when the light of truth is obscured. If we are not careful, we'll be marching in protest to things we have emotionally espoused only a short time ago.

Control of the shapers of our culture: *education, Hollywood, and the news media* are what the Enemy of our souls is after. Why? To control them, is to control how we think and, "As a man thinks in his heart, so is he" (Prov. 27:3).

News Media as the Fourth Branch

Our founders knew that the three branches of government might be the way to balance power, but they also knew that the news media could act as a watchdog for the people; hence the first amendment's freedom of the press. However, when the bias of the news media becomes so pronounced that they have an approval rating below that of Congress, their message is tuned out as being politically prejudiced. Not only must we have a free press, but their opinions cannot temper their reporting—it is up to a thinking public to decide for themselves if they are receiving the truth and how it should be applied.

What does the Bible say about news media? Doesn't the Lord expect me to know what's going on? What do I do with all the bad news out there? What can one person do anyway? How much news watching is too much? These and other questions are the ones thinking Christians should be asking themselves.

According to our culture today, *News Media* is the means by which what is going on in our world is transmitted; it includes print (newspapers and magazines), broadcast and cable (radio and television), and the internet (news organs, social media, and blogs).

Answering questions:

1. What does the Bible say about news media?

    The question might be more appropriately, "What does the Bible say about truth or rumor?" The Bible says much about both of them, but more pertinent even than that would be what the Bible says about those who purvey the truth as opposed to rumor. There are whole chapters that tell stories of prophets (the ancient equivalent of reporters—even if what they reported as accomplished fact had not yet occurred).

    Just as our president sometimes tries to control the media through a press secretary or political favors, so kings were often trying to get a prophet to prophesy in their favor. The classic example is the story of Balak, King of Moab, who tried to get the prophet Balaam to prophesy against Israel (curse them). He offered him money through messengers (Numbers 22:7), but Balaam at first refused to go with them. After much back and forth and the timely warning of God through Balaam's donkey (verses 28–34), Balaam finally said what God directed him to say (Numbers 23:6–10).

Since he refused to curse Israel as the king desired, he asked him to come to a different conclusion—thinking that if Balaam had a different perspective, he might arrive at a different conclusion. Sometimes the president tries the same ploy, thinking a ride on Air Force One will provide the needed different perspective. Balaam, however, famously replied,

> Rise up, Balak, and listen! Hear me, son of Zippor. God is not a man, so he does not lie. He is not human, so he does not change his mind. Has he ever spoken and failed to act? Has he ever promised and not carried it through? (Numbers 23:18–19, NLT)

As I've said before, "Truthful words stand the test of time; lies are soon exposed" (Prov. 12:19, NLT). The news media, through their various behind-the-scene sources, must be *truth detectors* and then *truth professors,* discerning between a rumor and the truth—even when a rumor sells better.

2. Doesn't the Lord expect *me* to know what's going on?

Of course, He does! He sure doesn't need another ignorant Christian doing something just because it's always been done that way or believing that way because somebody, somewhere said it was so. Blind faith may produce blind obedience, but that is not necessarily a good thing. Reasoning Christians who *don't* swallow the Kool-Aid merely because that is what is being served is what God needs and expects (1 Pet. 3:15).

Relevance is measured in the currency of the knowledge that is applicable to a certain circumstance. The more accurate, current, and practical a person's knowledge is, the more relevant he (or she) will be to a situation. That is the value of God's Word—forever relevant. And that is the informed Christian's value, too.

3. What do I do with all the bad news out there?

    The best way to handle all the "bad" news out there is to counter with the "good-news" perspective. Let me give you an example. I have a black T-shirt that has emblazoned in white letters on its front: "It is what it is." This was given to me to me right after I had two brain stem strokes in 2009. It was well-meaning, but the remaining truth should be printed on the back, "But it's not what it's going to be!" There are many ways of seeing the glass, but the half-full way is hopeful...and so should we be.

    I sneaked in quotation marks on the *bad* news in the paragraph above because much of what we call "bad" turns out, after the perspective of time has corrected our myopia, to be good, after all. Jesus's death on the cross seemed "bad" at the time but turned out to be the beginning of what the *Good News* is all about.

4. What can one person do anyway?

    Although the "by-one-vote" lists have been mostly debunked, the Bible records the significance of *singular* efforts by Noah (Genesis 6–9), Rahab (Joshua 2:4), Ruth (Ruth 1–4), Esther (Esther 2:7–9:32), David (First and Second Sam., First and Second Kings, First and Second Chron., most of the Psalms, etc.), and, of course, Jesus (see the entire New Testament). Without the efforts of these individuals, we would live very different lives indeed!

    The same could be said of less familiar but equally provident Christian personages down through the ages: Athanasius, Clement, and Origen (all early church fathers); Hus, Wycliffe, and Zwingli (less prominent but important reformers); Isaac

Newton (he wrote more books on theology than science), Galileo Galilei (he and Copernicus are responsible for us having a solar-centric celestial perspective), and Johannes Kepler (he and Tycho Brahe are responsible for our current elliptical orbit concepts); and I could go on with the contributions of our Founders (most were patently Christian), Albert Einstein or Billy Graham. The contributions of these Christian men are incalculable.

To this list, we could add the names of such women as Blandina, Perpetua, and Felicitas (early martyrs); Brigid, Clotilde, and Berta (played pivotal roles in the middle ages); Anne Hutchinson, Abigail Adams, Clara Barton, Catherine Booth, and Mother Teresa...and I could go on endlessly, but the point is that each of us has a vitally important role to play in history ("His" story). Although we may play behind-the-scenes parts—not as prominent as those listed above—our contributions are no less crucial. Everyone acknowledges the roles of John and Charles Wesley...but without a praying mother behind them—Susannah Wesley—where would they have been?

5.   How much news watching is too much?

You do have a family, a church, and perhaps a job which take precedence. When anything gets out of balance, it's just like a tire in the same condition...soon it will set up a vibration that threatens the very integrity of the vehicle it was meant to support. Even if you are watching something "fair and balanced," too much of a good thing may not be helpful. Limit your screen time in favor of face-time with God...and with those to whom He has sent you.

Recommended reading list:

*   *Prodigal Press: The Anti-Christian Bias of the American News Media*, Marvin Olasky

- *Culture Warrior,* Bill O'Reilly
- *Ruler of the Nations: Biblical Principles for Governments,* Gary DeMar

Web sites:

- www.mrc.org
- www.christianpost.com/news/media-watchdogs-accuse
- www.mediamatters.org

36

Outlook

Optimism, pessimism, pragmatism, and realism—these are our options. Some look at the glass half-empty, some half-full...some say the glass is too fragile a container. Our outlooks may be different, but they always determine how we view and experience life. When something difficult or destructive happens, some can only see the negative—"*Now* what are we going to do?" Others, with the same challenges, can only see the positive—"I wonder how God is going to turn this to our benefit?"

There is a story told about a mother who had spent thousands on therapy from psychologists for her twins. One was an incurable optimist—every cloud had a silver lining; the other was an incurable pessimist—every silver lining had a cloud. Finally, one doctor told her that she could solve her problem with the "$500 cure"—$499 spent on the pessimist, and $1 spent on the optimist. Since Christmas was imminent, he argued that her timing was perfect.

She shopped diligently and did as the professional had recommended. Christmas day came and after each child took their wrapped gifts to their respective rooms, she stood outside of each son's closed doors hoping to catch some exclamation that revealed the success of her experiment. Outside the pessimist's room, she heard such a clatter of destruction that she opened the door a crack to see her son bashing his new metal bat into the new green bicycle she had gotten him. "I wanted a red one!" she heard him scream.

Thinking one half—indeed the larger half—of her investment had failed, she stood outside the door of her other son. Since she could not make out the quiet muttering of her optimist son, she opened the door unobtrusively and crept close enough to hear him. She had spent the dollar at a garage sale on the only thing she could find that cheap: an empty cigar box. To make it more substantive... and repulsive...she had filled it with the heavy, fresh horse manure from a neighbor's field. Finally, almost upon him, she could barely make out his hopeful plea, as he stirred the contents of the box with his finger, "I know there's a pony in here, somewhere!"

I've had my share of tragedy. My mother died of Hodgkin's lymphoma when I was two; my older brother was diagnosed with hydrocephaly when he was two; my parents—my dad and first stepmother—divorced when I was sixteen; my second stepmother was a witch—a real one, I mean: tarot cards, crystal ball, astral projection, past-life regression through hypnosis, etc.; I was in a car wreck in 1986 where I broke my back, pelvis, shattered my heel, and separated the cartilage from all my ribs; I had my gall bladder removed in 2000...*and* the sponge they left in from the first surgery two years later; I suffered a brainstem stroke in 2009 and another one a week later; and had three adjacent rentals removed completely by an F3 tornado in 2011 But, "I know there is a pony in there, somewhere."

Which option do we *habitually* take? I am convinced of three things concerning *outlook*. First, that we all have a default view of life; that we have a *habit* of looking at things a certain way. Second, I believe that defaults are programmable; by us or by authority figures early in life. And third, that our outlook is a choice; it may be hard to overcome early wrong-headed programming, but sometimes it must be done.

Fortunately, I had a father who knew that an optimistic outlook would make life happier for his younger son...and it was easy to view my life more fortunate than my mentally handicapped brother. Even though my dad had a much more realistic or pragmatic view of life, he knew it had brought him no joy. So he had programmed me to be an optimist; *it's much easier to choose optimism when your programming has been in that direction*, anyway.

Optimism is God's way. The "man after God's own heart" (I Sam. 13:14) wrote, "Goodness and mercy shall follow me all the days of my life..." (Ps. 23:6). David was an optimist. It might have made him blind to his own lusts (his self-justified acts with Bathsheba), but he was quick to repent when confronted by his sin (2 Sam. 12:1–13).

As Christians, God expects us to choose the less traveled road of integrity and honor. It is not honorable for children of God, who have been the recipients of so much grace and mercy, to have any other than optimists' outlooks. As children of the Most High, whose default is to bless us, let our default be that whatever comes our way was intended as a blessing (James 1:17) or He will turn it for our good (Rom. 8:28).

Is our outlook biblical...I mean, does God even care what outlook we choose? If we have been programmed to look at life realistically, is that not better? Aren't pragmatists seeking solutions based on a more practical view of life...how can that be bad? How is life through rose-colored glasses—*optimism*—any better than seeing things 'as they really are'—*realism*? How come bad things happen to good people? These, and other questions, are the ones thinking Christians should be asking themselves.

According to a combination of what many dictionaries say, an *Outlook* is a perspective, a way of looking at things, a worldview, the lenses through which one sees events, things, and experiences. An outlook may be personal or corporate, unique to an individual or unique to an organization or group. An outlook helps the person possessing it to interpret other things by the same set of values.

Answering questions:

1. Is our outlook biblical...I mean, does God even care what outlook we choose?

    Of course He does; as Christians, we don't really have an option...or at least we have given up that option to Him. We are supposed to emulate Christ (John 13:15)—Christian actually means "little Christ"—to act like He would in every circumstance…obviously, it is something we grow into; salvation may occur at a moment in time, but redemption is a process— we are being "conformed" into His image (Rom. 8:29).

To emulate the nature of God—impossible without God within (Phil. 2:13)—we can only be optimists. Even when Christ struggled with His destiny in the Garden of Gethsemane (Lk. 22:42), His surrender had Him meet His betrayer head on, fully confident that His Father knew best. Whether the path we tread is pleasant or not, we are fully persuaded that "He who began a good work in us will perfect it" till He has finished it (Phil. 1:6; Heb. 12:2).

2. If we have been programmed to look at life realistically, is that not better?

Realism may seem like the right perspective, but we just don't have enough information to know what is really real… only what looks like reality at the moment or from "our perspective"…which is, no doubt, limited (read: *wrong*).

Listen to what the Lord says through the prophet Isaiah,

> "For My thoughts are not your thoughts, nor are your ways My ways," declares the Lord. "For as the heavens are higher than the earth, so are My ways higher than your ways and My thoughts than your thoughts." (Is. 55:8–9, NASU)

There is even a version that starts out that verse by rendering it: "For this plan of mine is not what you would work out…" (LB).

Occasionally, the Lord may open our eyes to see reality from His perspective (2 Kings 6:17), but most of the time He just expects us to see by faith…faith in His goodness…which is what optimism is.

3. Aren't pragmatists seeking solutions based on a more practical view of life...how can that be bad?

    Pragmatism can be defined as a belief that a *practical approach* to problems and circumstances will yield the best results. Such a view may be fine for most of life's problems...when things work out according to some neat formula...which they almost never do. No, usually God puts us in that circumstance that requires a kind of 'faith on the fly'—a total dependence on the kind of inside information that only a God Who sees the end from the beginning can give—otherwise we quit before we win.

    Pragmatism is only for those few people who have deceived themselves into thinking there is a 'Plan B.' God only has 'Plan A.' We don't fully understand God, but we're not supposed to. Pragmatism is not bad, but sometimes God does not do things to suit the pragmatist.

4. How is life through 'rose-colored glasses'—*optimism*, some say—any better than seeing things 'as they really are'—*realism*?

    Maybe that is a question better asked of Pollyanna. Young people may not remember that 1960 Disney movie that starred Haley Mills and Jane Wyman (as her Aunt Polly), but I do. In the movie, Pollyanna's indefatigable optimism maddened some, but when tragedy didn't dampen her general enthusiasm for life, they soon saw her optimism as an attractive and enviable quality.

    Rose-colored glasses? Maybe present optimism is really "hindsight realism." We have to trust that the end will justify the means...okay for God, not for us.

5. How come bad things happen to good people?

    The real question we should be asking is, how do we know it's *bad*? Many things happen to us that, at the moment, appear a curse. Later, in retrospect, we come to realize it was necessary for something that later turned out to be a blessing.

For the moment, I'm sure being kicked out of the Garden of Eden seemed harsh to Adam and Eve, but it kept them from immortalizing their sinful condition (Gen. 3:24). For the moment, confusing the tongues of even the closest of neighbors must have been frustrating to everyone involved, but it kept their evil from finding its mature self-destructive manifestation (Gen. 11:6–9).

Indeed the Bible is full of examples of God's intervention that, at first blush, appeared detrimental. Maybe His intervention in our lives is wiser than we give Him credit for.

The simple answer to that very probing question is, because He loves us more than the temporary discomfort He feels when we cry out…does not the Scripture say,

> No discipline is enjoyable while it is happening—it's painful! But afterward there will be a peaceful harvest of right living for those who are trained in this way. (Heb. 12:11, NLT)

If your parents had no good example to follow, or for whatever reason failed to train optimism into you, fortunately your Heavenly Parent has bequeathed to you a new nature. Receive from Him His perspective and let the eye of faith reign in the circumstances of your life.

Recommended reading list:

- *Faith and Optimism: Positive Expectation in the Christian Life*, M. Blaine Smith
- *Grattitude: Practicing Contagious Optimism for a Positive Change*, Ace Collins
- *Lord, Change My Attitude, Before It's Too Late, Revised*, James MacDonald

Web sites:

- www.gracegems.org/Pink/christian_outlook.htm
- www.christianoptimist.wordpress.com/category/christian-optimism
- www.josemariaescriva.info/article/christian-optimism

37

Patriotism

Both of my grandfathers were in the US Army. My grandfather on my father's side won the marksman medal...he was a sergeant, I think. My grandfather on my mother's side was a Lieutenant Colonel and a chaplain. This heritage of service made me a patriot, a man loyal and proud to be called an American. Though I may never be called on to serve my country as they did, I am willing to be numbered with those who have sacrificed much to let the rest of us enjoy the freedoms upon which this nation was built.

My dad used to tell me that one of the memorable moments of his life occurred watching the marching band come down our city streets during a parade playing that John Phillips Sousa tune, "Stars and Stripes Forever." Maybe it was seeing me in that band; maybe it was remembering that Veterans' Day his own father's service; maybe it was seeing Old Glory...who knows why his chest expanded and his heart fluttered, but we've all felt it. Perhaps at a football game when the "Star-Spangled Banner" was played; perhaps when you watched some American atop the podium during the Olympics... you've had those goose bumps of pride, something akin to the feeling a parent gets when he or she instinctively moves between a child and a perceived threat.

I remember going into Walmart and finding the aisle where the American flags were supposed to be...on September 13, 2001. It was empty, but crowded...empty of flags, but crowded with shoppers—presumably as disappointed as I. Loyalty and identifying with all those fellow Americans gave us all a desire to fly our flag everywhere—the highway looked like an unending presidential motorcade!

Actually, it's this familial loyalty for one's country that is the difficult-to-describe emotion of patriotism. For the Christian, who is trying to properly order the priorities of God, Family, Church, Personal Ministry, and Career, where does Love of Country fit in?

Contrary to the myopia of the average American Christian, this nation is no more guaranteed an on-going role is history than the Romans or the Aztecs were...by the way, there were those in both of these world-dominating cultures that felt that their position in the world was transcendent. The Bible teaches that, "...He made from one man every nation of mankind to live on all the face of the earth, *having determined their appointed times and the boundaries of their habitation...*" (Acts 17:26, NASU). In other words, as long as it satisfies the purposes of God...that's how long we—or anyone else—has.

We have another family that is even more transcendent than our family—or nation—it's called the Kingdom of God. We have dual citizenship—by God's design (John 17:14–16)—and we must consider ourselves aliens to this world and citizens of another (Eph. 2:19–22). Sure, while in this world, we should and must have our own family (and our nation) as a priority in our hierarchy of priorities. But in the background of our love for family and nation must be the knowledge that Jesus is returning for the purpose of erasing these temporary relationships in favor of an eternal one...with Him—and all those we will one day call our brothers and sisters.

This is what true *Christian patriotism* is. Not that we shouldn't be motivated to live and even die for family or country, but that there is a transcendent relationship that will extend beyond this life... and we should be moved by the plight of our brothers and sisters who are daily being persecuted by others. This *Christian patriotism* should make us look on them with the motivation to take the steps within our power to alleviate their suffering where possible.

America has a PR problem. Rather than apologize for our arrogance or spiritual pride, let us realize that everyone is proud of his or her country and/or religion. As American Christians, let us be neither apologetic for our benefits or our blessings—as if we deserved them—but rather recognize that this is our country's transitory moment on the stage which we must wisely use to further something less transitory and more everlasting—the Kingdom of God. Other nations before us have had their moments, we are having ours and there will likely be still others that will come after us—especially if we cannot lose this attitude that makes us so ugly to a reluctantly following world.

Is patriotism biblical? Is it possible to have a godly pride? Is it wrong to have the desire to lay my life down for my country? What about those who did…are they in heaven now? What about those who sincerely believe that their sacrifice is for a worthy cause? These, and other questions, are the ones thinking Christians should be asking themselves.

According to a combination of what many dictionaries say, *Patriotism* is the love and devoted loyalty one expresses toward his homeland. For the Christian, regardless of geography, a patriotic love of the Kingdom of God is both futuristic and very much in the present tense; *futuristic* in the sense that death and decay—the physical realities of the curse—are not to be vanquished until the end; and *present* because the Kingdom of God begins for each of us when we are born again.

Answering questions:

1. Is patriotism biblical?

    Of course it is; in the senses that sacrifice is often required for one's family, one's country, and one's God. There are ample biblical examples for all three.

    One of the best examples of sacrifice for one's family is the life of Joseph. Although he is often considered as an example of unwilling sacrifice or as a victim of his brothers' jealousy, he chose not to exact the revenge they were due—and within his power—becoming the source of their entire family's salvation

(Gen. 37:1–46:7). He did not lay down his life—in the sense of dying—but his future was forever altered in, what would seem to any casual observer, a negative way. He was sold into slavery, lived the life of a servant, was wrongfully accused of an abuse of his stewardship, spent eleven years in imprisonment, was forgotten by a man whom he thought would remember him to the Pharaoh, spent two more years in imprisonment...all before interpreting Pharaoh's dream and being elevated to a position that secured the future of the very family members who had betrayed him. Sounds vaguely familiar, doesn't it?

Then there's the example of Moses being overcome with the plight of his people (dare we say patriotism?) and murdering an abusive Egyptian overseer (Ex. 2:11–12). Although he no doubt deserved to be killed, Moses allowed his zeal to overcome his reason. Many justify their acts of vengeance by taking the matter into their own hands...and call it patriotism. Although God has accomplished His will in spite of well-meaning but sinful acts—did I hear someone say "the Crusades"?—it does not mean that He is pleased with us.

An example of laying down one's life for his *adopted* country can be found in Uriah the Hittite. His life was honorably sacrificed by him, although he was really the victim of a murderous plot hatched by the king (David) and the head of his army, Joab (2 Sam. 11:3–24). Uriah's act was one of patriotism, while David's was one of lust, murder, and conspiracy...an act that cost him his son's life (2 Sam. 12:14)...and much misery (2 Sam. 12 10). Again, I chose an act of patriotism that, in retrospect, is convoluted. The examples cited led to a mixed bag of motivations and results. Christian patriotism can never be used to justify sinful acts—it is never right to do wrong nor wrong to do right.

The sacrificial death of Christ is an example of Christian patriotism...for His family (us, the Body of Christ); for His country (at that time, Israel) and His God (Jehovah)—to save us; to save Israel; and to restore our relationship to His Father.

2. Is it possible to have a godly pride?

Yes, but it is not a good choice of words, in today's vernacular. Paul's words to the Corinthians are instructive:

> For our *proud* confidence is this: the testimony of our conscience, that in holiness and godly sincerity, not in fleshly wisdom but in the grace of God, we have conducted ourselves in the world, and especially toward you. For we write nothing else to you than what you read and understand, and I hope you will understand until the end; just as you also partially did understand us, that we are your reason to be proud as you also are ours, in the day of our Lord Jesus. (2 Cor. 1:12–14, NASU)

Most of our pride is "fleshly"; we do not listen to our "conscience"; we are not "in holiness and godly sincerity," but rather arrogantly pat ourselves on the back—this is what leads to *un*-Christian patriotism; it is this sentiment that leads us to reckless behavior that we justify as patriotic...idiotic might be more accurate.

3. Is it wrong to have the desire to lay my life down for my country?

No, not if you have been led to this conviction by God. Just remember, that many have been led to this "conviction" by circumstance, peer pressure, or because of a swell of emotion. We are emotional creatures and we should not think we should ever be led by God, devoid of emotions. At the same time, those who "feel" led should think more—a decision emotionally made and devoid of reason is usually without sufficient counsel and almost always regretted.

4. What about those who did...are they in heaven now?

Sacrifice is what gains a person admittance into heaven, to be sure...but His, not ours. There are those whose sacrifice is confirmative—only establishing what others already knew about them. And there are those whose sacrifice is an aberration to their otherwise selfish acts. Fortunately, we are not called to judge such matters. God alone sees the heart (Jer. 20:12). He does not measure the number of medals on the chest but the submission of what beats within.

5. What about those who sincerely believe that their sacrifice is for a worthy cause?

It is possible to act in "false patriotism," too; nineteen men were convinced they were doing their god's bidding by flying jets into the Trade Center, the Pentagon, and the Pennsylvania countryside—*sincerity is not the test of truth*.

What does God consider worthy? We are each to consider others as better than ourselves (Phil. 2:3). So it goes back to the leading of the Holy Spirit. Sometimes the needs of the many outweigh the needs of the few…but not necessarily so.

Patriotism, if it's Christian, is then led by the Holy Spirit, makes abundant sense to the sacrificer and is sometimes only considered wise in retrospect. Perhaps that is why heroes are rare and humble.

Recommended reading list:

- *Sundar Singh: Footprints Over the Mountains*, Janet Benge and Geoff Benge
- *Christian Patriotism*, Thomas Nelson Haskell
- *Reborn on the Fourth of July: The Challenge of Faith, Patriotism and Conscience (Kindle Book)*, Logan Mahl-Laituri

Web sites:

- www.patriot.embassyofheaven.com
- www.christianitytoday.com/.../patriotismchristian.html
- www.chalcedon.edu/research/articles/christian-patriotism

38

Political Correctness

Call it discretion, politeness, or self-control...political correctness is, by any other name, just bologna (baloney for the un-educated; BS for the red-necks, malarkey for the senior citizens, and a load of %#$*@& for the...uh, politically correct). Seriously, I think Christians should be careful with what they think, let alone what they let come out of their mouths (James 3:8–10), but when sensitivity and consideration become deception and distraction, the need to be un-offensive begins to assault common sense!

No longer is someone disabled, he is ambulatory challenged; a person is not white, he is melanin deficient; he is not short, he's just vertically challenged; he is not balding, he's just follicly challenged; he is not a heterosexual, he has just chosen to be oppositely oriented; he is not elderly, he is chronologically challenged. Are these language gyrations really efforts not to offend, or are they thinly veiled attempts to make socially sensitive subjects more acceptable? (By the way, I'm a disabled, white, squatty, balding, heterosexual, over sixty!)

Corporations are full of sensitivity-training seminars, our Congress is passing hate speech legislation, and teachers are trying to deal with bullying and name-calling. Whatever happened to parents teaching their children that old nursery rhyme: "Sticks and stones may break my bones, but names will never hurt me?" Of course there are things that civil people shouldn't say, but let's just chalk up their crude remarks to immaturity and get on with life.

Besides, what ever happened to free speech? Or is our skin too thin to allow for offense these days? The Christian believes he should let his yea be yea and his nay be nay (Matt. 5:37, 2 Cor. 1:17), but he also believes he learns patience by being tolerant of the immaturity of others (James 1:2–4).

Political correctness is to speech what fad and fashion are to clothing…never judge a book by its cover. Instead of constantly apologizing for imagined offenses, let us be a little less frivolous and a little more mature.

Is political correctness biblical? Shouldn't Christians defend their faith? What benefit is speaking the truth if your listener is offended? Jesus wasn't very politically correct and look where it got him…are you suggesting that we go *there*? These, and other questions, are the ones thinking Christians should be asking themselves.

According to a combination of what many dictionaries say, *Political Correctness* is the alteration of expressions to avoid real or imagined offenses (sometimes abbreviated PC). Political correctness has become so ridiculous as to deserve its own sarcasm humor genre. Have you heard the one where Santa gets suspended from his annual rounds because of his abuse of the term "Ho"?

Answering questions:

1. Is Political Correctness biblical?

    Of course not; as humans, even the universalists don't refer to us as the "siblinghood of persons under the Parentalhood of God"; rather we are the brotherhood of Man under the Fatherhood of God (Gen 1:26)—ladies, if you won't mind being called, with us collectively, "Mankind," We won't mind being referred to as part of the "Bride of Christ"!

2. Shouldn't Christians defend their faith?

    Absolutely! Of course we should, not by force of arms (Zech. 4:6; Matt. 26 52; Eph. 6:12), but by force of the "truth, spoken in love" (Eph. 4:15). This will take most of the offense right out…still, it's the truth and some folks are just determined to be offended. Jesus is called the "Rock of Offense" (Rom. 9:33; 1 Pet. 2:8), and some people are just going to be offended. Even love is offensive to the reprobate—he can't believe anyone could love him because he can't even love himself…therefore all love to him is insincere and mocking.

There is a whole field of the 'defense of the Gospel' called ironically, *Apologetics*. The original Latin word is *apologia* and it means "a defense of" or "an appeal to." Although this field is mostly dedicated to a study of the historicity of the resurrection, many have correctly used this term to supply the case for the Gospel in general.

3. What benefit is speaking the truth if your listener is offended?

    Talk is cheap. Sometimes much more can be done than said (1 John 3:18). In fact, many have said they "love," but do not show it in their actions. This "uncertain sound" (1 Cor. 14:8) will only serve to confuse and cause others to hold you in suspicion.

    The truth will always prevail (Prov. 12:19). Do not think that your witness is ever wasted. "So will My word be which goes forth from My mouth; it will not return to Me empty, without accomplishing what I desire, and without succeeding in the matter for which I sent it" (Isaiah 55:11, NASU). If you speak by His Spirit (Matt. 13:11), you can count on Him to fill your mouth. Our confidence should not come from our hours of study, the letters after our name, or the 'vast experience' we have in soul winning, but in Who is speaking through us.

4. Jesus wasn't very politically correct and look where it got him… are you suggesting that we go *there*?

    It is said that at the heart of all disappointment is unreasonable expectation. If you think your loving presentation of the Gospel is going to be warmly received (think: lost loved ones), are you in for a surprise! Persecution is not a possibility or even a probability, but a certainty. So much so, that one has to wonder if he is not being persecuted in some way, that perhaps he 'soft-pedaled' the message. After all, they killed Jesus to silence Him! Aren't we supposed to "take up our cross daily" (Matt. 10:38)?

Political correctness may be a temptation for the Christian who wants to be approved and loved by everyone…but if you're *for* everything, you're aren't really *for* anything; if you're loved by *everyone*, are you really loved by *anyone*?

Recommended reading list:

- *The Politically Incorrect Guide to the Bible*, Robert Hutchinson
- *The Next Nightmare: How Political Correctness Will Destroy America*, Peter Feaman
- *Soul Winning Made Easy*, C. S. Lovett

Web sites:

- www.christiananswers.net/q-eden/tolerance.html
- www.johnnyv.com/Politically.html (this is really a script for a free drama, but it is so instructive!)
- www.certainchristian.com/politically-correct-christians

39

Pornography

Hey, I was only ten, so I wasn't thinking too clearly concerning a good place to hide that Sears catalog. The women's lingerie' section was the only "pornography" I could get ahold of...though it was quite enough scintillating to me. The driveway culvert seemed a good enough stash-place to me till a peal of thunder awakened me. Suddenly, all I could think of was how cold and wet she must be...

Playboy and the pornography industry have made millions—with the internet, maybe billions—all catering to the curiosity or addiction of males from the age of eight to eighty-eight. I say male because porn is primarily a male problem; men, being visually aroused, are almost exclusively the objects of pornography...women are aroused more by touch (so, guys, you can quit dancing around in your skivvies).

When does natural curiosity become enslaving addiction? The simple answer is, when *opportunity* and *repetition over time* overcome training and self-control. And many a naturally curious young man has become shackled by an addiction that later threatens the marriage bed with unrighteous and unreasonable expectations. The endorphin release that is the God-given pleasure that drives husbands toward their wives gets perverted and a lucrative industry of evil is born.

True story: although I was there to secure advertising for a Christian radio station, the owner of a certain appliance store was seeking counsel and prayer from me for a habit of kinkiness that sadly threatened his marriage. Apparently, he was getting more and more aberrant in his behavior—his fantasies being fed by a guilt-ridden but grudgingly compliant wife—and he was ashamed by the increasingly weird costuming demands he was making of her. After answering sheepishly a couple of questions, he revealed a sexual addiction that had begun at a very early age. I did my best to counsel him, then we prayed.

To twist a scripture a little, "If thy computer screen offends thee, pluck it out (throw it away); better to enter heaven without social networking, than to enter hell addicted to pornography." (The scripture I'm butchering is from Matt. 5:29.)

King David didn't live in a time when pornography was as available as it is today, but his inopportune rooftop stroll (2 Sam. 11:2)—when he should have been with his troops (2 Sam. 11:1)—provided him all the opportunity that sinning with his eyes (Matt. 5:28) needed. Bathsheba was married to Uriah, but David used his authority as king to manipulate her...like some teachers are apt to do today. Authority figures must never use their influence to coerce those that are subservient. With increased power comes *increased* responsibility, not decreased.

But opportunity and repetition are only two of the three legs that make pornography so pernicious. The third leg of *vulnerability* is also a contributing factor. In addition to David's being a fallen man—every man is vulnerable—he also magnified his vulnerability by not being where he was supposed to be. It was spring and he was supposed to be with his troops on the battlefield. Instead, he chose the comfort of his palace...and its view! As the nursery rhyme ditty warns, "Be careful little eyes what you see..."

The internet today provides this elevated perspective which only magnifies our vulnerability. We have to make a decision to get on the battlefield where we belong, not in the computer chair in the privacy of our sin chamber. If we don't, we—like King David—may find ourselves raping, conspiring to commit murder, and all the while trying to cover up our dark deeds, convincing ourselves we are somehow justified in our actions.

Is pornography biblical? Why are men so visually aroused? Would my addiction be solved if I were blind? If my soul is the real problem, are you somehow recommending brain deadness? Is there hope for someone already addicted to a private life of internet porn? What would you do to protect your younger ones from pornography? These and other questions are the ones thinking Christians should be asking themselves.

According to a combination of what many dictionaries say, *Pornography* is the use of sexually explicit visual images to arouse. Also abbreviated "porn" or "porno," the hormonal release engendered in men (or, in some cases, women) makes habitual viewing physically and psychologically addictive. The more pornography is seen, the more it grabs the viewer demanding still more—a downward spiral that many seem powerless to overcome.

Answering questions:

1. Is pornography biblical?

    Of course it is; but only in a negative context and only from a reality-based perspective—harlots on street corners in pagan cultures were common back then (read Hosea)...so was forcible rape of both the heterosexual and the homosexual kind (Gen 19:1–11).

    The cure for lustful looking, whether you're talking rooftop or internet, is the same: Christians have to do the same as Job did and *"make a covenant with their eyes."*

    > I made a covenant with my eyes, that I would not so much as think upon a virgin. (Job 31:1)

2. Why are men so visually aroused?

    The simple answer is, that is the way God made us. I guess one could say that I'm laying the blame for lust upon God, but that would be misleading. Eyes that look lovingly and appreciatively upon beauty are a gift. Lust is the perversion of love. Here's how one distinguishes the difference: *love gives; lust takes.* The man who wants to give, will wait for marriage…his self-control wants to sacrifice as a demonstration of his love. The man who can't wait…only wants to take what is not his, and so demonstrates his lust.

3. Would my addiction be solved if I were blind?

It would if it were merely an eye problem; but it's not. The Scripture says (Jesus is talking), "…I say to you that everyone who looks at a woman with lust for her has already committed adultery with her in his heart" (Matt. 5:28, NASU). It's a heart issue; lust perverts the desire of the heart making it selfish and impatient.

Science tells us that certain perfumes have pheromones that excite the male (or men's cologne, the female) and arouse him (or her)…so cut off the nose, right? What about the sweet nothings whispered in the ear? Don't they arouse? So let's cut off the ears, right? And the taste of her sweet lips…off comes the tongue, right? How about the arousal that comes when the fingers run over naked skin? So cut off the hands, right?

Like I said, it's a heart issue (not the pumper of the blood; the *soul*). But fortunately, Christians have been given a new heart (Ezek. 36:26). We are not defaulted to lust…a new heart makes it possible to love…and keep your appendages!

4. If my soul is the real problem, are you somehow recommending brain deadness?

I'm not recommending you neutralize your brain any more than I'm suggesting cutting off the ears, nose, and hands or cutting out the tongue or eyes! The brain only processes the signals those appendages receive. The core problem is not reception or even perception; it's *conception*. Read what James has to say on the subject,

> Let no one say when he is tempted, "I am being tempted by God"; for God cannot be tempted by evil, and He

Himself does not tempt anyone. But each one is tempted when he is carried away and enticed by his own lust. Then when lust has *conceived*, it gives birth to sin; and when sin is accomplished, it brings forth death. (James 1:13–16, NASU)

5. Is there hope for someone already addicted to a private life of internet porn?

Of course there is; but, like many true triumphs, the path to victory lies through total surrender. One must unconditionally surrender to the Lordship of Christ.

For those who think they have already done that, let me ask you one question: Is there anything in your life that were the Lord to ask you to give it up, you'd have to say no? If there is, then you'd better give it up before He asks you! (You do realize that if you don't give it up, that thing—whatever it is—has become a god before Him (Ex. 20:3), right?

6. What would you do to protect your younger ones from pornography?

Like I said, all of us are vulnerable. However, we can reduce opportunity and eliminate the multiplier of time. As soon as your young men (or women) are old enough to appreciate the difference between boys and girls (I'd say when puberty begins, but sometimes that is too late), then the following simple rules may make sense:

A. Always put your TV or viewing screens (this includes laptops or desktops) in rooms that are public.
B. Have your kids make phone calls or other communications openly (this includes cellphones, tablets, or anything else with a screen and internet connectivity).
C. Privacy is for adults. All kids' bedroom doors are to be open at all times. Anyone wanting to enter someone's room must knock on the doorframe first and wait for permission. No

one is ever authorized admission to anyone else's room without their permission or that of an adult.

D. Only adults can have passwords and all the adults in one family have the *same* password. (This eliminates so many temptations for adults—husbands and wives should never have secrets.)

E. Parents should preview all movies.

Granted, these rules are more difficult to implement the older the kids are; and it is not always convenient to live by them. Children's innocence is, however, worth protecting.

The enemy has beaten men up long enough with the lie that they have a unique problem. Everyone, if he's red-blooded and male, struggles with the "second look" (you know, that thing many guys do when a pretty girl walks by). God wants men to admit they have a problem (to their pastors, their wives, and/or their accountability partners) and receive the help that will restore to them the self-esteem that has been stolen. His grace is sufficient.

Recommended reading list:

- *Conquering Pornography: Overcoming the Addiction*, Dennis Frederick, M. M. Div., Ph. D.
- *I Surrender All: Rebuilding a Marriage Broken by Pornography*, Clay Crosse, Renee Crosse, Mark Tabb
- *The Silent War: Ministering to Those Trapped in the Deception of Pornography*, Henry J. Rogers

Web sites:

- www.christianpost.com/news/porn-to-purity-christian
- www.befreeinchrist.com
- http://www.befreeinchrist.com/
- carm.org/pornography

40

Prayer

"Lord if you are really real it would be nothing for You to have it work out that I'd have exactly the right number of bulletins for the number of people that are left on this side of the sanctuary." Granted, my very first prayer as a new Christian was stupid, immature, and frivolous…but God, in His mercy, honored it. To my surprise and spiritual gratification, there were exactly enough!

Was God showing special favor to me? Had I prayed a prayer that was particularly righteous or had I tapped into His power over the physical universe? I would have to answer now, in a much more enlightened state, that none of these was the case. God was simply showing Himself to be God to a young man who needed some kind of concrete demonstration to overcome his rampant skepticism. Kind of like Gideon and the fleece, but I'm getting ahead of myself.

It is awesome, if not a little presumptuous, to think that puny man has access to the God Who created the universe…but that's what prayer, on its most basic level, is: communication with God. Of all the creatures that God made (Gen. 1:20–25), He gave communication access to Him only to angels (messengers from God) and to Man. And that communication is a right, a responsibility and a privilege.

Access to the Creator is the right of all of His creatures, but, placed by the Creator as the head of His creation (Gen. 1:26), we also have the creation looking to us for leadership. As goes the king, so goes the kingdom (Rom. 8:20–22). We not only have the right of access, but the *responsibility*, as kings (Rv. 1:6) to represent the interests of all of creation.

But not only is it a right and a responsibility; it is also a privilege. This is where we have a tendency to get things a little messed up. Case in point: "In the name of Jesus, I command these fish to bite!" Admittedly, I probably would have been a little more reticent to order God around like some sort of cosmic bellhop if I had had an audience, but my spiritual arrogance had no excuse.

I was alone fishing on Lake Tenkiller in 1975 in a bass boat that my dad and I had jointly purchased. It was nearly noon and I had already fished for nearly six hours...on a lake that I knew like the back of my hand. I knew where all the sand bass normally congregated at this time of year, had already trolled—a lazy man's fishing method where spinner bait is dragged behind the boat—by the points of dozens of schooling areas to no avail. I didn't even get the usual bump you get when you fish too shallow! I was to fish unsuccessfully for another ten hours!

As I was dejectedly motoring in after hours of confident, then desperate, and finally despondent prayer the Lord spoke to me as clearly as I've ever heard Him, "So now what? Are you going to deny me?"

I felt about two millimeters tall! What presumption! Just who did I think I was? Needless to say, I repented and sheepishly loaded my boat. I was embarrassed to have made such foolish demands then... and I'm a little embarrassed to share it now; but there it is. Prayer is also a privilege. God is not obligated to fulfill our petty desires...*our motive in prayer is almost as important as the petition itself.*

Is prayer biblical? Is there a right way or a wrong way to pray? Why are some prayers answered and some are not? What about the times when you don't know how to pray? What about 'praying in the Spirit'? These are the questions thinking Christians should be asking themselves.

In a combination of what many dictionaries say, *Prayer* is the means by which we communicate to God. Prayers can be long or short, but sincerity seems to be a universal ingredient in the effective prayer, as does the relationship of the petitioner to the One being petitioned (James 5:16).

Answering questions:

1. Is prayer biblical?

    On the surface, this seems a ridiculous question; but there is a prayer that is unbiblical; one that does not acknowledge the inferiority of the petitioner or the superiority of the One being petitioned is nonsensical and unbiblical. Prayer cannot be serious if it is prayed by someone who thinks he does God a favor to pray. Jesus gave us, in what we call "The Lord's Prayer," a pattern for all supplications to the Almighty. It begins with addressing God properly: "Our Father, Who art in heaven…" This appropriately acknowledges His superiority. Any prayer that doesn't do this is in danger of a deafening non-response.

2. Is there a right way or a wrong way to pray?

    Obviously, not all prayers are answered…at least in the way we would want. We should use the pattern mentioned above, but it is more than that. First, we must get a vision of what God is trying to do. Our prayers, to be successful, must be according to God's will.

    Secondly, they must be authoritative (according to His Word). But our own authority—our ability to get God to move on our behalf—comes from three things:

    A. Relationship
        Praying in the "Name of Jesus" and not being a Christian is truly taking the Lord's name in vain—nothing good will come of it (Ex. 20:7).
    B. Obedience
        If, as Christians, we are living in rebellion or sinfulness, God cannot give regard to our prayers. Why should He? Answering our prayers when we are in disobedience would

send the wrong message. We are being double-minded (James 1:6–8).

C. Sincerity

Volume or tone is no indication of the condition of the heart. We cannot fake sincerity with God. He knows our hearts (Lk. 16:15; Acts 15:8).

The effectual *fervent* prayer of a righteous man availeth much. (Ja. 5:16, KJV)

3. Why are some prayers answered and some are not?

All prayers *that are heard* are answered...now, not all prayers are heard—the Scriptures say that if we give sin a position of esteem in our lives, God does not hear our prayers (Ps. 66:18). Also, some of our prayers do not receive the answers we would like. Sometimes we get a yes, sometimes a no, and sometimes we get a wait.

This last answer requires more patience than we usually possess, so we get frustrated. Our world revolves around us, so we lack the patience for God to line up the other circumstances so that what He is orchestrating will occur (remember, He is answering others' prayers, too—God seldom does just one thing at a time; although God's will is singular, in His efficiency, His accomplishments are multiple).

Developing this patience is part of His *hidden* agenda. It is not that He is being deceptive; rather, He just doesn't want us to get in the way. Most of the time, however, we lack the patience to wait for His will; in our frustration, we take matters into our own hands—no surprise to Him—and we end up having to pray for rescue (Is. 55:8–9).

4. What about the times when we don't know how to pray?

I don't know about you, but I feel this way a lot! Fortunately that is no obstacle to God. The Scripture says something about that, too:

> Likewise the Spirit also helps in our weaknesses. For we do not know what we should pray for as we ought, *but the Spirit Himself makes intercession for us* with groanings which cannot be uttered. Now He who searches the hearts knows what the mind of the Spirit is, because He makes intercession for the saints according to the will of God. (Rom. 8:26–27, NKJV)

Some people say this refers to 'praying in the Spirit' (more about this later), but I think it may be more than that. Not knowing the will of God is no obstacle to God because He *does* know how we should pray. If we will pray anyway, He will often give us the words to pray…whether 'in our Spirit' or in our understanding (I Cor. 14:13–15).

5. What about 'praying in the Spirit'?
    This is an often misunderstood thing because many are not familiar with it. But, thank God, *He* is not limited to *our* understanding. Nor are we limited to use only things that are fully understood—otherwise we would never turn on the lights (we use electricity every day, but few are able to fully understand just how it works)!
    'Praying in the Spirit' is a gift of the Spirit as listed in I Corinthians 12. Some people call it speaking in an unknown tongue (or simply speaking in tongues) and say that they are not interested because Jesus never did it (of course, it is impossible for Him to ever speak in an unknown tongue, for all tongues are known to Him). Or they say that the gift passed away "when that which is perfect has come"—citing I Cor. 13:10—meaning the canonized Word. However, we didn't have the canonized Word until the mid-fourth century—actually first recorded in Athanasius' Thirty-Ninth Festal Letter of 367 AD. In fact, it is recorded in 1 Cor. 14:39, "do not forbid to speak in tongues."
    Although prayer is one of the four ways we can contribute to spiritual growth (along with witnessing, Bible study, and fellowship), it is the only one that is two way (God to man—

and man to God). Like my grandmother used to say, "The good Lord gave you two ears and only one mouth for a reason." We need to listen more to God, than speak to Him.

Finally, many cite Gideon's prayer as an example—remember, he prayed for a confirmation that he should lead his army of three hundred against the overwhelmingly large army of sixty thousand Midianites arrayed in the valley below—but his prayer (alternately for the fleece to be wet and the ground dry and the ground wet and the fleece dry) was not a testimony of faith (read the context in Judges 6 and 7), but of God's mercy in his immaturity!

Remember, we are called to let prayer change us!

Recommended reading list:

- *With Christ in the School of Prayer*, Andrew Murray
- *The Power of a Praying Wife*, Stormie Omartian
- *Fasting: Opening the Door to a Deeper, More Intimate, More Powerful Relationship with God*, Jentezen Franklin

Web sites:

- www.christianity.about.com/od/prayersverses
- www.ChristianPrayerCenter.com
- www.prayer.christian.com

41

Racism or Racial Prejudice

For some, Martin Luther King's "dream" was truly a nightmare. To treat another human as less than human is *inhumane*...prejudice of any kind is ungodly (Acts 10:34). However, "the content of their character" did not come into play in most of my classmates' consideration of my school's integration—they only did what the courts ordered. Central High School became Muskogee Central High School—and eventually just MHS—in 1970, the year I graduated. We were the transition class...in fact, my generation was the transition generation.

Now that I think about it, the Civil Rights Act of 1964 took, in some places, nearly a decade to implement (and in some remote places is still struggling). Forced integration was not pretty...school bussing, race riots, incidents of personal tragedy—on both sides—however, has finally resulted in a generation that knows little of the segregation that ruled the day in most southern cities. I am pretty well traveled and I don't recall the last time I saw a "Back-of-the-Bus" or "We-Reserve-the-Right-to-Refuse-Service-to-Anyone" sign.

Don't get me wrong, I am not naïve enough to believe that racial prejudice is dead. As recently as the mid-80s, we had a mixed-race couple get married in our home because their mid-western Bible college wouldn't allow it on campus. But in many cities of the south, a mixed-race couple now turns only the grayest head. And racism is so abhorred by so many that an accusation of that ilk can ruin the aspirations of any politician.

Although Hitler's designation of the Jews as "unter-menschen"— sub-humans—is akin to racial prejudice, we will take up "religious prejudice" and "nationalism" as separate issues elsewhere.

Is racial prejudice biblical? Where did the races come from, anyway? How should Christians act if someone of another race moves next door or our daughter brings home a boyfriend of another race? Why do races tend to vote monolithically? Are minorities prejudiced against majorities or does prejudice only go one way? Can a white man jump or dance or are some races really 'rhythmically challenged'? These and other questions need addressing.

According to the dictionary, *Racial prejudice or racism* is the view that there is some inherent superiority or inferiority attached to a distinct biological group or race. According to the United Nations convention, there is no difference between racial discrimination or ethnic discrimination; superiority based on racial differentiation is scientifically false, morally condemnable, socially unjust, and dangerous. According to the Bible, "God is no respecter of persons" (Acts 10:34, KJV).

Answering questions:

1. Is racial prejudice biblical?

    According to the biblical account of the creation, we are all descendants of the same two parents: Adam and Eve (see Genesis 4:1 and I Timothy 2:13). Even more recently, the gene pool got narrowed a little to Noah, his wife, their three sons and their wives—eight people in all—(Genesis 6:17–18). But the first evidence of racial prejudice probably came with the misunderstanding that must have come from the confusion of the tongues at Babel (Genesis 11:6–9).

    To say that something is biblical because it is mentioned in the Bible may give the wrong impression. To say that something is "biblical" implies an endorsement. Never has the Bible mentioned racism or racial prejudice (in fact, those expressions cannot be found in any Bible translation, anywhere) in anything other than a negative connotation. Although being God's chosen people may have given Israel every reason to feel superior, Exodus 12:49 is pretty clear: "One law shall be to him that is home-born, and unto the stranger that sojourneth among you" (Exodus 12:49, ASV).

The conscripting of Simon of Cyrene (he is believed by many to be black) by the Romans to carry the cross for Christ (Mark 15:31) may be an example of Roman prejudice, but it may also be an endorsement of honor from God. The Romans looked down on all slaves and regularly made slaves of conquered peoples regardless of skin color, so it may be that the prejudice was more cultural than racial.

The best example scripturally of God's attitude toward anyone—and everyone—may be, as mentioned above: "God is no respecter of persons" (Acts 10:34, ASV).

2. Where did the races come from, anyway?

After the flood—a flood account is almost universal in every culture history or legend—and the confusion of the tongues, the earth's contiguous land mass—modern science has termed this "Pangaea"—was broken up and the tectal plates began to radiate away from one another (Gen. 10:25; I Chronicles 1:19) to form the earth's continental geography as we know it today. Tribes and people groups were isolated from one another geographically by large and impassible oceans, deserts, and mountain ranges; land bridges became narrow isthmuses or imposing straights. Couple this geographic separation with the linguistic and cultural differences that must have developed and one sees the mechanism for the isolation of a gene pool.

Every species in gene pool isolation develops genetic distinctions. It is no accident that those that the world considers as distinct races have a continental geographic origin: The Oriental or "yellow" races come from Asia; the Caucasian or "white" races from Europe; the African or "black" races come from Africa; the Native American or "red" races come from

North America; the Native South Americans or "brown" races come from South America; and the Polynesian or "island" races from the islands of the Pacific.

There may be many places from which the races of the world hail, but there is only one God Who is the Father of all. As advancement in communication and transportation make our world smaller and as "mixed-race" marriages become more and more culturally acceptable, we may find these reasons for genetic isolation disappearing along with their genetic distinctions...to the end that we may all begin to look like one another.

Never mind, though. Prejudice will just appear in some other form. There will never be peace on earth until the Prince of Peace rules in the heart of every man.

3. How should Christians act if someone of another race moves next door or their daughter brings home a boyfriend of another race?

First of all, to be truly color blind, we have to stop seeing people as being from a race that is determined by color or some other ethnic characteristic—they are part of the *human* race.

As Christians, not just our actions, but our reactions should be governed by a set of principles to which we have subscribed; these principles must come from the source of truth: The Word of God. Having said that, anytime someone—whether of another race or not—moves next door, we should look on that "happenstance" as a divine appointment and see it for the opportunity in evangelism it represents. That person's color or background should not be the issue; the only relevant question is whether or not that person has accepted Jesus Christ as their personal Lord and Savior.

4. Why do races tend to vote monolithically?

In a word: Fear. Minorities have a tendency to gravitate toward the party that makes them feel secure. In 1976, when I was in Enugu, Nigeria, surrounded by a sea of faces unlike mine, I felt "uncomfortable." My "minority status" made me feel threatened. It was not a fear based on reason, but rather a fear based on a lack of familiarity. In reality, I felt less apprehension as the days wore on…proving my fear was unreasonable; never did anyone threaten me. Minorities want to feel that those who represent them will do so fairly and will protect their interests. When the media exploits those fears, they are feeding the bigotry and prejudice that makes minorities unreasonably assume the worst. Political parties that capitalize on this unreasoning fear will lose their following when they have their own ends exposed.

5. Are minorities prejudiced against majorities or does prejudice only go one way?

Unfortunately, prejudice goes both ways. Minorities are just as prejudiced against majorities as majorities are prejudiced against minorities. Everyone equally resists something perceived as different. And therein is the hope of the future. As students discover that those "other guys" have the same challenges, fears, motivations, etc., as they do, they begin accepting them on a more equal footing. Sure, they are taught by their parents to distrust anyone that looks different, but when time, personal experience, and right thinking cause them to doubt their training, their conclusions cause them to look within rather than without—to the "content of their character" (thank you, Dr. King).

6. Can a white man jump or dance or are some races really rhythmically challenged?

This cannot be a serious question…Pete Maravich and Fred Astaire proved the ridiculousness of that assumption long ago. Still, assumptions die hard.

Change comes slow, but most change to be sustainable must come that way. One cannot simply proclaim that racial prejudice is wrong and pretend that such a proclamation is truly the end of such a practice. Apartheid may have been a despicable practice, but no more so than slavery and we Americans should not expect the South Africans to rid themselves of this blight any faster than we did; a century separated the Emancipation Proclamation from the Civil Rights Act of 1964, when many of the abuses of racial prejudice were supposed to but did not end—in fact it has taken another fifty years…and it still rears its ugly head from time to time.

We as Christians must emulate our Father and prove our sonship, treating "others as better than ourselves" (Phil. 2:3) and doing "to others as we would have them do to us" (Luke 6:31).

Recommended reading list:

- *Becoming the Anti-racist Church: Journeying Toward Wholeness*, Joseph Barndt
- *Anti-Racism in U. S. History: The First Two Hundred Years*, Herbert Aptheker
- *Why Americans Hate Welfare: Race, Media, and the Politics of Antipoverty Policy*, Martin Gilens

Web sites:

- www.antiracistchurch.blogspot.com
- www.churchoftheservantcrc.org/ministries/anti-racism
- www.themennonite.org/.../articles/Racism_is_antiChristian

42

Raising Children—The Principle Approach

I've been harangued, emotionally and physically abused, punished for things others did…but always loved by a merciful and loving Lord Who took what I really deserved. I know what it is to be raised by a grandparent, a wicked stepmother, a single parent (and I even raised myself for a time)…but, arguably, I turned out alright. God's destiny for your life is never inexorably thwarted by obstacles He cannot overcome.

Before I go any further, let me say I was not a perfect parent… neither was my wife. In retrospect, many of the decisions we made we would, no doubt, now make differently. It seems strange that so many of the conclusions we've come to have arrived too late for our own children to benefit. Maybe that's why grandmas and grandpas, if they're available, should at least be consulted.

Children need to be raised by what I call *The Principle Approach*. Let me explain. Rules are rigid, concrete inviolable edicts. There must be exceptions because life is not lived in the black and white, but the gray of reality, where any deviation from a rule is another reason for a child to feel insecure by what he sees as a changing standard. Whereas principles are *guiding perspectives* that are equally as inviolable (that's where a child's security comes from) as they are varied in their application (that's where a child's sense of justice is refined and satisfied).

For example, a parent's *love principle* may one day overlook an infraction, but on another day see that same infraction has become a pattern of behavior and mete out a commensurate discipline to break the bad habit. The parent must see mercy and discipline as the opposite sides of the same coin, the *love principle*. Jesus was not being inconsistent when He alternately forgave the woman caught in the act of adultery and chased the money lenders out of the temple with a whip.

Here are a few principles we believe make sense:

Principle Perspectives

1. Punishment looks back at past incorrect behavior, discipline looks forward to future correct behavior. If you discipline well, punishment may be rare.
2. The wise parent is working himself (or herself) out of a job, slowly releasing reins of authority as a child learns to accept responsibility for his (or her) own acts.
3. Every child is different; possessing different gifts, approaching challenges differently and requiring different parenting solutions though the problems are similar.
4. When it's everyone's job, it's no one's job; everyone benefits from a little hard work.
5. Hands are for hugging and blessing, never for discipline... that's what a belt or wooden spoon is for (Prov. 13:24); angry discipline is always misunderstood; successful discipline is followed by forgiveness and restoration of relationship.
6. At the core of all disappointment is unreasonable expectation.
7. Regret is where the past meets the present to guide the future.
8. Everyone suffers a little injustice (Rom. 5:8)...you are not omniscient...only God is (Job 34:16–30), so cut yourselves some slack!

Is raising children biblical? What about the parent who's single? What about raising someone else's kids? Why are my kids so unruly and rebellious? What if I've made mistakes? Is it too late to do things right? These are the questions thinking Christians should be asking themselves.

It is important to true understanding of any topic to define your terms. According to a combination of what many dictionaries say, *Raising Children* is the means by which a parent or parental figure brings infants to maturity. *Principles* are fixed guidelines for direction. A *Perspective* is a viewpoint. Therefore, in the context of raising children, principle perspectives are certain ways of looking at the challenges of child-rearing that guide the parent in the raising of a child.

Answering questions:

1. Is raising children biblical?

Of course it is; what do you think God was doing when He walked with Adam and Eve in the "cool of the day"? (Gen. 3:8) Although it is not directly related, there seems to be a progression of revelation from God to Man, with knowledge imparted, choices given and made, consequences experienced, and new direction instituted…at the very least, we see that the raising of the progenitors of the human race by God is inferred.

A close study of Man from the creation to the arrival of Jesus reveals that Our Heavenly Father has taken a deep and personal interest in our raising. This process has been *involved* and is, ultimately, *quite costly*…much as parenting is known to be. The saga of God's parenting of mankind is what we call "history"—"His Story."

2. What about the parent who's single?

Whether you have arrived at single parenting though divorce, the death of a spouse or any one of a number of other circumstances, raising kids alone can be challenging. For the Christian, a realization that you are *not* alone (Heb. 13:5) is always comforting. God is only a prayer away and your children will keep you on your knees. Parents should have this bumper sticker on their car: "As long as there are children, there will be prayer in the home!"

However, not having another parent physically present to share the burden of raising children can be overwhelming at times. Let me help you be creative. Here are a few considerations that may make your task less daunting.

Single Parenting—Suggestions That Might Lighten the Load

A. Mother's Day Out—Many churches, realizing the need, offer this once-a-week half-day or all-day childcare service. It is clean and safe and it might make house cleaning, shopping, or just taking a break possible or at least more pleasant.

B. Au-pair or Nanny Service—There are professional, trained adults available and waiting for their services to be contracted. Though often expensive, it might pay for itself in sanity or therapy savings, if you know what I mean. Also, there are a surprising number of college-age young ladies wanting an American experience who, for the cost of a round-trip airfare, room-and-board, and a little spending money, might consider a live-in nanny position. Things to keep in mind: Do they have a valid driver's license? Training? Experience? References? Passport/Visa?

C. Extended Family—Often a local sister or brother (or sister-in-law or brother-in-law) or grandparent may offer both a family connection and an outlet for relief. Two things to note: (1) You should always offer to compensate them; they should always graciously refuse. (2) You can never be too sure that an otherwise circumspect relative (let alone a friend or neighbor) won't take advantage of the vulnerability of your children...just be sensitive AND sensible. God is holding you accountable for your children's well-being.

D. Nap-times are Me-times—Use your children's naptimes for cleaning, cooking, laundry, or breaks. Your wise use of these times can make all the difference.

I hope this section does not come across gender-specific. It surely was not my intent. One of my sons has four children and his role is "Mr. Mom"; he cleans, cooks, and home-schools his and three others, too. He is not a single parent, but since his wife works, many of the household responsibilities fall to him. There are probably others that are left alone with kids occasionally. The single parenting suggestions might come in handy for you, too.

3. What about raising someone else's kids?

In a sense, we all do...(they are really God's kids, on loan to you). Still, many *are* raising someone else's kids...or at least they feel like they are. Sometimes they're adopted, sometimes they're foster kids or the product of circumstances they did not choose...but they should never be collateral damage—the result of someone else's bad choices. They are *your* children, regardless of how they've come to live under your roof...and what happens from this point is entirely *your* responsibility.

Whether or not your DNA can be tied to theirs, the children in your care are a sacred trust, and the task with which you have been charged is the most important job in the universe. Children are not the "hope of the future"...they *are* the future!

Raising someone else's children is no different, then, than raising your own—the same love, care, provision, wisdom, and courage is required. And, as a Christian, you are tapped into the limitless Source of all that.

4. Why are my kids so unruly and rebellious?

How were you as a child? Maybe you are just reaping what you have sown! Still, the basic natures of children are different. Don't get me wrong—they are all fallen. Every child is the selfish center of his (or her) own world. Proof of that comes early...children are just naturally selfish with toys; they have to be taught to share—sharing is a self-sacrificing, loving, and caring act...and not natural in the least.

The Scriptures say, "All we like sheep have gone astray; we have turned everyone to his own way..." (Isaiah 53:6, ASV) and "All have sinned and fallen short of the glory of God" (Romans 3:23, KJV). *Until your children have their own knowledge of God, pleasing you will have to come with enough rewards and sanctions that the desire to obey is greater than the tendency to rebel.* Remember that the Scripture also says, "Foolishness is bound up in the heart of a child; the rod of discipline will remove it far from him" (Proverbs 22:15, NASU).

5. What if I've made mistakes?

    What parent hasn't? Remember, God is bigger than your mistakes and He will even turn them into something good for you and your child (Rom 8:28). Besides, the humbling experience of asking and receiving forgiveness can set a pattern that is both a good example for children and may humanize the parent in the child's eyes. It is good for your child to look up to you...but not as if you were God and never wrong. He (or she) needs to see that you, too, are submitted to Someone greater than yourself, and that He holds you accountable as a steward/parent.

    Mistakes are where you learn and as such are not to be entirely regretted. Remember the principle, "Regret is where the past meets the present to guide the future."

6. Is it too late to do things right?

    Time is a multiplier; the longer you wait, the more costly "doing things right" becomes. However, it is never too late, but it's always better for your young children to have a 'visit' from Mr. Belt or Mrs. Wooden Spoon than to for you to visit your adult children in jail.

Children pattern themselves after the role models you give them. Choose their caregivers wisely. A parent should be more concerned with what their children have caught than with what they have been taught...choose their teachers carefully. The wise parent looks for character, not credentials, but it is usually possible to find both. Even choose their friends until they are wise enough to begin making those choices themselves.

Finally, a word about screen time. There is much positive to be said about the convenience and capacity of technological advances. iPhones, iPads, and laptops are rapidly becoming essential for the person who wants to avail himself of the latest technology. A child's competitiveness may well depend on his (or her) ability to use these information management tools. But screen time is no substitute for face-time. Parents who allow violent games, Netflix, Hulu, or even social media to become the primary babysitter are cheating their children and themselves.

Parenting is as much a refiner of parents as it is of children.

> Iron sharpens iron, so one man sharpens another. (Prov. 27:17, NASU)

Recommended reading list:

- *Parenting Isn't for Cowards*, Dr. James Dobson
- *The New Dare to Discipline*, Dr. James Dobson
- *The Passionate Mom: Dare to Parent in Today's World*, Susan Merrill

Web sites:

- www. ezinearticles.com/?Christian-Parenting
- www. views-from-the-brook.blogspot.com/2013/06/Christian
- www.focusonthefamily.com

43

Recidivism

Having only spent the night in jail once when I was a broke college student who got pulled over by an over-zealous county mountie who noticed my missing taillight, I am, perhaps, not the best person to write on chronic offenders…but then again, everyone struggles with the tendency to repeat past mistakes; recidivism is not just a criminal tendency but it's a personal tendency as well. Besides, that's what I really want to deal with—the insanity that thinks doing the wrong thing again will garner different results.

The Devil keeps files, so to speak, on all of us—just as the Lord has a wonderful (and personal) plan for our lives, so also the Enemy of Our Souls has a terrible (and personal) plan. Whatever tripped us up in the past is a proven area of weakness. The Devil may have been kicked in the head (Gen. 3:16), but he isn't stupid. Why try something new when the old temptations or trials will do just fine?

The familiar is a default position for all of us "criminals," whether we've been incarcerated by bars of steel or of our own making. Beth Moore wrote a book on *Breaking Free* (I even wrote one entitled *Changing Your Stars – Empowerment for a Different Destiny*); we all have a tendency to be bound by a past that threatens to keep us imprisoned. We all have areas of weakness the Lord wants us to surrender to Him. That is what the purpose of trials is…we don't know of an area that is flawed until failure reveals it to us (I Cor. 10:13; James 1:2).

Instead of "…and lead us not into temptation" (Matt. 6:13), I think that a good contemporary interpretation of that portion of the Lord's Prayer is, "Lord, let there not be anything in my heart that will cause You to have to test it out." The Scripture attests to the universality of this problem. It says, "All we like sheep have gone astray…" (Isaiah 53:6). Also, "Misery loves company"…this may be worldly wisdom, but it is reflected in the rest of that verse in Isaiah 53:6—"we've turned everyone to his own way." Recidivism is always our default, unless we 'break free' from the rest of the flock.

That was what made David a "man after God's own heart" (1 Sam. 13:13; Acts 13 22). Not that David never sinned, but that he *quickly acknowledged* his sin, took his discipline, and *did not let the past be prologue*. That is the key; we must recognize our sin, acknowledge that we deserve our discipline, and get over it! That is why the recidivism rate is so high (in many states, over 60 percent!). Nobody is ever guilty of what they have been convicted. Ask around the prison—nobody committed a crime…they are all 'unjustly' incarcerated—nobody is serving the time because they did the crime. I am reminded of the Scripture, "What is that bleating of the sheep?" (1 Sam. 15:14). Without admitting to the crime, Saul was condemned to repeat his offense over and over again.

Why not admit to it? In a word, pride. Humility is a prerequisite for change.

Is recidivism biblical? Shouldn't Christians live lives that are beyond the baser drives that put men in jail? Prison is for the criminal; so why are we talking about "repeat offenders"? (I haven't even committed the first crime!) I don't mind visiting them, but should I be lumped in with them in a discussion? Am I imprisoned by my own chronic behavior? These, and other questions, are the ones thinking Christians should be asking themselves.

According to a combination of what many dictionaries say, *Recidivism* is the tendency to chronically relapse; relevant to this article, it could be any habitual activity, but especially crime. Rehabilitation depends on the re-*habit*uation of individuals—is the subject capable of learning new habits or defaults?

This brings into question the very concept of most of the prison methods. Are people being sequestered from the rest of society, quarantined because their behavior is unacceptable to a peaceable world *or* are they being rehabilitated so that their defaults change *or* are they paying for their criminal behavior by being denied their freedoms for a specific period of time? (Usually a combination… perhaps our ambiguity of goal is part of the problem with recidivism…both criminal and personal).

Answering questions:

1. Is recidivism biblical?

    No, in the sense that it is an authorized behavior; yes, in the sense that it is everywhere in the Bible—Abraham repeatedly caved to the temptation to claim the half-truth that his wife was his sister (Gen. 12 13; 20:2), Jacob continued to take matters into his own hands (Gen. 25:31–33; Gen. 27:5–29; Gen. 30:35–43) and, in the New Testament, Simon Peter defaulted to the impetuous (Matt. 14:28; Matt. 17:4; Matt. 26:34) and the list could go on.

    Interestingly, all three of the biblical personages I mentioned had one thing in common—they all got a name change (Abram to Abraham, Jacob to Israel, and Simon to Peter). Their changed names indicate a change in nature, too. Maybe that's what we all need—unless a *nature* change occurs, recidivism is inevitable. In fact, Paul says as much in Romans 7.

    > I have discovered this principle of life—that when I want to do what is right, I inevitably do what is wrong. I love God's law with all my heart. But there is another power within me that is at war with my mind. This power makes me a slave to the sin that is still within me. Oh, what a miserable person I am! Who will free me from this life that is dominated by sin and death? Thank God! The answer is in Jesus Christ our Lord. So you see how it is: In my mind I really want to obey God's law, but because

of my sinful *nature* I am a slave to sin. (Rom. 7:21–25, NLT)

For our past *not* to be prologue, for recidivism *not* to rule the day—whether personal or criminal—a nature change is required. Maybe that's the reason programs like Chuck Colson's Prison Ministries Fellowship International has been so successful in lowering recidivism rates.

2.   Shouldn't Christians live lives that are beyond the baser drives that put men in jail?
      Of course, we are supposed to live exemplary lives (I 1 Thess. 1:6–7; 1 Pet. 5:3), but many who think they're Christians are really just nominal (in name only) or traditional—born to church-attending parents—Christians…they've had no real nature change.

3.   Prison is for the criminal; so why are we talking about "repeat offenders"? (I haven't even committed the first crime!)
      Just because you haven't been caught doesn't mean you haven't committed the crime. Besides, most people have at least been angry enough to kill, and to have murder in your heart makes you no less guilty of sin before God than someone who has committed the act (Matt. 5:21–22). None of us, in ourselves, are a match for the desires of the flesh. We would "just say no," if we could!

> I can anticipate the response that is coming: "I know that all God's commands are spiritual, but I'm not. Isn't this also your experience?" Yes. I'm full of myself—after all, I've spent a long time in *sin's prison*. What I don't understand about myself is that I decide one way, but then I act another, doing things I absolutely despise. So if I can't be trusted to figure out what is best for myself and then do it, it becomes obvious that God's command is necessary. (Rom. 7:14–16, The Message)

Christians are "repeat offenders" if they keep disappointing God in the same way. Before we Christians look down our pious noses in judgment, we need to realize that the cure for *criminal* and *personal* recidivism is the same...a nature change. Not possible apart from God.

4. I don't mind visiting them, but should I be lumped in with them in a discussion?

Yes, we are supposed to visit them (Matt. 25:36–39); and yes, you should be lumped in with them! There, but for the grace of God, go I! The bumper sticker that is so trite is also so true. "Christians aren't perfect, just forgiven." I am not qualified to throw the first stone—are you?

5. Am I imprisoned by my own chronic behavior?

Anything you can't say no to has become a god before Him (Exodus 20:3). We default to much because it is familiar to us...but it's not any more right for us this time than it was last time. Let's unlock the prison door and throw away the key—the prison we've made for ourselves by our lack of forgiveness of others, ourselves, and God.

Recidivism does not have to be our chronic default. Dogs always return to their vomit and pigs, no matter if you educate them or change their environment—both very helpful steps in the right direction—still return to wallow in the mud when released (2 Peter 2:22). After all, they are dogs and pigs...what do we expect? Only when the pigs and dogs have a basic nature change can we expect anything different.

Recommended reading list:

*   *Breaking Free*, Beth Moore
*   *Changing Your Stars: Empowerment for a Different Destiny*, Alan E. Sargent
*   *Unconditional Surrender*, Dr. Gary North

Web sites:

- www.prisonfellowship.org
- www.mykairos.org
- www.prisonfellowship.org/resources

44

Sacred Texts

Admittedly, I was a geek. I wasn't popular enough to be a sosh—short for 'socialite,' I think—not athletic enough to be a jock, as I was only 4'7" as a seventh grader; the basketball coach politely suppressed a chuckle when I showed up for tryouts—and I definitely didn't smoke cigarettes, so being a greaser was out of the question. So I spent a lot of my time reading books. The bookmobile stopped at my school twice a week, and, by summer's end, I had read nearly every book they carried. Soon the public library was my favorite haunt.

In those days, it wasn't as un-cool as it is now to be academic. I don't recall making less than an A till I got to high school—except for the C in wood shop, where old man York didn't like my project for that semester…I still have it in my office…yep, you guessed it, *a bookshelf.* In high school, girls discovered me (I had discovered them in the seventh grade; just couldn't do much about it)—right after they announced over the school intercom that I had gotten appointments to the Air Force Academy, Naval Academy, and Coast Guard Academy—but it was my senior year already and I didn't have much opportunity to take advantage of my new-found celebrity status.

I didn't have much regard for sacred texts, unless you consider the *Rubaiyat of Omar Khayyam* a sacred text…I had whole sections of that thousand-year-old Persian poem memorized. If you had to categorize my belief system, you probably would call me a humanist.

I regularly read Khalil Gibran, Byron, Keats, and Thoreau, and, while the Jocks all got trophies for their athletic prowess, I managed to bring home State Science Fair trophies and the Elizabeth Cosgrove Poetry Cup.

Then it happened. One week I was coming home and chuckling with my dad about "crutch"—my pet name for the service I attended at First Methodist (where all the pretty girls went)—the next week I was virtually *floating* home, full of a new-found faith. I couldn't get enough of the New English Version of the *Bible* Katy gave me for Christmas.

Since then, I've read many sacred texts: the Muslims' *Quran*, the Hindus' *Upanishads*, the Mormons' *Pearl of Great Price*...and I don't think that Christians should be afraid of those books; they have no more power over us than we ascribe. "Truth stands the test of time, lies are soon exposed" (Prov. 12:17). All of them have some wise counsel to give, but when you compare them with Scripture...well let's just say I know that their authors are still in their graves.

Truth must be absolute or it's of no use. If there is nothing that is sure, then everything is a matter of interpretation, subjective, and circumstantial. Imagine a mariner trying to navigate a certain course to arrive at a certain destination, but all his measurements were off because he had not chosen a fixed reference point! As the North Star—the star that shines from a position in space directly above the north axis of the earth—is the fixed reference point for navigators, so also is truth for philosophers and leaders.

For the Christian, truth is the Scripture, the Bible, the Word of God. It is the fixed reference point by which we judge all human behavior. For other religious peoples—the Hindu, the Muslim, the Jew—the Upanishads, the Quran, and the Torah are the "fixed references." Having a fixed reference may be a good thing...you may feel with comfort that you are making progress toward a desired end...but the test of truth will be in the destination at which you arrive. "Many will say 'Lord, Lord...,' but I will say, 'Depart from Me, you workers of iniquity. I never knew you'" (Matt. 7:22–23).

If the Bible, the Word of God, is represented as a fixed line, all truth is then parallel. Any proposed action can be compared with that fixed line to determine whether it is convergent, divergent, or co-destinational. All truth will take you to the same end: absolute reality.

Every line, if it is short enough, can appear to be parallel. Only if a line is made up of many points—consecutive events over a long period of time—can truth be determined. In other words, we must extend the line if we are to judge aright.

It has been said, "The falseness of a lie is measured in its nearness to the truth." One who is practiced in deception learns quickly that he must sow much of what is true in what is false, if his tale is to be believed. The best training, however, for recognizing the counterfeit is to never handle it; for when you do encounter it, you will instantly know something just doesn't feel right.

The problem with choosing the wrong set of fixed references is that by the time you learn that you have chosen poorly, it's too late. Does God cast into hell the sincere but deceived person? In a sense, God casts no one into hell, but a man casts himself there when his choices lead him to an absolute reality that is eternally undesirable. Some say that hell's greatest pain is seeing the tear in the eye of God over the consequences of our choices.

Are sacred texts biblical? What if what I believe is wrong? What if what I believe is right? Don't writings other than the Bible have some good things to say? Who's to say you are right…I mean, who died and left you king? These and other questions are the ones thinking Christians should be asking themselves.

According to a combination of what many dictionaries say, a *Sacred Text* is a writing, usually of a religious nature, whose adherents believe is divinely inspired or supernaturally revealed. Most religions have a founder and his (or her) writings are usually considered pivotal to those who ascribe to its tenets.

Answering questions:

1. Are sacred texts biblical?

   That is almost a ridiculous question. The Scriptures them-selves make it self-evident.

However, the concept of following a certain written code of behavior is ancient. The Code of Hammurabi may predate the writings of Moses (who authored the first five books of the Bible—actually Job, although most of its subject matter deals with a time frame that post-dates the earlier chapters of Genesis, may have been written earlier). But the Israelites certainly had the advantage that their texts claimed divine origin. Think of the moral authority that would give them!

2. What if what I believe is wrong?

Certainly, to have arrived at the conclusion that what you have always believed is wrong can be, to say the least, disheartening. Still, arriving at that conclusion usually means that you have arrived at the right belief system; often in the nick of time. In any case, Einstein is often credited with saying that "the definition for insanity is continuing to do the same thing, but expecting different results." If what you believe is not taking you where you want to go, you had better change course!

To believe wrongly can have resulted from only two possible courses:

A. You have deviated from the right course...in which case, you can either get back on course by retracing your steps to the point of deviation OR you may take the path that leads you from where you are to the right path. Take whichever course is the shortest...of course, maybe it's easier to go back than to go on.

B. You were never on the right course to begin with... in which case, finding the right path may have been a "Eureka! moment" for you. Probably the path found you, not the other way around (1 John 4:19). Just rejoice and begin walking!

3. What if what I believe is right?

Then hallelujah! You have discovered the treasure (Matt. 13:44)! Now, like Don Francisco says in one of his songs, you've "just got to tell somebody." For you to not share would be selfish! Imagine yourself having found someone downtown giving away hundred-dollar bills. Would you stuff your pockets full *and then tell no one?* No; you'd probably call everyone you knew and say to them, "There's a crazy man giving away hundred-dollar bills downtown; go get yourself some!" (I mean, *after* you had stuffed your *own* pockets full…let's be realistic here!)

4. Don't writings other than the Bible have some good things to say?

    Of course they do. God has bestowed His wisdom on many. But, like the Scriptures say,

    > "For My thoughts are not your thoughts, nor are your ways My ways," declares the Lord. "For as the heavens are higher than the earth, so are My ways higher than your ways, and My thoughts than your thoughts." (Isaiah 55:8–9, NASU)

    There is man's wisdom and then there is God's wisdom… and a huge chasm in between. A lot of good wisdom comes from Confucius, Muhammad, Gautama Buddha, Joseph Smith, and Khalil Gibran…but none of them have been seen to make a bodily resurrection! Jesus was seen alive after His resurrection by His disciples (Luke 24:33–39), Mary Magdalene (John 20:14–17), and by over five hundred at one time (1 Cor. 15:6)!

5. Who's to say you are right…I mean, who died and left you king?

    Actually, Jesus (Rom. 8:17; Rev. 1:6)! Besides, don't take my word for it. In fact, all 1.6 billion of us may be wrong. Experience Him for yourself.

    Hopefully, you will read something that I have written and find the same anointing flows through me that has flowed through countless others who, down through the ages, have written words inspired by the King of Kings.

Recommended reading list:

- *Sacred Texts of the World: A Universal Anthology*, Ninian Smart and Richard D. Hecht (Editors)
- *Church History in Plain Language*, Bruce L. Shelley
- *The Story of Christianity, Volumes 1 & 2*, Justo Gonzales

Web sites:

- www.bl.uk/learning/cult/sacredbooks/sacredintro.html
- www.religionfacts.com/christianity/texts.htm
- www.sacred-texts.com/bib/index.htm

45

Smoking, Alcohol Consumption, and Other "Salvation" Issues

You know the old saying, "Don't smoke, drink, or chew…or go with the girls that do!" Needless to say, in this day of situational ethics, it is a little outmoded. Still, it would be good to know what behavior is acceptable to other Christians and, more importantly, to God. Surprisingly, God is a lot more forgiving than we. For us, in our state of perpetual spiritual arrogance, the list of "salvation" issues is quite long…for God, not so much.

First of all, let me tell you why I put "salvation" in quotes. There are many behaviors we consider reprehensible which may indeed be unapproved in some circles, but since salvation is our entrance into *His* heaven, we should let *Him* make the final determination, shouldn't we? Some things are forgivable, some things are not *absolutely* wrong, and some things are only wrong in certain contexts.

I guess I had my first serious temptation to smoke when I was sixteen. Our Boy Scout troop had embarked on a canoe trip into the Quettico National Provincial Park in Canada north of Ely, Minnesota, and we had already made camp for the night. The tents had mosquito-proof zip-down netting doors and we had already sprayed inside them in preparation for another decent night's sleep. Our guide, an experienced canoeist of twenty-something, had chosen a large rock outcropping from which to gaze at the descending sun.

As dusk came on, he, to my surprise, lit up a cigar and began to gently puff a surrounding cloud of hazy smoke. Noticing my raised eyebrow, he handed me a cigar and a lighter. "You had better arm yourself; they take no prisoners," he warned. He pointed at an approaching cloud of mosquitos advancing across the lake toward us like an incoming fog bank. I hurriedly lit and coughed my way to protection. Two weeks later and back home, I had taken up the habit because it looked cool and had an attendant tough-man story.

But eventually my teenage need for French fries overcame my financially draining new-found habit…and the fries seemed to taste progressively better. My own self-confidence didn't seem to need bolstering as much as my desire for tasty food. At least that was my one and only bout with tobacco.

Oh, and I tried chewing tobacco once. I had discovered an abandoned half-pouch of Red Man behind the pavilion at the Scout Camp on Lake Ft. Gibson. The friend I was with instructionally placed a wad of it between his cheek and gum and motioned for me to do likewise. I did so and suddenly felt a growing nausea that had me spitting it out and choking completely out of control. Needless to say, I never made that mistake again. Sure, I played baseball, but I found the bulge in my cheek looked just as cool—and was a lot more pleasant—if made by a Jolly Rancher or a wad of Double Bubble.

Although there are many "salvation" issues, I chose smoking and drinking as representative samples because they are—at least in the "Christian" west—so universally considered to be morally questionable. Smoking is more of a *lung issue* than a salvation issue. C. S. Lewis smoked, as do many people whose relationship with the Lord I do not question. Alcohol consumption, overeating, and use of non-prescription drugs are all questionable behaviors… but I have three problems with critics who like to think they are "salvation" issues:

1. They are more likely to become *addiction issues,* and anything you can't say no to may become a god in your life (Ex. 20:3).

2. Life, especially the life of a Christian, is not a snapshot; it is more of a video—as we effectively surrender more of ourselves to Him, many acts we had excused before have become reprehensible to us.

3. Besides, can we see the heart (Jer. 20:12)? We need to let Him be the Final Judge of all things.

To this list we can add many denominational preferences: dancing (I guess King David's in trouble—2 Sam. 6:14), caffeine consumption, skin color, ethnic background (I thought we were all from the Human Race), musical instruments in the church, rock music (what about when Gregorian chants were the latest craze?), etc. The key word here is *preference*.

Are smoking and alcohol consumption biblical? Is anything a "salvation" issue? What about those things we do even though we know we shouldn't? Is "judge not" a consideration here? These are the questions thinking Christians should be asking themselves.

According to a combination of what many dictionaries say, *Smoking* is the means by which active ingredients—like nicotine—are released by combustion to be absorbed in the lungs. *Drinking*, if it has a negative connotation, usually refers to the consumption of alcohol. Some people consider such activities as proof that those who do them are not Christians, while others do not see a *necessary* link.

Answering questions:

1. Are smoking and alcohol consumption biblical?

   Of course they are, haven't you read the scripture? "And Rebekah lifted up her eyes, and when she saw Isaac, she lighted off the camel" (Gen. 24:64, KJV). And maybe you think Jesus changed water into grape juice?! (John 4:46). Seriously, smoking is not mentioned unless you are talking about the lake of fire, and drinking alcohol is mentioned many times, but usually in a positive context, if not done to excess.

That is the key to many of what we might call *questionable* practices. Duration of exposure or quantity in the bloodstream (or age) may determine what is legal or even healthy, but what is healthy soul-wise to you or someone else is more determined by the impression it leaves on others...in other words, it may be hard for a Christian to witness with a cigarette or a bottle in his hand. For the Christian, the rightness or wrongness of an activity may not be determined by his own estimation, but by the estimation of others (1 Cor. 8:13).

That may seem like a harsh standard, but are you living for your own pleasure or for the salvation of others? As the old saying goes, "If you can't say 'Amen,' say 'Ouch!'"

2. Is *anything* a "salvation" issue?

    Of course, but Romans 10:9–10 covers that, not your personal theology. Let's let God determine what is or is not a salvation issue. The scripture referred to is below.

    > That if you confess with your mouth Jesus as Lord, and believe in your heart that God raised Him from the dead, you will be saved; for with the heart a person believes, resulting in righteousness, and with the mouth he confesses, resulting in salvation. (Rom. 10:9–10, NASU)

3. What about those things we do even though we know we shouldn't?

    The Scripture is very plain about this. The Holy Spirit convicts us of sin—or as one translation puts it, "our hearts condemn us"—what may be right for one person may be wrong for another.

    > We know love by this, that He laid down His life for us; and we ought to lay down our lives for the brethren. But whoever has the world's goods, and sees his brother in need and closes his heart against him, how does the love of God abide in him? Little children, let us not love with

word or with tongue, but in deed and truth. We will know
by this that we are of the truth, and will assure our heart
before Him in whatever *our heart condemns us*; for God
is greater than our heart and knows all things. Beloved,
if our heart does not condemn us, we have confidence
before God; and whatever we ask we receive from Him,
because we keep His commandments and do the things
that are pleasing in His sight. (I Jn. 3:16–23, NASU)

4.   Is "judge not" a consideration here?

In fact, this scripture is the most oft-quoted one in the
Bible...usually to justify our behavior by pointing at someone
else's. The actual verse, *not* taken out of context, calls us to
integrity—never hypocritically condemning others of the
things we ourselves may be guilty.

> Judge not, that ye be not judged. For with what judgment
> ye judge, ye shall be judged: and with what measure ye
> mete, it shall be measured to you again. (Matt. 7:1–2, KJV)

We are not to call things good that are really bad or vice
versa; besides, what may seem bad might not be as bad as the
alternative or something that appears to be good may end up
being detrimental. We simply cannot see the end from the
beginning, so let's leave the final judgment to He Who can.

Before we condemn someone for an act we think is a
"salvation" issue, let us look at our own lives. We are to work
out "*own* salvation with fear and trembling" (Phil. 2:12), not
someone else's.

Recommended reading list:

- *I Want to Stop Smoking...So Help Me God!: A Christian-based Approach to Use When Quitting*, Judy Murphy Simpson
- *Take Control of Your Drinking...And You May Not Need to Quit!*, Michael S. Levy

- *Unconditional Surrender*, Gary North

Web sites:

- www.gotquestions.org/quit-smoking-Christian.html
- www.thechristiantreatmentcenter.com/.../how-to-quit-drinking
- www.achristiancounselor.com/habits.html

46

Star Trek, Star Wars, and the Search for Extraterrestrial Life

By the time I had reached high school, I had already read most of Jules Verne, Robert Heinlein, Ray Bradbury, and Isaac Asimov. Throw in Arthur C. Clarke's *2001-Space Odyssey* and some H. Ryder Haggard (for fantasy's sake) and you'd have a pretty science-fiction-oriented teenager. It didn't help that I had won a NASA science fair award as an eighth grader, been their guest (with forty-nine other geekly award winners) at Houston's Manned Spacecraft Center; and President Kennedy had made it a national goal to put an American on the moon before the decade was out. To say I was a young man with my "head in the clouds" would not only be accurate geographically and anatomically, but an understatement.

It seemed to me quite natural to contact Dr. Carl Sagan (I actually received a hand-signed response from him) when I chose to attempt growing some bacteria in a simulated Martian atmosphere as my science fair experiment. Although getting ahold of liquid nitrogen appeared a daunting challenge, recreating the surface pressures was harder, still. Even though I won a first place in the Oklahoma State Science Fair that year, it wasn't till I entered the application process for an appointment to the US Air Force Academy that I seriously considered that there might be something—or someone—out there…and I might get to meet him (or it) someday. I have met Someone other-worldly, but it was an experience I didn't expect.

The names of the Mercury, Gemini, and Apollo astronauts were household words then. Everyone knows that even in 1977, George Lucas had to have some very special effects in *Star Wars* before there could be something like a Wookiee or Jabba-the-Hut. But, did you know that the entire Air Force Academy in 1970 suspended activity from 4:30–5:00 p.m. to watch *Star Trek*? Yep, every cadet knew he'd be going to Mars someday...or to the hills surrounding Saigon.

Yes, "The Quest For Extraterrestrial Life" was more than the title to my research paper that accompanied my science fair project. It represented the drive and imagination that continues to spawn the surreal—TV series like *Star Trek* and its myriad spin-offs have made the acting careers of William Shatner (Capt. Kirk) and Leonard Nimoy (Spock); eight movies later, *Star Wars* continues to be a box-office phenomenon; and movies like *ET, Independence Day, Close Encounters, Mission to Mars, First Contact* (actually dedicated to Carl Sagan) and the TV series *The 4400* keep terms like "alien abduction" and "interstellar space travel" in today's vernacular.

Is extraterrestrial life biblical? Are we, as science fiction (and some in the field of genetics) postulates, the offspring of some superior race of beings? Will they find life on Mars? What about recent discoveries of planets outside our Solar System? Are UFOs real? These and other questions are the ones thinking Christians should be asking themselves.

According to a combination of what many dictionaries say, *Extraterrestrial Life* is the existence of non-Earth life (Latin: *extra*—outside of, or beyond; and *terrestris*—things pertaining to Earth). Alien life, while not proven, is considered by many in the scientific community to be plausible. Science fiction writers have long toyed with the possibility of extraterrestrial life and evolutionists, with their help, have created the quasi-science of exobiology, the study of alien life. In fact, SETI (the Search for *Extra*terrestrial *I*ntelligence) is a collaboration of a sometimes-government-funded array of radio telescopes and personal computers sharing their excess computing power. Although no direct evidence for extraterrestrial life exists, a considerable amount of mostly private funds continues to be spent chasing what many think is a "romantic" concept.

Answering questions:

1. Is extraterrestrial life biblical?

    Of course it is; but only if you consider the inhabitants of heaven extraterrestrial (Rev. 5:3) which, of course, they are.

    Most of the Bible's references to all things astronomical can be found in Job 38. Interestingly, the word "mazzaroth" can be found as a transliterated word—a word that goes straight from the original language into English; like "hallelujah"—in the King James; it is translated by some versions into the word "constellations." In the Greek Septuagint—the Old Testament translated into Greek about the time of Alexander the Great; literally *the Bible Jesus used*—the word "mazzaroth" is translated "zodiakos" or Zodiac in English.

2. Are we, as science fiction (and some in the field of genetics) postulates, the offspring of some superior race of beings?

    In spite of what pop culture, the Darwin-gone-wild group or the *Stargate* crowd (fans of the movie or TV series spin-offs) may say, man is the product of God's creativity (Gen. 1:26), not the product of the procreativity of some ancient superior extraterrestrial culture. Besides, the last time I checked Mendel's Law, things don't automatically get better. Things don't fall together, they fall apart.

    I know the arguments for evolution and the survival of the fittest and all, but I also know there are no fossils of transitional species, no present-day examples of mutational survivors and that mutations leave their victims dead or sterile. It takes a lot more faith to believe Darwin's account than God's.

3. Will they find life on Mars?

    Probably not; it's a lot more likely they'll find the necessary ingredients—water, oxygen, etc.—proving just how special Earth really is. In fact, though they search the cosmos—and astronomers have located other planets surrounding other stars with the Hubbell Space Telescope (HST)—I doubt they will find any life.

But, if they do, and it is life created in free moral agency, then Jesus will only have to die for them, too. Read the first chapter of John's gospel and you'll see that Jesus is the active Agent of the Godhead in creation. Did He make all this knowing the choice Man would make? Yes. Before Man ever ate of the Tree of the Knowledge of Good and Evil (Gen. 3:6)...before He even made trees from which to eat (Gen. 2:29)...before he even made the land upon which a tree could grow (Gen. 1:9)...God, Who is love (1 John 4:8), died for His creation (1 Pet. 1:19–21).

4. What about recent discoveries of planets outside our Solar System?

Like I said, the HST *has* discovered planets outside our Solar System. But, as C. S. Lewis postulates in his science fiction trilogy (*Out of the Silent Planet, Perelandra*, and *That Hideous Strength*), even life on other planets, if it's sentient, will struggle with the temptation to disobey and, without Divine intervention (supplied by our hero in Perelandra, Dr. Ransom), will ultimately fail—innocence always yields to experience.

You can tell only a little from a telescope, but subsequent exploration will doubtlessly reveal that the created life on this planet is unique and instructive...that God created Man in His image (Gen. 1:26), gave him a home in the image of God's home (Rev. 21:3-NLT) and a job in the image of God's job (Gen. 2:15; Col. 1:17). Whether He's done it once or countless times, the results are always the same...temptation always defeats innocence leading to sin, sin always separates, a worthy sacrifice always pays for sin, and love always restores.

5. Are UFOs real?

Of course, at least initially, there are many things that fly or appear to fly that are not identified or are not identified correctly. But after you subtract the logical explanations and the atmospheric phenomenon, there are really only a few inexplicable objects left. Of these, it takes a lot more than multiple sightings and questionable photographic evidence to believe these are not intentional deceptions or government clandestine experiments gone awry. It takes more faith to believe the remaining UFOs are something truly alien than I have. Besides, do you think something as truly newsworthy as proof positive of alien life could be kept a secret for very long?

The real problem with Christians and the popularity of alien theories and UFO conspiracies is what I call today's "culture of gullibility." Ignorance is the willing and hapless accomplice of tantalizing superstition; with the people of today feeding their mental susceptibility with a lack of education, common sense or logic, it's no wonder. Whether one blames demons for UFO and apparent alien manifestations or something else, the distraction from the more practical aspects of everyday living is just as effective. We need to be too focused on things earthly to get side-tracked by the extraterrestrial.

Recommended reading list:

- *Out of the Silent Planet*, C.S. Lewis
- *UFO's and the Christian Worldview*, Jeff Gerke
- *Cosmic Deception: Christian Answers on UFO's and Aliens*, Steve McGee

Web sites:

- www.khouse.org/pages/special_events/alien_encounters
- www.christian-faith.com/...aliens-and-ufos-a-short-answer
- www.examiner.com/article/first-christian-ufo-alien-symposium

47

Suicide and Euthanasia

Not a continental youth movement, euthanasia is a barbaric practice that may be fine for animals that have no souls—sorry, all dogs don't go to heaven; although there will be animals in heaven, Buffy won't be there—but people must never play God with the life of another human being. Except where He has given us the responsibility and wisdom to judge where someone might be a risk to others' lives or worthy of the severest punishment, suicide or assisting someone else to commit suicide is morally wrong. The Scripture clearly says, "You are not your own; you have been bought with a price" (I Cor. 6:19–20)

My mother died at twenty-four of Hodgkin's lymphoma. I was two and much as I've tried to conjure up an image of her in my remembrance, when I look at a photo of her, there is simply no recognition. In a moment of painful reflection, my dad related how my mom had begged him to give her a lethal overdose of the morphine she was on. He told me of the three jobs he had worked to pay for the medical bills, the faith healers he went to…and of her begging him to just make it all go away.

But in those days, you never even considered such an option. Till the day my dad passed away, he missed her and spoke of her only in the most tender of ways. He was sorry for her pain but just couldn't take out of God's hands what was clearly only in His authority. Although it might have eased her suffering, it certainly would have increased his regret.

Dr. Kevorkian (known by some as "Dr. Death") changed all that. He assisted over 130 people to commit suicide before he was tried, convicted of second-degree murder, and served eight years of a ten- to twenty-five-year sentence. Dying in 2011, he famously said "Dying is not a crime." To which I would reply, "Yeah, but murder is!"

Is suicide or euthanasia biblical? What should my attitude as a Christian be toward those who suffer extreme pain? It's my life and I can call it quits anytime I want to, can't I? Isn't it more merciful to end someone's suffering than to let them languish in unbearable pain? What about those who for one reason or another have taken their own lives? These are the questions thinking Christians must answer.

Suicide comes from the Latin *suicidium* (to take one's own life). According to a dictionary amalgamation, it is the act of intentionally killing oneself. In some oriental cultures, it is the "honorable way out," ending what may have been a shameful episode in life or business. The Romans were known to end political defeats by poison or venomous snakes, the Japanese committed *hari kari* or *Seppuku*—"stomach-cutting"—a ritual suicide by disembowelment originally reserved for Samurai and even King Saul "fell on his sword" (1 Sam. 31:4), so suicide has been with us for a long time. However, the customariness of a practice does not guarantee its acceptability to God, the giver of life (Eph. 2:5).

Answering questions:

1. Is suicide or euthanasia biblical?

    Although suicide and euthanasia are mentioned—not the words, but the practice—it is always with a negative connotation. Again, just because something is mentioned in the Bible does not mean it is endorsed by God. Actually, King Saul committed suicide because his armor-bearer refused to fulfill Saul's request to assist him. Then he fell on his own sword, too. Read the context...both were acts of pride (1 Sam. 31:2–6).

2. What should my attitude as a Christian be toward those who suffer extreme pain?

No one has endured—except Christ on the cross—the pain and agony of Job, yet because the Lord was merciful to him, we ought also to be merciful (Luke 6:36).

> You have heard of the endurance of Job and have seen the outcome of the Lord's dealings, that the Lord is full of compassion and is merciful. (James 5:11, NASU)

Besides, He knows how weak we are (Ps. 103:14); just as He takes that into consideration, so should we. Just as He will not allow us to be tested beyond our ability and will with the trial provide the grace to bear it (1 Cor. 10:13), so He expects us to be understanding of those who are called to great suffering.

There are many Christians who have no room in their theology for a God who allows suffering, but we would have a small God indeed if we kept Him within the boundaries of our puny understanding. Besides, what about the following Scriptures?

> When the heavens are shut up and there is no rain, because they have sinned against You, and they pray toward this place and confess Your name and turn from their sin *when You afflict them*, then hear in heaven and forgive the sin of Your servants and of Your people Israel, indeed, teach them the good way in which they should walk. And send rain on Your land, which You have given Your people for an inheritance. (1 Kings 8:35–36, NASU)

They have a saying in Arkansas that goes something like this:

> We shouldn't fix the fix He fixed to fix the fix we're in.

Make no mistake, God is *for* us (Rom 8:31); everything was designed to be a blessing to us (3 John 2); even the things we think are not good, God will turn around for our good in some way (Rom. 8:28). We just have to trust that He will give us the grace sufficient for the moment (2 Cor. 12:9).

Individual responsibility was, however, the rule of the day. If people could provide for themselves, they were encouraged to do so. Even those who had taken someone into their household to provide for them had the responsibility for them, in order that the Church, who provided for everyone else, would not be burdened.

> If any man or woman that believeth have widows, let them relieve them, and let not the church be charged; that it may relieve them that are widows indeed. (1 Tim. 5:16, KJV)

3. It's my life and I can call it quits anytime I want to, can't I?

The fallacy of that argument is its false premise. It isn't *your* life. Like the Word says,

> Or do you not know that your body is a temple of the Holy Spirit Who is in you, whom you have from God, and that *you are not your own*? For you have been bought with a price: therefore glorify God in your body. (1 Cor. 6:19–20, NASU)

How glorifying to God do you think it is when you take what does not belong to you? It is either stealing or murder (taking someone else's life). Besides to refuse to live the life that cost God His only Son is the height of rejection.

4. Isn't it more merciful to end someone's suffering than to let them languish in unbearable pain?

Do you know what tomorrow holds? I don't…only God does; since you are not Him, why don't you trust Him with the final outcome? Perhaps He's going to heal him…think of the man born blind (John 9:1–11); he sat and begged all his life;

what if someone had assessed his quality of life and thought to do him a 'favor' the day before Jesus healed him?

5. What about those who for one reason or another have taken their own lives?

That's why he is called the Judge of all the earth (Gen. 18:25). He alone knows the heart (Acts 15:8). He knows *why* we do the things we do and judges accordingly; and we know His judgment is righteous (2 Thess. 1:5). The sin of suicide is like every other sin; it, too, is under the blood.

Sometimes mental anguish is even more difficult to bear than physical pain. Chemical imbalances in the brain can make it difficult for the sufferer to determine reality. And then there's the whole realm of the truly spiritual. Some have inadvertently or purposefully opened a window of opportunity for demonic tormentors to gain access and, as a result, have contemplated or accomplished self-destruction. We can trust that God, the righteous judge will mete out His rewards and punishments where they are due.

Recommended reading list:

- *When God Doesn't Make Sense*, Dr. James Dobson and R. T. Kendall
- *Where is God When it Hurts*, Philip Yancey
- *Suicide: A Christian Response: Crucial Considerations for Choosing Life*, Timothy J. Demy

Web sites:

- www.christiananswers.net/q-dml/suicide-and-heaven
- www.christianitytoday.com/ct/2000/july10/30.61.html
- www.religionfacts.com/euthanasia/christianity.htm

48

Terrorism

Almost everyone remembers where they were and what they were doing when they first learned of the terror attack on the World Trade Center on September 11, 2001. I was at home; I had just said good-bye to my wife who had to teach a class that morning. She called as soon as she heard about it, and I turned on the TV and watched in disbelief as the second jet hit.

The thing that stunned me the most was watching all those people choosing to jump rather than succumb to a jet-fuel fire. That's when it became obvious that it wasn't just a wayward pilot. Then came the news that the Pentagon was hit...then the revelation that the Capitol Building or the White House might be next...we didn't know what the day might yet hold.

For weeks after that series of events, you couldn't buy an American flag. The store shelves were empty. People were flying flags from everywhere they would flutter. Parking lots looked as though like dignitaries were in town, and every vehicle was carrying an American VIP. Patriotism was rife and everyone put up with the new security measures at airports as if it were their civic duty.

But that was over a decade ago and we've been lulled into a false sense of security. We have forgotten the patriotism and the dire warnings that we had embarked on a multi-generational "War on Terror." That is until 4/15/2013. The people of Boston will remember that date like New Yorkers remember 9/11; the whole nation mourned the three killed and the more than 170 that were wounded by those two bombs set off near the finish line of the Boston Marathon.

The senselessness and unpredictability of acts of terrorism are what makes them so…well, terrorizing!

Is terrorism biblical? Wasn't the original Tea Party with all those Bostonians dumping crates of tea into the harbor an act of terrorism? Are terroristic acts justified by the ends they accomplish? Are Christians justified by their enthusiasm or zeal? What about non-violent protest…isn't rebellion "as the sin of witchcraft" (1 Sam. 15:23)? These and other questions are the ones thinking Christians should be asking themselves.

According to a dictionary amalgamation, *terrorism* is a pejorative term that depends on the perspective of the historian…just like "one man's trash is another man's treasure," so also terrorists are to those who send them out "freedom fighters." Liberators, vigilantes, and revolutionaries often justify violence and threats of violence to achieve their political agenda…like people making a losing argument often increase their volume. According to the Bible, terrorism only has strength because of its power to move people to fear: "Fear hath torment" (1 John 4:18, KJV).

In that same verse is the key to defusing (to use a bombing term) terrorism. "There is no fear in love; but perfect love casteth out fear…" (1 John 4:18, KJV). Fear gives terrorism its power. If folks continue to react in faith, like America did on 9/11 and Bostonians did on 4/15, "running to the battle" (I Sam. 17:48), then terrorism would lose its terror. David was not terrorized by the size or weaponry of Goliath because he knew he had a secret weapon: a God Who loved him. When you know God loves you; when you are armed with a covenantal relationship, even a slingshot is enough.

Answering questions:

1. Is terrorism biblical?

    One could argue that the inhabitants of Jericho were terrorized by the Israelites when they were marching around the walls (Joshua 6). Certainly the Bible records they were afraid (Josh. 6:1). Still, fear was *their* choice. But it isn't what brought the walls down. Hebrews 11:30 records that is was *faith*. Only when they had faith was the power of God's love activated. Having a covenantal relationship wasn't enough. Knowing that God loved them was not what made them victorious; it was *faith* that brought the walls down…and made David run.

2. Wasn't the original Tea Party with all those Bostonians dumping crates of tea into the harbor an act of terrorism?

    No, it was an act of vandalism. Of course, some would call that "economic terrorism." By any name, it was the acts of desperate men…and it was wrong. Patiently enduring hardship is the Christian way. Anything else is impatience or at the least making a way for yourself. (I'm reminded of David's refusal to kill Saul when he was vulnerable [1 Sam. 16:23]; instead, he waited for God to sort him out…and He did [1 Sam. 31:4–6]). Who knows what miraculous interventions have been negated by impatience?

3. Are terroristic acts justified by the ends they accomplish?

    The nineteen Islamic terrorists that flew planes into buildings were promised seventy virgins in paradise, but the sincerity of their zeal did not justify their acts any more than the atrocities committed during the crusades by "Christians" were justified by theirs. The means are not justified by the end (at least so says Heroides in the *Ovid*).

4. Are Christians justified by their enthusiasm or zeal?

    Professing one ideology over another is a good thing, if you are on the right side (which assumes there is a "right side"…but you would have to believe in absolutes; which I do…and I'm *absolutely* right!). But one's vociferousness of statement does not justify one's method of argument.

There was a Christian consensus in America at the time of the revolution—which should come as no surprise considering that many immigrants were fleeing religious persecution in Europe and the colonies had just gone through a spiritual revival (the Great Awakening, 1725–1775). Consequently, it should not be surprising either that many of those early Americans justified rebelling against "mother" England on moral issues—violation of their charters of land grants, an attempt to enforce Anglicanism in the colonies, and of course, taxation without representation.

The early colonists were quite literate and they had a commitment to education (Harvard was founded in 1637; just sixteen years after the Pilgrims landed!). Many of them read Junius Brutus's 1536 edition of "A Defense of Liberty Against Tyrants." An overview of this will quickly yield its primary tenet: "We must obey God rather than men" (Acts 5:29, KJV). This was their justification, atrocities, and improprieties notwithstanding—Gen. Sherman was right; war is hell—the colonists were righteously defending their homeland and their right to worship from an invading force.

Christians must find the will of God and the moral high ground from which to fight any war. Failure to do so will ultimately end in defeat. God will see to it. It is difficult to win the battle and lose the war or win a war and lose a country. The only thing worse than being on the wrong side of history is being on the wrong side against God...many times they are one and the same.

5. What about non-violent protest...isn't rebellion "as the sin of witchcraft" (1 Sam. 15:23)?

Non-violent protest seems to be preferable, at least Jesus seemed to be saying so when he healed Malchus's ear (John 18:10; Luke 22:49–51). Of course He used force to drive the moneylenders from the temple (John 2:13–17); that is where you had better be "rightly dividing the Word of Truth" (2 Tim. 2:15, kjv).

As far as whether your protest is rebellious or not, you had better find scriptural justification as "Truthful words stand the test of time; lies are soon exposed" (Prov. 12:19, nlt).

The ultimate defeat of terrorism only occurs when you take the fear out of it. "Do not fear those who kill the body but are unable to kill the soul; but rather fear Him who is able to destroy both soul and body in hell" (Matt. 10:28, nasu). By the way, if you haven't read the "Anti-terrorism Psalm" lately, do so (Ps. 46).

Recommended reading list:

- *A Defense of Liberty Against Tyrants* (originally under the title in Latin, *Vindicae Contra Tyrannos*), Junius Brutus
- *This Independent Republic*, Rousas J. Rushdoony
- *God and Government: A Biblical, Historical and Constitutional Perspective*, Gary De Mar and James Kennedy

Web sites:

- www.clashdaily.com/2013/04/purpose-of-terrorism-and-our-response
- www.terrorism.about.com/od/christianmilitancy/Terrorism
- http://carm.org/religious-movements/islam/islam-religion-peace-and-terrorism

49

Tornadoes, Hurricanes, and Other Unexpected Disasters

I think you would have to search long and hard to find many people who have experienced personally both a hurricane *and* a tornado, especially if they also experienced those disasters from different storm systems. My wife, however, has. Hurricane Erin, which made landfall in Pensacola, Florida, on August 3, 1995, during her attendance at a teacher's conference at PCC, came ashore as a category 2 hurricane—with winds in excess of 100 mph—and she survived a direct hit from an EF-3 tornado on April 25, 2011— this same storm system spawned 3-EF5 tornadoes, 13-EF4's and 23-EF3's: the largest outbreak of tornadoes in US history. Although the only personal damages we sustained from the hurricane were to our van—all the windows were blown out—the tornado completely destroyed three of our rentals and killed one of our tenants' children…we only lost our roof and a few out-buildings.

To say we are acquainted with disaster might be an understatement, but many have undergone tragedy that we can only imagine. (I'm not going to bring any focus to the two brainstem strokes I had in July and August of 2009.) When you think about the shootings at Columbine, the theatre in Colorado, or the more recent Sandy Hook Elementary, or the storm tragedies at Joplin, the Jersey Shore or at Moore, Oklahoma, our little tragedies pale by comparison. But we're Christians—stuff like that is not supposed to happen to us...right? We must have been in sin or at least near-rebellion, right?

I had been in the ministry since 1974 (ordained in 1976), taught at a Christian College since 1987...although I will not claim anything close to an exemplary lifestyle; my wife had been a teacher in a Christian school for over twenty years and had to put up with me for thirty-seven years (when the tornado hit). As the Scripture says, for neither my sin nor my wife's sin, "*...but that the works of God should be made manifest...*" (John 9:2, ASV).

Why do bad things happen to good people? If God is in control, how come evil still happens? Don't the good things I do count for something? What about the law of sowing and reaping—doesn't God weigh the bad against the good? Since I am a King's kid, don't I get special ("royal") treatment—is it wrong to expect this? Isn't Satan the "prince and power of the air" and isn't he responsible for the destructive forces at work on the earth? These and other questions are the ones thinking Christians should be asking.

According to a combination of what many dictionaries say, a *Tornado* is a violently rotating column of air that connects the ground to its source cumuliform cloud and occurs when a cold air mass, accompanied by a low pressure center, encounters a warm front and the conditions (measured now by a TORCON index) of the atmosphere—the jet stream, the moisture content, the instability of opposing air masses, etc.—are conducive to their spawning. Tornadoes, also called cyclones, rotate counterclockwise in the northern hemisphere and clockwise in the southern hemisphere. *Hurricanes* usually start as a tropical depression over water and sometimes intensify enough to become a named tropical storm and occasionally reach hurricane status—sustained winds in excess of 75 mph. A typhoon is a Western-Pacific-generated cyclone.

Answering questions:

1. Why do bad things happen to good people?

Firstly, not everything that at first blush appears to be bad is actually, in the long run, detrimental. A lot of things appear at first to have undesirable outcomes...the burned legs of a child, for instance...at eight, doctors recommended that Glenn Cunningham have his legs amputated, they were burned so badly—yet he ended up being a world champion runner who set the world record in the mile and 1,500 meter runs and was on the 1932 and 1936 Olympic teams!

Secondly, because only God can see the end from the beginning (Rev. 1:8), He is the only One to be trusted with final outcomes. Many have looked on their present calamity and thought things could not get any worse...only to have them get truly disastrous by comparison. There will come a day when it will all make sense—until then, we just have to trust. The Scripture puts it well:

> "They will be my people," says the Lord of Heaven's Armies. "On the day when I act in judgment, they will be my own special treasure. I will spare them as a father spares an obedient child. Then you will again see the difference between the righteous and the wicked, between those who serve God and those who do not." (Mal. 3:17–18, NLT)

Finally, perspective is an interesting thing...it helps us see our situation unclouded by the fog of our personal pain or circumstance. Like the old missionary story goes, "I complained about the shoes I didn't have till I met a man who had no feet."

2. If God is in control, how come evil still happens?

God created Angels and Man in free moral agency—a fancy way of saying, "with the right to choose" (Joshua 1:8). It's not God's fault that we have almost always chosen poorly (Isaiah 53:6; Rom. 3:23). I say almost because the one good choice some have made is to make Jesus the Lord of our lives. We, who have made that choice, have yielded up all our other choices to His ultimate wisdom.

Evil still happens not just because Adam sinned and we have that proclivity (Roman 7), but because we live in a fallen world (Rom. 8:19–23). Although sin and the evil consequences may become a habit, it is much more than that. It is our *un*natural bent. Whereas we might have once done the right thing—before the fall that was our natural bent—after the fall, we all had the tendency to sin. That's why Jesus died *and* sent His Holy Spirit. His death took care of our sins (lower case—plural), our individual infractions of the law—and His Holy Spirit began the process of sanctification, dealing with our Sin (upper case—singular), our bent natural tendency to disobey.

God may know which course you will choose, but His foreknowledge is not His fore control.

3. Don't the good things I do count for something?

Of course they do; they just don't cancel out the bad things we have done. Although good works prove faith (Titus 2:7), they don't *produce* it (Eph. 2:9). Only Christ's death on the cross pays in full for our "bad works" (sins).

There are many rewards promised to believers that do good works (Ps. 58:11; Mk. 10:29–30), but doing good works is not enough; we must first believe (Heb. 11:6). We must remember the sobering warning of Scripture:

> Many will say to Me on that day, "Lord, Lord, did we not prophesy in Your name, and in Your name cast out demons, and in Your name perform many miracles?" And then I will declare to them, "I never knew you; DEPART FROM ME, YOU WHO PRACTICE LAWLESSNESS." (Matt. 7:22–23, NASU)

Not only must we do good works, but the *ones* He has appointed us to do, *when* He has appointed them. In other words, we must be led by the Spirit.

4. What about the law of sowing and reaping—doesn't God weigh the bad against the good?

    The law of sowing and reaping (Gal. 6:7) is immutable (unchangeable); that is why Christ had to die—He reaped where we sowed. But God judges in an absolute sense, not as man judges (Isaiah 16:7); His balance scales weigh not only the deed but the intent behind the deed.

5. Since I am a King's kid, don't I get special ("royal") treatment—is it wrong to expect this?

    There is a difficult balance between wrath and mercy... justice can sometimes be hard to determine...at least for us. On the one hand, we are "joint heirs" with Christ (Rom. 8:17), and therefore "royalty"; and it is not wrong to expect to be treated differently. On the other hand, this "royalty" does not decrease God's expectation of us...if anything, it increases it. "For everyone to whom much is given, from him much will be required" (Luke 12:48, NKJV).

6. Isn't Satan the "prince of the power of the air" and isn't he responsible for the destructive forces at work on the earth?

    Yes, he is (Eph. 2:22), and there will come a time when he and his destructive devices will be incarcerated (2 Pet. 2:4) forever; and he has come to destroy (John 10:10), but God allows these "calamities" to provide for us some greater good (3 John 2). Although we may not understand these things from our own perspective, He encourages us to see with the eyes of faith and from *His eternal perspective.*

    Disasters can come in many forms: tornadoes, hurricanes, sickness, injury, bankruptcy...sometimes from our sin, sometimes from the collateral damage to other people's stupidity, sometimes just because we live in a fallen world...but He is Lord of all!

Recommended reading list:

- *When God Doesn't Make Sense*, James Dobson
- *One Call Away: Answering Life's Challenges with Unshakable Faith*, Brenda Warner
- *I Beat the Odds*, Michael Oher

Web sites:

- www.christianemergencynetwork.org
- www.jsyuille.blogspot.com/2011/03/christian-response-to

50

Witnessing

March 14, 1970 will go down as a day I will never forget. It was a Saturday and I was involved in a Lay Witness Mission in my church. The only reason I went to this weekend-long event is that I, as the elected president of the youth group, had an obligation. All I really felt for the church was contempt. In fact, my dad and I, who had moved into a rent house across the street from the church, would often refer to the church by our derogatory code name, the "crutch."

I had signed up to house one of the visiting "witnesses" (Craig, do you remember this?) and I felt obliged to be at the kick-off for the weekend, Friday night's potluck dinner. As I got in line opposite one of the cuter visitors (I may have been hypocritical, but I wasn't stupid!), she and I happened to reach for the same fried chicken leg at the same time. The ensuing conversation went something like this.

"Oh, I'm sorry. You were obviously going for that piece. Go ahead," she offered.

Looking at her intently, I said, "No, you go ahead. You are our guests."

"Okay. I won't wrestle you for it. Besides, God loves you and so do I."

I must have looked shocked, but managed to cover it up. Continuing to go through the line, I thought to myself, *This is not going to be too bad a weekend, after all!* Of course, I chose a seat close to hers and she introduced her brother who said, "Hi! God loves you and so do I." I accepted his outstretched hand somewhat reluctantly. *Oh,* I thought, *one of "those."*

After dinner, several of the visiting "lay witnesses" got up and shared how they had "come to the Lord." I only half-paid attention, because I was distracted; but I did notice that these folks were regular people…a plumber, a lawyer, a businessman, a secretary, a housewife…each of them spoke about Jesus as if He were a real person, not some historical religious leader.

As we adjourned to small groups, we cleaned up a little, but the girl I had found so attractive introduced me to her parents. "This is my mom and dad."

"We are so glad to be here at your beautiful church." Then, sticking out his hand, her father said, "God loves you and so do we."

I didn't know how to respond, so I just shook his hand and smiled. By then I had figured out that the greeting was just some sort of slogan, but there was no faking the sincerity with which it was delivered. That night I went to sleep with those haunting words echoing in my memory.

The next day, the youth met together all day long and had just plain fun; we played interactive games that had everyone laughing at themselves. That evening, after another "general session," the youth again were sequestered for more youth "testimonies."

Then Craig got up and hauled his chair out to the center of the circle. "Someone dim the lights, please. I don't want anyone to feel embarrassed; that's why I dimmed the lights. The chair I have put in the center of the circle is the 'prayer chair.' Anyone who wants prayer for anything may get up and sit in the chair. Anyone who wants to may get up to pray for that person."

Sitting in that circle in the near-dark, a lot went through my mind…not the least of which was the recent divorce my folks had gone through. I was relieved when a young girl got up and sat in the chair and requested prayer for her dog. Several got up and prayed for her. Then the chair was empty again.

All of a sudden, I found my feet were moving toward the chair. I sat down and opened my mouth with what had to be the "if-i-est" prayer that you've ever heard: "Lord, if you're there, and I really doubt that You are; and if what these people say is true, and I really doubt that it is; then forgive me of my sins and come into my heart to be Lord of my life."

I then literally—and spiritually—crossed my arms, as if defiantly daring Him to do anything. The curtains on the window didn't flutter, the floor didn't quake nor did the streetlight outside vary its steady stream of light into the room. Just as I had said to myself: *see!* Suddenly, I knew what John Wesley must have meant when he said "I felt my heart grow strangely warm."

Don't ask me how a questioning young man of seventeen suddenly knew, but I did...and I have known ever since that God was (and is) real and the Bible was (and is) true. Oh, I still had a lot of questions, and still do. But I know that He will give me every answer in due season...and He has (and continues to do so)!

What has ensued from that point is a walk of grace...God continually showing me areas I have yet to yield to Him; revealing to me first the obvious and then, the not-so-obvious, sins and forgiving them as I come to realize more and more just how much His blood has bought. Slowly, I am coming to the place where I am realizing His love for me knows no bounds.

As I've led hundreds (and perhaps thousands) to the Lord, ministered as an ordained evangelist on three continents and discipled dozens in The Way, I have come to this conclusion: *Jesus Christ alone can save the world, but He can't save the world alone.* Perhaps I should say: He *won't* save the world alone; we are His only hands and feet. There is no "Plan B," for the very rocks and stones will cry out if we don't (Luke 19:40).

The Lord Jesus Himself said, "The words that I say to you, I do not speak on My own initiative, but the Father abiding in Me does His works. Believe Me that I am in the Father and the Father is in Me; otherwise believe because of the works themselves" (John

14:10–11, NASU). Witnessing is nothing other than the living out of what you profess, to make your words line up with your work.

Is witnessing biblical? Are Christians obligated to witness? What if I'm too scared of reprisal or persecution? What about bumper stickers and cross medallions and necklaces? Aren't we warned against offending? These are the questions Christians should be asking themselves.

According to a dictionary amalgamation, witnessing is the act of giving a first-hand account of something one has seen, heard, or experienced. According to the Bible, witnessing is usually referring to an eye-witness account of the resurrection or of Jesus' acts or miracles.

Answering questions:

1. Is witnessing biblical?

   Three times in the Book of Acts a leader of the Church makes the pronouncement, "We are witnesses of these things…" (Acts 3:15, 5:32, 10:39). There is nothing more powerful in a courtroom or before a listening world than an eyewitness account. Evidence may be to the contrary, but sworn eyewitness testimony will always trump everything else.

   We are not just encouraged, but commanded to, "Tell someone each day that He saves" (Psalms 96:2, LB). In fact, we are told that, "He that winneth souls is wise" (Prov. 11:30, KJV).

2. Are Christians obligated to witness?

   Yes, but it should be a joy. Considering all that Jesus has done for us…dying for us (Rom. 5:8), healing us (1 Pet. 2:24), binding up our broken hearts (Psalms 147:3; Isaiah 61:1; Luke 4:18), etc.…isn't it a small thing to bear witness of His goodness in our lives? Besides, *obligation* has a bad reputation undeservedly. Obligation may not be the most pleasant of motivations, but more done out of obligation is not necessarily a bad thing. Many times obligation must suffice until love takes over.

3. What if I'm too scared of reprisal or persecution?

You are not the first to feel that way. The Apostle Peter, who had professed to Jesus that even if everybody else left Him, he would be there to support the Savior, folded like a cheap tent under the accusations of a mere servant girl (Matt. 26:34–75). The same Holy Spirit that emboldened the otherwise timid Peter on the day of Pentecost (Acts 2:14–40) will give you the strength and boldness you need.

> And the special gift of ministry you received when I laid hands on you and prayed—keep that ablaze! God doesn't want us to be shy with his gifts, but bold and loving and sensible. So don't be embarrassed to speak up for our Master or for me, his prisoner. (2 Tim. 1:6–8, The Message)

Recent laws that have been passed or contemplated make workplace proselytizing forbidden. *No coercion should ever be used or needed.* Witnessing the truth of what God has done in our lives—especially when asked—may make us the objects of ire, ridicule, or persecution but the truth will prevail...even without our help.

Peter and John, after healing the lame beggar and leading five thousand to the Lord from their witnessing were threatened by the religious leaders (Acts 4:1–21). Do you think that shut them up? Read their response:

> But Peter and John answered and said unto them, Whether it be right in the sight of God to hearken unto you more than unto God, judge ye. For we cannot but speak the things which we have seen and heard. (Acts 4:19, KJV)

4. What about bumper stickers, Christian T-shirts, and cross medallions or necklaces?

As long as you're willing to drive under the speed limit and live Christianly—24/7—I see no problem. Most Christians are not willing to commit to that level of integrity, but what message does it send when we say one thing and do another?

We must have lives that match our witness...*it is our acts that give our words their power.* The bumper sticker, "Christians aren't perfect; just forgiven" may be a theologically accurate statement, but it does not give the driver license to obey only those laws that are convenient.

I used to lead a drama team called "God's Army." We wore military camouflage to identify with the concept of a "Christian Soldier." Although we had ranks and lines of authority within our group, the greatest recognition we could give was to award shoulder patches that said "Follow Me." Could you invite others to follow your example in everything? Only by His grace could we even attempt such a thing...but this is what He calls us all to do.

5. Aren't we warned against offending?

Yes (Matt. 18:7; 2 Cor. 6:3), but we must be careful that we don't compromise our message, either. Remember, we must obey God, not men (Acts 4:19).

God doesn't want us to button-hole people on the street, but to live lives that demand explanation. If you haven't had someone come up to you and say, "I want what you've got," perhaps you're too concerned about offending to let your light shine.

> So let your light shine before men, that they may see your good works, and may glorify your Father who [is] in the heavens. (Matt. 5:16, YLT)

Recommended reading list:

- *Larry Moyer's How-To Book on Personal Evangelism*, Larry Moyer
- *The Christian and Witnessing: Bringing Words of Hope to the World Around You*, Bill Bright
- *Witnessing Without Fear*, Bill Bright and Billy Graham

Web sites:

- www.allaboutgod.com/christian-witnessing.htm
- www.knowthebible.net
- www.christianwitnessingtools.com/tips.html

51

Women in Combat

When I was a senior in high school (1970—Muskogee, Oklahoma), we were told that we were one of only six all-boy marching bands left in the country. I don't know if that was true or not, but I do know that there were no women in the United States Air Force Academy when I entered as a basic cadet that same summer. I also know that when my son Jeremy entered the same institution in the summer of 1994, he trained alongside women. Somewhere between 1970 and 1994, there was obviously a fundamental change in the way the genders were viewed in America.

My grandmother Sargent was a crack shot and her favorite slide-action 22 caliber Remington sits in my gun cabinet awaiting my daughter…who is also a crack shot. Still, I have never in my life thought my daughter, as capable as she is, was someone I had to be concerned with serving her country as a soldier on the front lines of battle.

Don't get me wrong; I think women have every bit as much right to lay down their lives for their country (my hat is off and my hand extended in thanks for all those women who have fought: almost three hundred thousand have been deployed since 2001); and they are certainly capable of doing many of the military's most rigorous functions…*indeed some of those functions they are* better suited *to accomplish with as much or more success than their male counterparts*. It's just that the front-line battle combat of modern warfare is not best served by the wives or future-wives, mothers or future-mothers…or for that matter even by those women who are committedly single.

Are women in combat biblical? Should women, by virtue of their gender alone, be considered less fit for front-line combat? Is a man trained to be protective of women or can he be retrained to ignore those tendencies? Does a woman's slighter build make her more or less capable of the physical demands of combat? Should "barefoot and pregnant" be the role of women in a male-dominated society? These are the questions that the thinking Christian must answer.

Women in Combat, the practice of opening up what have been traditional roles for men—over 230,000 positions in the Army and Marines, mostly in the infantry; much fewer in the Air Force and the Navy—to women. An order by the Secretary of Defense, encouraged by the Joint Chiefs, gave the military services just a few months to come up with plans integrating women into combat roles or for seeking certain exemptions from doing so. These are the facts "on the ground."

There can be a lively discussion on the pros and cons of women serving in combat roles…and I've read much of that debate. What about the increased incidence rate of pregnancy to avoid deployment or the rate of STDs or the rate of unwed pregnancies or the emotional ties that decrease unit effectiveness or the ability of women to carry wounded men from a vehicle hit by IUDs or their ability to carry the heavy packs required for combat or the increased vulnerability of a captured or wounded woman? Great questions…but not greater than the military's ability to adapt. However, the question is not whether the military can make the adjustments without sacrificing effectiveness, but should women even be allowed to occupy combat roles?

Answering questions:

1. Is it biblical?

While it might be politically correct to ignore this aspect (after all, doesn't the IDF—the Israeli Defense Force—

have women in combat roles?), the Christian has to answer this question.

There are a few of the exploits of women in leadership, even in quasi-military roles—the example of the prophetess Deborah, who judged Israel before Gideon (Judges 4 and 5) and Jael the wife of Heber, the Kennite who took a hammer and a tent peg to the temple of a sleeping enemy (Judges 4:21); also one could say that Rahab, who hid the Israeli spies (Joshua 2:1–7) was operating in a military capacity—but there are no mentions of women in combat in the Bible.

Contrast that with the high regard for women that Christendom has bestowed. In fact, today wherever you find women being given the equal station they enjoy with men, you will find some Christian influence. Admittedly, western civilization has been slow to come to that conclusion—the Women's Suffrage Movement and the equalization of education and pay being embarrassingly good examples of a tardily appropriate recognition—but you will find few examples of such a high regard for women among those cultures that have not been 'Christianized.' Indeed, there is still room for improvement, but to force women into a role for which no biblical example can be found is to make illegitimate policy.

2. Should women, by virtue of their gender alone, be considered less fit for front-line combat?

Yes, by virtue of their unique ability to be wives and mothers, women should be protected as the counselors and nurturers that their natures—both physical and emotional—singularly enable them to be. They should not be exposed to the rigors of combat, though it might not be politically correct to say it; they alone possess the ability to replenish the fallen—as high birth rates after world conflicts will attest.

This is not to say that women should never play roles as defenders of their homes or their country—just not while there are able-bodied men to take up that task. A woman may find herself having to defend her home in the absence of a man, just as a man may have to be the nurturer should his wife be the bread-winner. While the task of being the Protector and Provider of his home may be temporarily delegated to the wife, the ultimate responsibility for these roles belongs squarely on the husband's shoulders (Ephesians 5:25; 1 Timothy 5:8).

3. Is a man trained to be protective of women or can he be retrained to ignore those tendencies?

Maybe it's cultural...or maybe it's instinctive; whether it is one or the other, a man *can* be trained to resist a 'natural' urge. The human male, like the female, is first a spirit with a soul; he only lives in a body...although present science may want him to be merely a higher order animal—a mammal at the top of the food chain—he is a soul creature, created reasoning by a reasoning God, not just instinctively following his drives and passions. A man is hard-wired to be protective of women and kids. Why go against his programming?

Just because our culture has blurred the roles of men and women, doesn't mean Christians have to do so—chivalry may be on life-support, but that fact is not a justification for perpetuation of a non-biblical practice or attitude. The feminization of our culture may have helped women to attain to new heights in the corporate world, but women in combat may have been the undesirable and unintended consequence. Vast and sudden cultural change often results in collateral damage. When do you know whether or not this collateral damage is justified by the change wrought? *When it goes against biblical principle.*

4. Does a woman's slighter build make her more or less capable of the physical demands of combat?

Less capable, of course. There will still be jobs that are off limits to women—Navy Seals or Army Rangers, for instance— but handling fifty-five-pound artillery rounds in a tank may be beyond a woman's usual abilities. Of course, it can be argued that all women may not qualify, but some would. I argue, that just because some can doesn't mean any should. We wouldn't even be having this discussion if our nation were trying to preserve the femininity of women, rather than trying to denigrate them.

Call me old-fashioned, but isn't it the tradition for men to carry women across the threshold, not the other way around?

5.   Should "barefoot and pregnant" be the role of women in a male-dominated society?

Let's hope not! Women can handle nearly everything in today's modern world that can be thrown against a man…and a few things he can't handle. That most women assume a support role to men is no sign of weakness or inferiority. Rather it is a choice that makes them indispensable.

You might argue with the rightness of a "male-dominated society" premise or think the Bible needs to be amended to make God non-gender-specific but anything with two heads is a monster!

Recommended reading list:

- *Women in Leadership*, Bob Briner
- *The Role of Women*, Jeannette Nedoma
- *Twelve Extraordinary Women: How God Shaped Women of the Bible, and What He Wants to Do with You*, John MacArthur

Web sites:

Women in combat a dangerous experiment—CNN.com
- http://www.cnn.com/2013/01/25/opinion/boykin-women-in-combat
Women in Combat? Some Marines React—NYTimes.com
- http://atwar.blogs.nytimes.com/2013/01/29/women-in-combat-so

52

Work

When my tenth birthday rolled around, my dad took me to an old gas station that had been converted to a small-engine repair shop and loaned me enough money to buy a rebuilt 20"-cut Snark. This gasoline-type push-mower was much more modern than my grandmother's kinetic model—truly a "push" mower. I'll never forget it. It cost me $22.00...$20.00, which is what my father paid for it, and the $2.00 interest he charged me. This was my favorite birthday present from him because it said so much I needed to hear as a young boy growing up in Muskogee, Oklahoma. First, it said that he trusted me—to repay him, that I would take care of the mower, that I was man enough to work, and that I could handle the "great wealth" I was sure this money-making machine would soon garner me.

And I learned a lot; that gas was expensive—sometimes as much as 25 cents per gallon, that mowing was hot, hard work—that's why most of the old ladies in the neighborhood were willing to pay so much (sometimes $3.00 or $3.50 for a large lawn), and that with enough effort over a long enough period, I could earn just about anything a ten-year-old heart could desire.

Since this first foray into working for myself—the hardest boss I've ever faced—I have done many things...sometimes working for others, sometimes for myself; sometimes as an entry-level worker making minimum wage, sometimes as a consultant making more per hour than my dad used to make in a month. I've learned some valuable lessons along the way; I'll share seven of the bigger ones here:

- WORK may have four letters, but it is not a 'four-letter word'
- Impressing a boss is easy: Just show up for work five minutes early, and work five minutes after you've clocked out (today it's even easier: JUST SHOW UP)
- Anybody who really wants work can find it
- Never give up a job until you've got another one
- If you don't have time to do it right, when will you have time to do it over?
- 'Good enough' never is
- If you cannot meet your obligations with your present income, you have three choices:
  1. Get a higher paying job
  2. Take a second or third job
  3. Reduce your standard of living to match your income

NOTE: It is never good to borrow your way out of your financial problems (too bad, the government isn't reading this).

As Christians, our efforts are not rendered in a vacuum. There is always someone watching...either to follow our example or to excuse their own shortcomings...hopefully not both. Since we must give an account for every idle word we speak (Matthew 12:36), how much more so our actions? It was Geoffrey Chaucer who said it first (twelfth century), "Idle hands are the devil's workshop." God expects us to work and He holds a dim view of those who do not labor for their sustenance (II Thessalonians 3:10).

Work, according to *Wikipedia*: in physics, a force is said to do *work* when it acts on a body so that there is a displacement of the point of application. Work, according to modern usage, is the effort expended by people who have to survive, in order to meet the basic needs of a family or an individual. According to Maynard G Krebs, the quintessential beatnik of Dobie Gillis's (and Gilligan's Island') fame, "*work!*" is an epithet for all productive activity that requires effort. Work may be something that means different things to different people, but to Christians it is not what produces faith, but what proves it (Ephesians 2:9; James 2:18).

Is work biblical? Isn't work part of the "curse"? What is God's attitude toward unemployment? If work is good, why isn't works? Does God work? Does God really care how I work? These and other questions need addressing.

Answering questions:

1. Is it biblical?

    One of the greatest examples of work in the Old Testament is a little building project assigned to Noah—the ark—designed by God, but commissioned to Noah to build (Genesis 6:14). This 'little' work project some say only took Noah sixty years to build. It is a great example of working with God. A great example of working against God might be the Tower of Babel (Genesis 11:4). Truly, the only thing worse than working against God and failing, is working against God and succeeding. Sometimes our growth interests are better served by God giving us *our* way—even if it goes against His desired will for our lives.

    Another example is the portable temple (the tabernacle and ark). The detailed instructions for its construction (Exodus 25–27), how it was to be moved (Exodus 25:14), who moved it (I Chronicles 15:2), and when it was to be moved (Exodus 40:33–38) etc....were all examples of man *working* with God. The redemptive work of Christ on the cross was so that another portable temple—the heart of man—might be a suitable dwelling place for the presence of God (2 Corinthians 4:6–7; 2 Corinthians 5:1; Hebrews 9:2–8).

    Work is definitely biblical!

2. Isn't work part of the "curse"?

    Man had a job before the fall (Genesis 1:26–28). He was to "tend and keep" the earth (Genesis 2:15), and specifically a garden God had Himself planted (Genesis 2:8). This all happened before the "Fall" of chapter three (Genesis 3:1–19).

God set a good example for man in the six days of creation (Genesis 1:1–31). He even set a good example, by resting from His creative works by resting on the seventh day (Genesis 2:2). What *did* come as a curse for man's disobedience was the sweat—the toil of the earth's non-cooperation with man's efforts—and the frustration that whatever we do produce will ultimately wear out or decay. Have you ever noticed that the only thing that grows with no effort is weeds?

To summarize: God created Man in His image (Gen. 1:26), placed him in a home in the image of God's home (Gen. 2:8–15), and gave him a job (Gen. 2:8) in the image of God's job (Col. 1:16–17).

3. What is God's attitude toward unemployment?

Employment is necessary for survival; according to the Word, if we don't work, we shouldn't eat (2 Thess. 3:10).

There was an actuarial study done by an insurance company once where one hundred men age sixty-five were compared with another group of men age sixty-five...ten years was allowed to elapse. One group retired at age sixty-five—all one hundred of them...there were only ten left alive at age seventy-five! Of the other group, who kept working, ninety of them were alive at age seventy-five! It was as if God had agreed with them. Done? Okay.

The former Soviet Union had a law called the "parasite law." If you were unemployed, you were considered a "parasite to the state" and you were imprisoned! Of course the state used this law to coerce the people into doing their bidding...and there was much cronyism going on...but the concept—absent the coercion and the political spoils—is more productive.

There is no such thing biblically as retirement—unless you are a priest (Num. 8:25)...we might slow down some...maybe a lot...but unproductivity is as unbiblical as a five-day work week

(Exodus 20:9). Many work (and get paid) 20 percent less than they should. Of course, doing those 'honey-do jobs' around the house on Saturday may pay dividends, too.

4. If work is good, why isn't works?

    "Works" is associated with those efforts expended to earn God's approval...when we, who have applied His blood to the 'lentils and doorposts' (Ex. 12:22) of our hearts, already have it (2 Cor. 10:18). They make the statement that Christ's work on the cross was somehow insufficient; that our own efforts will add to those He already performed in winning our souls for God's kingdom; in other words, His blood was just not enough. We can readily see how this might be offensive to Jesus, or the Father Who sent Him.

The truth is,

> We reckon therefore that a man is justified by faith *apart from the works* of the law. (Romans 3:28, ASV)

> For by grace are ye saved through faith; and that not of yourselves: it is the gift of God: *Not of works*, lest any man should boast. For we are his workmanship, created in Christ Jesus unto good works, which God hath before ordained that we should walk in them. (Ephesians 2:8–10, KJV)

5. Does God work?

    Yes, but being God, He is not diminished by the effort of it. God, being the alpha and omega, the beginning and the end (Revelations 1:8), He is outside of time (which means that He existed before there was any matter and will exist after all matter has given up its energy...indeed, all energy is sourced in Him).

    The greatest question of Scripture concerns the connection between God's works and the efforts of Man: "What shall we do that we might work the works of God?" (John 6:28, NKJV).

Jesus was asked this question by His disciples who had just seen Him multiply the loaves and fishes, but He did not give them the answer they were seeking.

Rather, He defines what the work of God is, "This is the work of God, that you believe in Him whom He sent" (John 6:29, NKJV). Jesus equated belief or faith with the work of God.

Satan's purpose is to steal, kill, and destroy (John 10:10). But what does he want to destroy? Faith. Why? Because it is through faith that men come to believe God. That is why Jesus's and Satan's purposes are juxtaposed. He came to destroy the works of the Devil (I John 3:8).

Does God work? Yes, but He never tires.

6. Does God really care how I work?

Of course He cares; His Word gives us specific instructions: "Whatsoever ye do, work heartily, as unto the Lord, and not unto men;" (Col. 3:23, KJV).

The Lord deserves nothing less than our best effort. Once this was a 'given.' But the Puritan work ethic has given way to selfish half-heartedness. Excellence should not be rendered for self-respect's sake or even pride, but because the efforts of the creature reflect on the Creator.

Thoughts about work for Christians should be all about *What Would Jesus Do*? What business am I in? The Lord's business!

Recommended reading list:

- *Your Brain at Work: Strategies for Overcoming Distraction, Retaining Focus, and Working Smarter All Day Long*, David Rock
- *The Seven Habits of Highly Effective People*, Stephen R. Covey
- *Getting Things Done: A Time Saving Summary of David Allen's Book on Productivity*, Shortcut Summaries

Web sites:

- www.top3workathome.com
- www.jobs.com
- www.workethic.org

Index

A Partial Listing of Some Significant Words and Phrases